Proto-Phenomenology and the Nature of Language

New Heidegger Research

Series Editors:
Gregory Fried, Professor of Philosophy, Suffolk University, USA
Richard Polt, Professor of Philosophy, Xavier University, USA

The *New Heidegger Research* series promotes informed and critical dialogue that breaks new philosophical ground by taking into account the full range of Heidegger's thought, as well as the enduring questions raised by his work.

Titles in the Series

Making Sense of Heidegger: A Paradigm Shift, by Thomas Sheehan
Heidegger and the Environment, by Casey Rentmeester
Correspondence 1949–1975, by Martin Heidegger and Ernst Jünger, translated by Timothy Sean Quinn
After the Greeks: Following Heidegger, by Laurence Paul Hemming (forthcoming)
The Question Concerning the Thing: On Kant's Doctrine of the Transcendental Principles, by Martin Heidegger, translated by Benjamin D. Crowe and James D. Reid
Heidegger's Gods: An Ecofeminist Perspective, by Susanne Claxton
Proto-Phenomenology and the Nature of Language: Dwelling in Speech I, by Lawrence J. Hatab

Proto-Phenomenology and the Nature of Language

Dwelling in Speech I

Lawrence J. Hatab

**ROWMAN &
LITTLEFIELD**
───────── INTERNATIONAL
London • New York

Published by Rowman & Littlefield International, Ltd.
Unit A, Whitacre Mews, 26-34 Stannary Street, London SE11 4AB
www.rowmaninternational.com

Rowman & Littlefield International, Ltd. is an affiliate of Rowman & Littlefield
4501 Forbes Boulevard, Suite 200, Lanham, Maryland 20706, USA
With additional offices in Boulder, New York, Toronto (Canada), and London (UK)
www.rowman.com

Copyright © 2017 by Lawrence J. Hatab

All rights reserved. No part of this book may be reproduced in any form or by any electronic or mechanical means, including information storage and retrieval systems, without written permission from the publisher, except by a reviewer who may quote passages in a review.

British Library Cataloguing in Publication Information Available
A catalogue record for this book is available from the British Library

ISBN: HB 978-1-7834-8818-6
ISBN: PB 978-1-7834-8819-3

Library of Congress Cataloging-in-Publication Data Available

978-1-78348-818-6 (cloth : alk. paper)
978-1-78348-819-3 (pbk. : alk. paper)
978-1-78348-820-9 (electronic)

∞™ The paper used in this publication meets the minimum requirements of American National Standard for Information Sciences Permanence of Paper for Printed Library Materials, ANSI/NISO Z39.48-1992.

Printed in the United States of America

For Elliot and Ethan.

Contents

Preface — xi
   Notes — xiv

Introduction — 1
   1. Representation and Presentation — 2
   2. A Sketch of the Investigation — 4
   3. Proto-Phenomenology — 8
      3.1. The Lived World — 8
   4. Plato and Descartes — 11
   5. The Priority of the Lived World — 12
   6. Indicative Concepts — 14
   Notes — 17

1 Proto-Phenomenology and the Lived World — 19
   1. Ecstatic Dwelling — 19
      1.1. Skepticism — 20
   2. The Personal-World — 22
   3. The Environing-World — 23
      3.1. Immersion and Exposition — 24
      3.2. Exposition and Contravention — 25
      3.3. Everyday Exposition — 28
      3.4. The Scope of Immersion — 29
      3.5. Consciousness — 31
      3.6. Representation — 32
      3.7. Know-How — 36

	3.8. Tacit Knowledge and Habit	39
	3.9. Immersion and Conscious Direction	40
	3.10. The Scope of Proto-Phenomenology	41
	3.11. Meaning and Value	42
	4. The Social-World	44
	4.1. Empathy	47
	4.2. Persons and Things	49
	4.3. Socialization and Individuation	50
	5. Projection	51
	6. Temporality	53
	6.1. The Derivation of Objective Time	56
	6.2. History	58
	6.3. Improvisation and Creativity	59
	7. Embodiment	61
	7.1. Place and Space	62
	Notes	64
2	Disclosure, Interpretation, and Philosophy	73
	1. World Disclosure	73
	1.1. Affective Attunement	73
	1.2. Intimation	75
	1.3. Language	78
	2. The Scope and Importance of Exposition	78
	3. Interpretation	79
	3.1. Pluralism	80
	3.2. Enactive Interpretation	82
	3.3. Reductive Naturalism	83
	4. Phenomenology and Cognitive Science	90
	4.1. Mirror Neurons	92
	4.2. Representation Revisited	94
	4.3. Embodied Cognition	96
	4.4. Proto-Phenomenology and Artificial Intelligence	98
	5. Philosophy and the Lived World	102
	5.1. Disposition and Exposition	103
	5.2. Philosophy and History	104
	5.3. Philosophy and Contravention	106
	5.4. The Importance of Philosophy	107
	Notes	109
3	Proto-Phenomenology and Language	117
	1. Natural Language	117

	2. The Phenomenological Priority of Language	118
	3. Language and the Lived World	120
	3.1. Ecstatic Dwelling	121
	3.2. Existential Meaning	122
	3.3. The Personal-Social-Environing-World	122
	3.4. The Disclosive Field of Language	126
	3.5. Temporality	127
	3.6. Representation Revisited	129
	4. Language and Embodiment	132
	4.1. Gesture	132
	4.2. Sound	134
	5. Differential Fitness	136
	6. Natural Language and Convention	141
	7. Ordinary Language Philosophy and Pragmatics	144
	8. Language and Thought	146
	8.1. Language and Thinking	147
	8.2. Language, World, and Relativism	152
	8.3. Language Deprivation	157
	9. Language and Artificial Intelligence	159
	10. Evolution and Language	162
	10.1. Nature and Culture	165
	10.2. Language and Evolution	168
	Notes	172
4	**Language and Truth**	**183**
	1. Presentational Truth	183
	2. Phenomenology and Truth	187
	2.1. Objectivity and Realism	188
	2.2. Truth Conditions	191
	2.3. Rationality	193
	2.4. Ethics and Truth	195
	3. Philosophy and Reason	199
	4. Pluralism	203
	5. The Mind-Body Question and Linguistic Pluralism	207
	5.1. Selfhood	213
	Notes	216
5	**Transition to Volume 2**	**223**
	1. Language Acquisition and Child Development	225
	2. Oral and Written Language	230
	2.1. Sound and Sight	233

2.2. Time and Space 233
　　　2.3. Modification and Identity 234
　　　2.4. Embodiment and Disembodiment 234
　　　2.5. Lived Context and Decontextualization 234
　　　2.6. Enchantment and Disengagement 235
　　　2.7. Performance and Reflection 235
　　　2.8. Narration and Abstraction 236
　　　2.9. Tradition and Innovation 236
　　　2.10. Presentational and Representational Truth 237
　　Note 238

Bibliography 239

Index 253

Preface

I originally planned to write this book from the standpoint of Heidegger's approach to language, particularly in his early phenomenological works. For a number of reasons I decided to find my own voice on the question of language rather than do a "Heideggerian" treatment. I was coming up with many angles and tributaries that diverted from Heidegger's own agenda. Taking my own path freed me from the burdens of Heideggerian exegesis, and I would not be bound by Heidegger's language, which can be daunting. I could express things in a vocabulary more to my liking and perhaps more digestible for readers outside Heidegger studies. Finally, I could choose what to include and exclude with respect to Heidegger's approach. In particular, I could leave aside his lofty ontological concerns launched in *Being and Time* in order to focus on more pedestrian matters illuminated in early parts of that masterwork. I could concentrate on what I found philosophically stimulating in Heidegger's phenomenology of being-in-the-world, with special attention to language.

Heidegger was a typical philosopher in that his agenda was to think through and reformulate the classic grounding concept of "being." The phenomenological analysis of being-in-the-world aimed to supplant objective and present-centered notions of being with a more original sense of meaning-laden temporality. The phenomenological account was therefore preparatory for a meditation on the meaning of being itself. Yet Heidegger's preliminary account advanced many interesting and important findings that can address standard philosophical questions in a novel way, such as matters pertaining to cognition, meaning, values, selfhood, social relations, ethics, action, and language.[1] It is this dimension of *Being and Time* that has always been attractive to me, rather than Heidegger's later ruminations on being as such, the history of being, and the dramatic story of the forgetting of being that is brought to a climax in modern technology. It is not that I entirely reject such things, but I find that level of thinking unnerving and overheated. But I do turn away from Heidegger's apparent need to focus on something "original" and "bestowing" behind all manifestations of being.[2] Nevertheless, anyone who is familiar with Heidegger's writings will see his significant influence on my thinking, and it is important that other readers know this. Yet I believe I have put together something viable in my own way that might make a contribution to the questions at hand, perhaps in a manner that would resonate with more readers than would a strictly Heideggerian venture.

My notion of proto-phenomenology offers a new way to zero in on how Heidegger's early thinking is different from other approaches to phenomenology, especially Husserl's. Even many Heidegger scholars miss the unique sense in which his analysis begins with the everyday world of concerns, involvements, and practices, rather than cognitive structures or even some overformalized renditions of Heidegger's language in *Being and Time*. The terminology I offer aims to be more faithful to Heidegger's phenomenology and perhaps more illuminating than many treatments of his thought, at least more so for those who might otherwise be put off or mystified by Heidegger's texts. My concentration on the lived world, which Heidegger called facticity and being-in-the-world, puts off larger questions that occupy his writings and aims to detail how proto-phenomenology applies to many familiar philosophical topics, especially the nature of language. In any case, whenever I deploy my own terminology or approach to a Heideggerian concept, I will note which concept I am revising.

I appreciate how difficult it can be to understand Heidegger. For most of my career I have been the only continental philosopher in my immediate professional environment, and conversations about my work have required much outreach that would not be needed within my own tribe. I still believe in philosophy as one common discipline (perhaps naïvely) and I have always been predisposed to bridging differences. Hence my book is pitched a bit more to readers outside the continental tradition because I find it more challenging and interesting to venture outside of home territory and attract strangers to something worthy than to simply converse with neighbors on familiar ground. The hope is that experimenting with my own language can achieve some effective outreach without losing the distinctive posture of Heidegger's critical assessment of traditional philosophical assumptions, terms, and methods.

There are a number of developments outside of continental thought that can provide good avenues for bridge building. Many references in the text will involve such sources, but with the purpose of facilitating possible bridgework—without necessarily countenancing all aspects of these sources. My book is an attempt to expose important Heideggerian insights to a wider audience and to engage many familiar philosophical topics, but the main focus of investigation is a joint exploration of phenomenology and the nature of language. When certain topics outside of the phenomenological tradition are engaged—pertaining to research in epistemology, philosophy of mind, and linguistics, among others—the scope of discussion will be more a sketch than a detailed treatment of the matters at hand. The aim is to open doors for further research on such topics.

I am gratified that the editors for the New Heidegger Research series have embraced the inclusion of my book because it is drawn from fifty years of exposure to Heidegger's thought. Yet the wide ambitions of the series are surely at work here as well because I am stretching a Heideggerian orientation beyond what some scholars would want or expect and my vocabulary, emphases, omissions, and departures from much of Heidegger's agenda might strike some as too much of a stretch. Indeed, since I am going my own way, not everything in this study will accord with Heidegger's own output. But the power of Heidegger's thinking should not be restricted to its own domain—and such openness of interpretation is a laudable feature of the New Heidegger Research series.

Accordingly, I would like to thank editors Richard Polt and Gregory Fried, as well as Sarah Campbell of Rowman & Littlefield International, for supporting and nurturing my project. Likewise, I want to thank the many professional colleagues (too numerous to name) who have helped and influenced me along the way. I also thank graduate students Tamyka Brown, Amanda Franco, Joseph Ponthieux, Ryan Elza, Shaun Respass, and Lee Welch, who slogged through a course I offered on this material. Finally, as always, thanks to my wife, Chelsy, for everything important in my life.

NOTES

1. I pursued the matter of ethics in my *Ethics and Finitude: Heideggerian Contributions to Moral Philosophy* (Lanham, MD: Rowman & Littlefield, 2000).

2. See my essay, "The Point of Language in Heidegger's Thinking: A Call for the Revival of Formal Indication," *Gatherings: The Heidegger Circle Annual* 6 (2016): 1–22.

Introduction

I answer the phone and hear my father tell me, "Your mother died last night." I ask my girlfriend a question and she answers, "Yes, I will marry you." I receive a letter that says, "Your manuscript has been approved for publication." The effect of these words is an immediate disclosure of important meanings in my life, constituted by a range of comprehensions and feelings. Right away my world is altered. How is it that sounds from the mouth or marks on a page—which by themselves are nothing like things or events in the world—can be so world-disclosive in such an automatic manner? Think of how natural it is to be absorbed in or moved by a story or verbal account of something important without any current experience of what is described. If we can suspend our pervasive familiarity with language, its operation appears almost magical, or at least exceedingly strange. Philosophy, as Plato and Aristotle tell us, begins with wonderment at seemingly familiar things, and from the beginning philosophy has sought to understand the nature of language (with refined executions of language). Philosophical reflection *on* language differs markedly from normal usage because now language itself becomes something to talk about. We step back from engaged linguistic milieus (like the ones I opened with) and quite naturally turn elements of such scenarios into objects of investigation: sounds, words, meanings, things, thoughts, feelings, speech, speakers, and communication between speakers. With such delineations there arise questions concerning how (or whether) words can be linked to things, meanings, or thoughts and how (or whether) different speakers can be joined in communication about things, meanings, or thoughts. The manifest differences exhibited in such elements (words and things, different minds) make it difficult to navigate or answer such questions.

1. REPRESENTATION AND PRESENTATION

To a large extent philosophical treatments of language in the West have proceeded by way of these delineations that follow from the reflective objectification of language. I call this mode of thinking *representational*, which is especially evident when language is thought to "represent" or "signify" things, meanings, or thoughts and when communication is accomplished by a transfer of representations from one speaker to another by way of verbal conveyance. Representational delineations of language, reality, and speakers have informed most of the topics and guiding questions in the philosophy of language. Here we find a basic distinction between reference and meaning, where reference pertains to the language-reality relation (with particular attention to truth conditions) and where meaning pertains to either semantic meaning or a speaker's meaning (especially with regard to intention). Then there is the question of communication, which involves speaker-to-speaker relations, causal accounts of communication, and the interplay of individual speech and social patterns. Finally, there are models of linguistic structure, which take up the relation between words and sentences, grammatical rules, and the formal/logical schematics of language as distinct from particular acts of speech. Within the representational approach there also looms the problem of skepticism, which challenges the veracity of the language-reality relation or the very possibility of genuine communication.

The representational model of language is anchored in the subject-object distinction, which was clinched in modern philosophy, beginning with Descartes. Here there persists a differentiation between the interior mental space of the subject and the exterior space of physical objects, a division that prompts all the questions concerning the relations between thoughts and things, mind and world, mind and other minds. The alternative approach in this investigation is anchored in the concept of *dwelling*, which is meant to capture the pre-reflective character of the *lived world*, which is not perceived as a subject-object transaction but an engaged *field* of experience that precedes delineations of mind and world, of internal and external spheres.[1] Along these lines, language is taken to be a mode of dwelling, which is indicated in the examples at the beginning of this introduction. In such cases I am not experiencing transactions between words and things or transfers between linguistic agents and recipients. There is simply an immediate, direct disclosure of meaning—and here it is not a matter of semantic meaning but existential meaningfulness, how such moments figure in the meaning of my life. In this respect the "world" disclosed by language is not the brute sense of an "external world" but settings of meaningful import (as in the world of art or people coming from different worlds). Such experiences of meaning are not simply subjective states because they are absorbed in natural, social, and cultural *environments*.

The concept of dwelling is not meant to reject representational thinking but to situate it in a more original environment that precedes, and makes possible, representational distinctions—which, I aim to show, emerge out of disruptions in pre-reflective occasions of dwelling. My account, therefore, cannot be labeled anti-representational. The precedence of dwelling will, however, inform a critique of representational models of language that presume to be sufficient accounts or that reduce the phenomenon of language to representational distinctions, arrangements, and operations. Such critique especially pertains when moments of dwelling illustrated in my examples are "reverse engineered" as transactions between signs and referents, intentions and signs, agents and recipients, etc. The immediate disclosive effects of language in occasions of dwelling have what I call a *presentational* character that precedes them being re-presented as subject-object and subject-subject relations. Language at a more original level *presents* a meaningful world rather than a procedure "representing" something in the world. Presentation will mark the use of the term *disclosure* and its variations. The word *dis-closure* is a double-negative (like un-cover) that captures the positive sense of presentation as well as the process-character of linguistic manifestation, an unfolding or coming forth from absence to presence.[2]

The notions of dwelling and presentation are meant to challenge representational divisions drawn from the subject-object split. This can help resolve longstanding debates that stem from such divisional thinking, as in disputes between realism and idealism, externalism and internalism, intellectualism and anti-intellectualism, objectivism and relativism, dogmatism and skepticism. A resolution of these debates will not involve choosing one side over the other, or even a negotiated settlement between the two sides, because the very construction of the *sides* is a reflective polarization of pre-reflective modes of dwelling, which cannot be sliced into discrete spheres that prompt the terms of the debate in the first place. If philosophy begins with finding things strange, representational approaches to language in some respects make language even stranger when explanatory or descriptive theories are detached from lived speech, from the way in which language functions and is directly experienced in everyday life.

2. A SKETCH OF THE INVESTIGATION

The representational model of language depends on a host of philosophical assumptions, and so a presentational account must confront these assumptions with an alternative orientation. That is the task of chapter 1, which establishes a phenomenology of dwelling. A phenomenological approach aims to describe the way in which the world *appears* in lived experience in a manner that is faithful to appearances without importing alien or inappropriate theories. A phenomenology of the lived world examines what it is like to directly engage the world in a pre-theoretical manner before it becomes an object of reflection. This *first* world is the domain of what I am calling proto-phenomenology, which is distinguished from some models of phenomenology that are still caught up in reflective or representational prejudices. Here I mean the tradition inspired by Husserl, which contributes much to overcoming subject-object divisions but which emphasizes cognition and foundational structures and misses the presentational immediacy of dwelling.[3] At times Husserl's thought has been designated as proto-phenomenology, in the sense of being the discipline's origin. The same designation has been given to pre-Husserlian sources or instances of phenomenological thinking before its formal identification as a discipline, for instance in Aristotle, Kant, or Brentano. What is "first" in my usage is not a matter of chronological or historical origins, but rather the pre-reflective character of the lived world that precedes objectification and even some formal constructions operating in phenomenology.

Chapter 1 works out the basic features of dwelling in the lived world, which will be shown to have environmental structures and modes of involvement that cannot be captured by subject-object delineations because it is saturated with existential meaningfulness. Dwelling exhibits a threefold constellation of the personal-, social-, and environing-world, together showing the world as intrinsically meaningful (not at first objective), socially engaged (not at first individual), and extended into natural, cultural, and social environments (not at first an interior mind).

Chapter 2 spells out a phenomenological account of disclosure, interpretation, and philosophy. Disclosure is meant to capture ways in which the world is opened up that precede representational models of cognition, particularly affective attunement and tacit understanding. Interpretation carries this discussion further with a pluralized, enactive sense of disclosure that is counter-posed to metaphysical realism and reductive naturalism. Also covered is how proto-phenomenology bears on research in cognitive science and artificial intelligence. Finally, philosophy itself is examined in terms of its own mode of dwelling.

The most important feature of the lived world is the disclosive capacity of language. That is the subject of chapter 3, which applies the various findings of proto-phenomenology to the nature of language. The specific treatment of language does not take place until chapter 3, but this is not an undue delay. The phenomenology of dwelling and the nature of language are co-equal treatments in this investigation, especially because of their reciprocal relationship, which will be more evident in chapter 3. In any case a good deal of philosophical preparation must be in place before a proper treatment of language can ensue. That is the job of chapters 1 and 2.

One crucial element of the phenomenological setup for this investigation is situating language in the lived *world*, thus avoiding any kind of linguistic idealism, determinism, or formalism. Language too is shown to be an environment in which we dwell—indeed it is the core mode of dwelling that animates all the others. Face-to-face speech serves as the most illuminating gateway to my approach. The notion of "dwelling in speech" becomes a guiding concept indicating an environing field that cannot be reduced to, or sufficiently addressed by, representational divisions of words and things, words and thoughts, or separate linguistic agents. Before any such distinction, language is an engaged, social, communicative practice-field with a disclosive function that informs the full range of human inhabitance. Chapter 3 also examines the correlation of language and embodiment, as well as the classic question of whether thought is constituted by language. I argue in the affirmative, but not in terms of a reduction to verbal tokens; the environmental/embodied approach to language is better suited to answering this question than are subject-based models of cognition and language. Finally, the proto-phenomenological account of language is applied to central assumptions in artificial intelligence and evolution theory.

In the light of chapter 3, chapter 4 explores the concept of truth as a matter of appropriate disclosure of phenomena, which is distinguished from theories grounded in correspondence and indefeasibility. A presentational sense of truth takes precedence over representational schemas, as does pluralism over unitary models. Also treated is how a phenomenological approach to language can offer its own take on objectivity, realism, and rationality. Finally, the classic mind-body question is examined by way of linguistic pluralism.

As indicated in the preface, my approach owes much of its inspiration to Heidegger's early phenomenology. There are other writers in the continental tradition that are congenial with, or have influenced, my account, such as Gadamer, Ricoeur, Merleau-Ponty, and Hubert Dreyfus. The same can be said for pragmatic approaches to language, ordinary language philosophy, and thinkers in the analytic tradition such as Wittgenstein, Austin, and McDowell. I will not engage in detailed accounts of these sources because I am trying to find my own voice and I do not want to get bogged down in exegetical matters. There will be some reference to sources that can help bridge the gap between analytic and continental philosophy. In addition, there are developments in contemporary cognitive science that will be noted as complementary to my approach, yet such convergence will be treated with caution, owing to an insistence on the difference between phenomenological description and causal explanation. The distinctiveness of my account is its proto-phenomenological method and a presentational alternative to representational models—which involves some divergence from congenial sources mentioned above.[4]

I cannot pretend to have broken entirely new ground, but what may be unique in my approach is the subject of volume 2, *Language Acquisition, Orality, and Literacy*, which will take up child development and the differences between oral language (face-to-face speech) and literacy (writing and reading). Chapter 5 in the present volume will serve as a bridge to volume 2, but here I can give a brief forecast. Child development is usually not given extensive treatment in philosophy, but it helps my argument by grounding proto-phenomenological features of language in the environment of early childhood and the emergence of speech, the original nexus of social, behavioral, and practical forces that shape all of us as language users and that are not left behind in maturity. A good deal of research on child development and language acquisition can supply a kind of empirical complement to chapters 1 and 3 of volume 1, and in turn a phenomenological account of dwelling in speech can help illuminate the research in question and dispel problematic assumptions therein that in fact are based in representational and subject-object frameworks. In any case, all the phenomenological features of the lived world are well grounded and evident in the experiences of children and their enculturation.

The question of orality and literacy has also received little attention in philosophy, but it reinforces my argument even further with another kind of empirical supplement. I claim that reading and writing skills are a necessary condition for philosophy as we understand it. The case history for such a claim is ancient Greece, where philosophy was born in a culture that had previously been a strictly oral tradition before the discovery and use of alphabetic script. I rely on research that has shown how literacy altered the Greek world and made philosophy possible. What we are able to surmise about the pre-literate character of Greek life shows that an oral culture embodies much of what I lay out as dwelling in speech, which thus can be exhibited as the primary orientation in an entire adult world, not simply in childhood. The lived world precedes philosophical reflection not only phenomenologically, but historically as well. The analysis will show 1) how an oral culture embodies the various elements of dwelling and 2) how philosophical disengagement from lived experience that reversed this precedence was gradually achieved by skills and avenues of thought generated by writing. Not only will I show how philosophy was made possible by literacy in ancient Greece, I will also try to demonstrate how the representational model of language could only have arisen in a literate domain—where language *literally* can be objectified in a visual, physical medium. Finally, at the end of volume 2 I will survey how literacy has figured in and shaped various philosophical approaches to language and how attention to orality can enrich an alternative phenomenological account.

In effect my overall study amounts to a specific kind of metaphilosophical analysis by engaging basic differences between philosophical thinking and pre-philosophical existence: with respect to the lived world (volume 1), childhood, and orality (volume 2). These three areas are "borderlands" of philosophy. Obviously, none of us are natives to philosophy-land; we are immigrants from the borderlands. Proto-phenomenology is an alert about overassimilation in philosophy-land, which dims the memory of native habitats; it is also a call for open rather than protected borders, which can serve to benefit philosophy-land. Opening borders can identify problems in philosophy that could be resolved by attending to pre-philosophical life.[5] This is surely a precarious endeavor because my book is a philosophical work—perhaps I write in the manner of a "double agent." But the hope is that my text will convince readers that the endeavor is worthy and viable. The basic problem is this: How can philosophical reflection duly attend to a pre-reflective world?

3. PROTO-PHENOMENOLOGY

Here I prepare what is meant by a phenomenological analysis and its preliminary features that will be fleshed out further in chapters to come. As indicated earlier, phenomenology generally examines how things appear, without assuming that appearance is *mere* appearance hiding some "reality." Appearance denotes something emerging or showing-forth (the actor appearing on stage). Phenomenology attends to the positive sense of how things show themselves in the way they show themselves, without presuppositions that are unfaithful to phenomena. Unlike some versions of phenomenology, my approach does not begin with abstract notions of consciousness, intentionality, intuition, constitution, synthesis, qualia, or any such philosophical construct, but simply with what life is like in normal experience, in a way that would be evident to any human being. Such is the lived world we already inhabit before philosophical reflection or scientific analysis. This world is the domain of *factical* experience, and I use this word not in reference to the "factual" but the concrete embeddedness and engagement in meaningful activities that mark pre-reflective existence.[6]

3.1. The Lived World

The lived world is the first setting in which we find ourselves, and its proto-phenomenological analysis amounts to a kind of naturalism, not in the current philosophical sense of being grounded in the findings of natural science, but in a manner consistent with the Greek and Latin words *phusis* and *natura*, having to do with birth and emergence, and thus a "nativism" referring to the world in which we are born and raised, that which comes "naturally" to us. For much of Western philosophy, this approach would be deemed naïve, but that is why such a phenomenology is implicitly a critique of much that has transpired in philosophy.[7] I begin with a *presumption of immanence*, which means that the world into which we are born is from a phenomenological standpoint the primary reality, and nothing in thought can be divorced from it. This world of engagement has first-order priority over any reflective construct because all realms of thought emerge out of factical life and cannot presume a more original status. The lived world includes, of course, the larger cosmos and even the possibility of alternative universes as entertained in astrophysics. Yet the gateway to any such extraterrestrial reality is opened by our sentient experience of natural life. It must be stressed that immanence cannot be confined to a philosophical "position" on the nature of reality because it points to a mode of existence that is *already* in place and functioning before philosophical analysis—and that as such can *never* be fully captured as a philosophical "posit," especially because philosophizing itself is a mode of factical existence. Immanence therefore confronts philosophy with an inextricable circularity that eludes objectification or explication. Here the explanatory urge of philosophy must simply recognize a limit that cannot be surmounted.

A central feature of proto-phenomenology is its common sense ontology. Immediate reality is life in the midst of a world of perceptible things—that is, our occupation with natural and artificial entities like animals, plants, rivers, houses, tools, cars, and so on, along with all the activities involved with these things and their significance. Even "elements" such as air, fire, and water are perceptible entities in this phenomenological sense. The presumption of immanence surely puts aside any transcendent reality beyond earthly life, but the "thingly" character of the lived world also assigns a secondary status to analytical reductions that have marked many philosophical projects, wherein the various entities in experience are bracketed in favor of ingredient components that make up or explain anything whatsoever (sense data, concepts, elements, atoms, etc.).[8] As I write this sentence, what is most real are my room, chair, desk, pen, and the concrete act of writing—not a God who created me, not a scheme of form and matter or concepts and percepts, not even the atomic structure of all these things. Atomic accounts *can* have priority if the context pertains to explanatory questions ("What are things composed of?") rather than phenomenological description. In proto-phenomenology, however, the first order of being involves how we normally exist in the world. Something like scientific accounts of material composition, natural causation, or mathematical structure would pertain to subsequent (usually explanatory) orders that are emergent out of, and derived from, the lived world. More on this in due course, but a central feature of this investigation is the *coexistence* of scientific and nonscientific domains in a contextual manner. All told, proto-phenomenology amounts to an *existential naturalism*, having to do with the factual meaningfulness of the world into which we are born, in which we already find ourselves before we examine it philosophically.

What are the characteristics of the lived world? I do not want to limit the discussion simply to the "everyday" world or normal experience because factual life exhibits extraordinary moments and dramatic concerns as well. Nevertheless, we must begin with evident conditions that anyone would recognize as normally pertaining to human existence. Therein we are embodied beings surrounded by natural and cultural environments. We have desires, needs, concerns, and interests driven by the assignments of life. We possess habits, capacities, and practical skills that enable dealings with things and other people. Aspects of the world are opened up by a host of feelings, moods, perceptions, and comprehensions. Normative guidance and a wide range of valuations pervade every dimension of life. From the beginning, individual existence is shaped and furthered by social relations. Everyone is born into a world not of their choosing and shaped by inherited customs and traditions. And everything so far described is saturated with language usage. Finally, factual life is finite in being temporal, ever changing, and subject to chance, and in pressing limits on knowledge, agency, achievement, and well-being, all consummated by the ultimate limit of death. In summation, the lived world is embodied, environed, meaningful, active, capacious, felt, understood, social, inherited, and finite. I assume that the elements here described are evident to anyone and would cut across all human cultures, with obvious differences in how these common features are specified.[9]

With the presumption of immanence there is nothing more original than the lived world. So whatever the character and findings of philosophy and science, these disciplines have necessarily arisen out of this first world. That should be evident with respect to the historical inception of philosophy and science, as well as the lives of philosophers and scientists. The question concerns the relationship between the lived world and its emergent disciplines. No thought system has ever denied that factual life is our first orientation. How could it? Even if one believed in a spiritual realm to come or that the existence of the world is subject to doubt or even illusory, the original setting of any such belief will always be the lived world, in that we initially find ourselves or seem to find ourselves in such a setting.[10] In much of the Western tradition, the relationship between philosophical thinking and factical experience involved a corrective or progressive narrative—that there is something essentially problematic about the lived world and that rational thought will either liberate us from its defects or perfect us by overcoming its confused, disordered, unenlightened condition.

4. PLATO AND DESCARTES

For Plato, the lived world is symbolized by the cave allegory in the *Republic*. There the realm of the body, passions, and senses is a dark confinement from which we must escape if we are to discover the truth found in eternal Forms, the timeless, universal principles that serve as a stable foundation for knowledge. Embodied life on its own terms suffers from intrinsic intellectual and existential limits because it is marked by change, variation, disorder, degeneration, and death. In the *Phaedo* (63bff), Socrates gathers such limits as 1) the forces of embodiment that block true knowledge because of sensory errors and confusion, the endless needs of appetite and nurturance, passion-driven strife, and the lure of pleasure, honor, and wealth, and 2) the locus of the soul's descent from its pre-existence in the eternal realm of the Forms. Philosophy, then, involves the discipline of disengagement from this world and even the welcoming of death as liberation from bodily life and a restoration of the soul's immortal condition (*Phaedo* 80–81).

The thought of Descartes represents some of the most fundamental elements of modern philosophy, especially its connection with the emergence of modern science. Mind-body dualism in Descartes has some resonance with Platonism, but it also highlights a defining feature of modern thought that shaped much of philosophy to this day: the subject-object/mind-world dichotomy. Descartes was in large part aiming to ground the mechanical-mathematical character of the new physics and defend its dissonance with common sense, religious doctrine, and most of philosophy since Aristotle. His method of radical doubt put everything in question except the *cogito*, the self-conscious thinking subject. The certainty of the reflective subject opened space for the priority of abstract mathematization over sense experience and embodiment. Now nature could be understood simply as units of matter in motion measured by mechanical laws and quantified space-time coordinates. The external world was thus stripped of customary meanings and values, particularity, common sense beliefs, and practical involvement—accomplished by an "internalized" reflective detachment from the immediacy of factual experience. The abstract mindscape of the thinking subject thereby set up space for framing external "objects" measured by the now familiar standard of objectivity, namely *independence* from desires, interests, values, and purposes—which is best exemplified by mathematical physics and marked by universal principles, uniformity, causal regularity, and predictability.[11] Descartes's pathway of radical doubt in its way dramatizes the fact that modern science does indeed have to disengage from the lived world in order to shape its findings (for instance, the heliocentric theory versus the normal experience of the sun's motion across the sky, and in general the mathematical framework that grounds the work of physics). The question concerns whether modern *philosophy* was overly bound up with natural science and thus presumed that philosophical questions could be adequately addressed with constructs divorced from ordinary life.

With the obvious simplification and compression in this historical sketch, I only want to put in place certain assumptions and ideals born in the thinking of Plato and Descartes that have influenced much of philosophy since, no matter the many disagreements with parts of their philosophies that have come to pass. These are the authority of theoretical reason, the appeal to stable foundations that can ground and govern thinking, the standard of indefeasibility that can survive doubt and disputation, the division of mind and world into a thinking subject and external objects, and "nature" conceived as the sphere of material things divorced from interests and values. Each of these assumptions finds the lived world falling short, which accounts for the remedial attitude of traditional philosophy. I aim to turn things around by arguing for the priority of factical life, not only as our first world, but also as a region of truth that cannot be dismissed or set aside in philosophical thinking.[12]

5. THE PRIORITY OF THE LIVED WORLD

How can the priority of the lived world be defended? As noted, a presumption of immanence at least must accept the fact that this world comes first in our lives, that it is natural in the sense of our being natives in this terrain. The degree to which philosophy has been beholden to modern science—especially in current conceptions of "naturalism"—can be interrogated by considering basic orientations of science that modern philosophers adopted in their intellectual work. Physics does indeed depart from common sense and a host of normal bearings, but this fact alone can put in question the presumption of this departure as the proper lens for viewing philosophical topics. Descartes's methodic doubt entailed a withdrawal from ordinary life and beliefs—in fact he had to fight off the force of these beliefs, as we will see. Modern science exhibits a similar kind of contested disposition toward native experience, which a number of thinkers saw from the start. Consider Bacon's understanding that experimental science investigates "nature under constraint and vexed; that is to say, when by art and the hand of man she is forced out of her natural state, and squeezed and molded."[13] Kant similarly claimed that scientific reason "has insight only into what it itself produces according to its own plan" and that, armed with necessary laws, it must "compel nature to answer reason's own questions."[14] Accordingly, modern science in many ways emerged as a struggle with erstwhile conceptions of the world. This suggests that the construal of the natural world as a set of scientific "objects" is itself not an objective discovery. For such a scheme to emerge, the rational subject must disengage from natural (native) experience to reconstitute the *being* of nature by way of scientific and mathematical constructs. Science does not simply "report" its findings about nature. The active character of modern science is shown in methodological guidelines set up *before* inquiry and in experimental interventions that *reconfigure* natural events to test a preconceived theory.

The point is not to invalidate scientific disengagement or to think of science in purely constructivist terms, but to ask whether this orientation should extend to all philosophical matters, and especially whether this orientation can be taken as a "correction" of factual experience generally. How is it that our first world would come up short with respect to truth? How is it that human existence could be in ignorance or at least in a backward condition so easily and for so long before philosophy and scientific knowledge came to correct it? A presumption of immanence certainly renders such a script strange. It would *not* be so strange if we committed to some fanciful story about some original deficient condition followed by an enlightened deliverance—a notion that indeed has been alive in the Western tradition, given the Platonic myth of recollection and the Christian doctrine of the fall. Could modern philosophy and its legacy be an echo of such a notion?[15] In what follows I am not challenging science but scientism, and I am not dismissing all elements of modern philosophy. I am simply calling into question the supposed deficient status of factical experience and exploring how philosophical analysis can benefit from this interrogation. Philosophy itself emerges out of the lived world, and if it departs too much from its first environment, it is less a correction and more an insurrection.

The presumption of immanence entails that human beings fully belong in the world and that factical life has ontological and veridical primacy on its own terms and cannot be set aside or thought to require rationalized explanation to be intelligible. In this analysis, the lived world is gathered around the term *dwelling*, which captures in its verb sense active living and in its noun sense the natural and cultural environments in which we live. The hope is that the features of dwelling examined in chapter 1 will allow a more situated philosophical vocabulary and expose the shortcomings in much of traditional philosophical language. Human dwelling *inhabits* the world in an irreducible and inextricable manner, a "field" concept that precedes the dichotomy of subject and object, of reflective consciousness and external things. Dwelling "in" the world is not like spatial location ("in the box"), but more like being "in love" or "in pain." Writing "in my room" can certainly indicate location, but also dwelling in *meaningful* space, the *place* where I write. A phenomenological account of dwelling cannot begin with, or be limited to, the third-person standpoint. It begins with the first-person standpoint and what it is like to actively engage in the affairs of life—before such engagement is subjected to reflective analysis.[16] Here of course we confront the difficulty of attending reflectively (as I am now) to pre-reflective experience, which runs up against the circular problem of immanence noted earlier. But if we can give first-person attention to a recognizable difference between engaged actions and reflective disengagement, we should be able to intimate a vocabulary that is faithful to this difference.

6. INDICATIVE CONCEPTS

Phenomenological reflection on the pre-reflective world will employ what I call *indicative* concepts.[17] As concepts they gather the sense of lived experience, but primarily in concrete, performative terms rather than abstract, constative terms. As "indicative" concepts they simply *point* back to factical experience for their realization. In this way, phenomenological concepts are nominal in nature, as verbal experiments in sense making that simply *show* rather than define, that are not meant to satisfy traditional conceptual criteria presumed to govern or ground thinking (definitions, universals, essences, necessary and sufficient conditions). Rather than *giving* sense to inchoate experience, indicative concepts are meant to gather the already implicit sense of factical dwelling. That is why ostensive exemplification can be appropriate in the operation of proto-phenomenological concepts.[18]

The everyday usage of words shows the proto-operation of concepts, but in an indicative manner that does not fit squarely with the sophisticated philosophical sense of concepts, namely mental constructions that organize, classify, unify, or define particulars. Everyday indicative concepts span a range of uses and make sense *in* usage rather than through abstract classifications. So a competent speaker of English *knows how to use* words like "tree," "friend," "know," "good," and so on, without having gone through advanced procedures of collection and division. That is why students can be perplexed or frustrated when asked philosophical questions (What is friendship? knowledge? goodness?). Knowing how to use the word "friend" means that it already has indicative sense, and the *capacity* to differentiate things (say, trees from bushes) can be called proto-conceptual, not as an ideational construct but more a perceptual, pragmatic aptitude. Indicative sense *can* benefit from philosophical interrogation, but not always, especially if factical understanding is presumed to be essentially problematic and needful of correction or codification. Proto-concepts can be refined, expanded, classified, organized, even delimited in mathematical abstraction, and productively so, but such operations have contextual limitations and are derived from the original milieu of indicative sense. That is why the perennial philosophical aim to "purify" concepts cannot go all the way down.

Much of traditional philosophy has focused on concepts as formal entities unto themselves, apart from an indicative function. Accordingly, philosophical sentences have provided a grammar wherein abstractions mimic natural language descriptions and seem to have a life of their own, as in the following: the soul governs the body, time is the measure of motion, knowledge is the conceptual organization of sense data, and the good is the maximization of well-being. Such accounts can be disclosive, especially if an indicative function points to processes and activities rather than "faculties," "ideas," or other constative designations. Such designations become formal reifications that then prompt descriptions mimicking normal discourse about things and their aspects (the mind cannot be divided; ideas are different from the things they represent; desire precedes action), which then issues questions or problems concerning the reference of such terms, whether they can be verified, and how they function or relate to each other. Indicative concepts, on the other hand, are simply nominal notions showing phenomenological regions of life that are not "objects" of investigation but *ways* of engaging the world—so that if a manner of experience appears to have both cognitive and sensory aspects, there is no need to wonder how "concepts" and "percepts" can coincide. Indicative concepts are like a pointing finger that focuses attention on something in the lived world. The focusing function of such concepts can be called their *focal meaning*, which is like the hub of a wheel from which spokes radiate and retain their distinct space without being reduced to one common form. Indicative concepts are nothing more than their focal, pointing function. Consequently, if they point away from themselves toward concrete engagements, we need not face the puzzle of how reflective concepts can capture pre-reflective experience. The success or failure of indicative concepts will be measured not by theoretical principles or rules of inference but by whether or not they resonate (with readers) in opening up the lived world. All the coming chapters have a certain indicative character in that the aim is not a compelling logical argument that can defeat all comers but an attempt to illuminate the existential background of philosophical and scientific thinking and how reflective inquiry can benefit from attending to this background. There *is* a case to be made in this investigation, especially regarding the cogency of a proto-phenomenological account, its conceptual organization of the lived world, and its first-order primacy. As an indicative endeavor, however, readers will have to actively participate by suspending many philosophical habits and attending to factical experience on its own terms if the book is to make its case effectively. One way to highlight the indicative character of this investigation is that it honors the circularity of immanence. It does not propose to "explain" or even propose "transcendental conditions" for dwelling in the world. It points to what is already in play and not in need of explanation or schematics in order to be intelligible.

NOTES

1. The lived world stands for Heidegger's concept of being-in-the-world.
2. Disclosure is my term for what Heidegger called unconcealment.
3. I will have more to say about this in chapter 2.
4. At the completion of my manuscript, I came across two books that seem to fit my approach in significant ways: Andrew Inkpin, *Disclosing the World: On the Phenomenology of Language* (Cambridge, MA: MIT Press, 2016), and Charles Taylor, *The Language Animal: The Full Shape of the Human Linguistic Capacity* (Cambridge, MA: Belknap Press of Harvard University Press, 2016). I will be able to address these works in volume 2.
5. This is the kind of thing that marks the writings of Nietzsche, Heidegger, and Wittgenstein.
6. The Latin word *factum* did not denote the modern sense of "facts" but simply something done or performed. The term *factical* stems from Heidegger's concept of *Faktizität*.
7. In some respects, proto-phenomenology can be traced back to Aristotle, who seems unique in the Western tradition up until the nineteenth century. For Aristotle, human beings belong in the natural world and are at home in it. There is no other reality than the world we inhabit. Unlike Platonism, medieval philosophy, or even modern philosophy, human existence is not subject to some fundamental flaw (respectively: embodiment, the fall, or common sense) that philosophy is called upon to repair. For Aristotle, the ordinary world of our experience is fully prepared and meant to elicit philosophical understanding. Philosophy therefore will begin with how the world already appears to us in various ways *before* we philosophize (*Physics* 184a16–21; *Parts of Animals*, 640a15ff), and phenomena should be understood essentially as perceptible wholes (*Physics* 184a 22–27; *Parts of Animals* 645a31–37) in the way that things (like trees) present themselves to us in ordinary experience—an orientation that distinguished Aristotle's thinking from Platonic transcendence and the elemental reductions of earlier natural philosophers and atomists. For an account of the relevance of Aristotle's thinking even today, see David Roochnik, *Retrieving Aristotle in an Age of Crisis* (Albany, NY: SUNY Press, 2013).
8. Starting with the thingly character of the world in this manner was Aristotle's orientation. See *Physics* 184a14ff, *Metaphysics* I.10, and 1061a30ff.
9. I fear that some readers will find my work philosophically uninteresting because it deals with so much that is "obvious." But that is part of my point: Philosophical analysis *should* begin with what is obvious and *implicated* in what philosophy is all about. At any rate, too much finery in philosophy has caused me to find the obvious interesting.
10. The presumption of immanence can include an examination of religion, not in terms of transcendent domains or metaphysical claims but religious existence, the human impulse toward spiritual meanings, and the factical way of life animated by such meanings.
11. This constitution of objects *by way of* the thinking subject was clarified and completed in the work of Kant. For an account of how Kant's philosophy applies to modern natural science in specific terms, see Michael Friedman, *Kant's Construction of Nature: A Reading of the* Metaphysical Foundations of Natural Science (Cambridge: Cambridge University Press, 2013).
12. The "common sense" philosophy of Thomas Reid challenged the remedial and skeptical posture of modern philosophy toward normal beliefs and everyday assumptions. A helpful overview is John Greco, "Common Sense in Thomas Reid," *Canadian Journal of Philosophy* 41, no. S1 (2014): 142–55.

13. *Novum Organum*, in *The Philosophical Works of Francis Bacon*, trans. Robert L. Ellis and James Spedding, ed. John M. Robinson (London: Routledge, 1905), 27.

14. Immanuel Kant, *The Critique of Pure Reason*, trans. Werner S. Pluhar (Indianapolis, IN: Hackett, 1996), Bxiii. This is a route toward understanding what has been called the theory-ladenness of scientific findings, the selective preconditions setting out what will be looked for and how it will be investigated.

15. Charles Taylor sees a connection between modern thought and traditional fall-and-return narratives. See *Sources of the Self: The Making of Modern Identity* (Cambridge, MA: Harvard University Press, 1989), 351. A less fanciful way to advance a remedial script would be to assume that early human cultures were pursuing explanatory aims but in a defective manner that science came to repair (for instance, belief in gods as causes of natural phenomena). To whatever extent this is the case, science can be seen as an advance, but the notion that early cultural beliefs were nothing more than explanatory gropings is tenuous at best. For an account of mythical thinking as less an explanatory project and more an expression of the lived world, see my *Myth and Philosophy: A Contest of Truths* (Chicago, IL: Open Court, 1995), especially chaps. 1–2.

16. The notions of lived experience and pre-reflective experience differ from the empiricist notion of "sense experience," which is examined from the third-person standpoint and by way of abstract categories such as data, impressions, and qualia.

17. The notion of indicative concepts is a rendition of what Heidegger called formal indication.

18. In his search for definitions, Socrates was looking for essences that could not be satisfied by citing particular instances. That is why he would not accept examples of courageous behavior in trying to define courage. The essence of courage will unify particulars by way of a governing principle that no example can suffice to capture. It should be noted that my sense of nominal indication is different from traditional theories of "nominalism," which do not reject essences but simply their ontological status apart from the organizing functions of language. In my use, indicative concepts are not "essences."

Chapter One

Proto-Phenomenology and the Lived World

1. ECSTATIC DWELLING

I begin a proto-phenomenological account by characterizing pre-reflective experience as *ecstatic*. I use this word in connection with the ancient Greek word *ekstasis*, literally "standing-outside" and carrying a meaning of absorbed captivation.[1] Ecstatic experience involves an *immersion* in activity that is not experienced as conscious reflection on a "self" relating to an external action scene; there is simply the *doing*, an absorbed involvement with the world, without being self-conscious about it. The "standing-out" connotation is meant to capture immersion *in an environment*, in something outside the self and not simply a psychological state. There is also ecstatic immersion in simply experiencing something, shown in various circumstances of engaged attention or fascination, as in "suspension of disbelief," when we get absorbed in an artistic performance as though it were a real event or inhabit an imaginary world in reading literature.[2] We can also be immersed in a conversation or even in thinking something through without reflective attention to "speech" or "thought." Naturally, ecstatic immersion can be and often is interrupted by conscious reflection standing back from involvement. But I argue that ecstatic dwelling has a certain precedence over conscious reflection, and I hope the details of the coming analysis will be persuasive of that. In any case, ecstatic dwelling precedes the subject-object binary and may be able to resolve or dissolve a host of philosophical problems that stem from dividing reflective thought (beliefs, ideas, concepts) from its supposedly external environment (things, events, activities). One key problem in this regard is radical skepticism.

1.1. Skepticism

The problem of skepticism is a central element in modern thought, as shown in the writings of Descartes and Hume. Doubt can be a healthy disposition, but in modern philosophy skepticism reaches further than specific doubts of this or that idea, all the way to doubts about the very possibility of knowledge or the existence of the external world. Three related assumptions seem basic to this kind of radical skepticism: 1) the principle of indefeasibility, in which no belief can be warranted unless immune from doubt, unless proven to a strict certainty; 2) the division of self and world into subject and object; and 3) the realm of thinking understood as "representing" things in the world. Yet since dwelling is not originally an internal consciousness over against an external world but rather *is* world-involvement, the notion that subjective consciousness should pursue a demonstration that its environment exists shows that here reflection has disengaged from a prior mode of existence that makes it possible to pose such a question in the first place.[3]

A critique of skepticism from the standpoint of dwelling might be confirmed by considering some telling admissions in the arguments of Descartes and Hume. Descartes was not a skeptic in the end, but he used a rigorous method of doubt in the pursuit of certainty so that any possibility of error or deception could be weeded out of cognition. In *Meditations* I,[4] Descartes confesses that his attempt to subject normal beliefs to radical doubt meets stiff resistance: "For long-standing opinions keep returning, and, almost against my will, they take advantage of my credulity." He admits that he will never get out of the "habit" of believing in them as long as he takes them to be what they are, "highly probable, so that it is much more consonant with reason to believe them than to deny them." But in order that no such "bad habit" should turn his judgment "from the correct perception of things," he decides to *deceive* himself and *pretend* "for a while that these judgments are wholly false and imaginary." One could say that here Descartes is haunted by the lived world, and so the quest for certainty must deploy self-deception and pretense to overcome the intimacies of normal experience (which surely is an honest and revealing admission by Descartes). He goes on to mitigate his pretense of excessive doubt with the assurance that he will not fall into error because here he is "concentrating only on knowledge, not on action." The division between knowledge and action, theory and practice, is familiar in the history of philosophy and becomes perfected in the hyper-reflective posture of radical skepticism. Because dwelling, however, involves an essential practical engagement with its environment, "knowing" cannot be utterly detached from "doing." Accordingly, Descartes's "pretense" might not be a justified methodological tactic but rather a *philosophical* deception.

Hume's skepticism can be read in a similar manner. In the *Enquiry* IV.2,[5] after the critique of causal thinking, Hume considers the objection that his practices in ordinary life would betray his skeptical conclusion. Yet he says that the objection is a misunderstanding of his project. As an *agent* he is "quite satisfied that the future will be like the past; but as a *philosopher* [my emphasis] . . . I want to know what this confidence is based on. Nothing . . . has yet been able to remove my difficulty." Later in the text (XII.2), while reiterating the validity of skeptical challenges to basic beliefs and conceding its disconnection from normal existence, Hume says that "the great subverter of excessive skepticism is *action*, practical projects, the occupations of everyday life." Yet skepticism still flourishes and triumphs "in the philosophy lecture-room"—because as he had said earlier (XII.1), "the slightest philosophy is enough to destroy" common beliefs in things like the real existence of external objects. What Hume calls habit and custom are the living antidotes to skepticism, but such ways of being cannot be decisive for *philosophy*.

In the course of their skeptical projects, both Descartes and Hume admit that the factical world is existentially compelling but not philosophically decisive or even relevant to philosophy. But when philosophy disengages from this pre-philosophical environment it can run astray, especially when we consider the fact that skepticism itself is a practice in the lived world, a written or spoken offering to an audience, with the aim of having an effect on people's thinking. Accordingly, if skeptics are sincerely uncertain about the external world or other minds, they have to put in doubt the very setting and point of their own endeavor. So philosophy itself (*as* a communicative practice) undermines radical doubt. Once dwelling in the world is presumed, radical skepticism is dissolved as a problem because skepticism itself is a move in the world.[6]

In dwelling, we inhabit the world as a familiar extension of ourselves; we know our way around, so to speak. Naturally there are unfamiliar elements of experience and in extreme cases familiarity can be utterly undone. But human life could never function well or prosper without a bedrock of comprehension and customary practices that fit us for coping with the world and pursuing what we care about. Because dwelling and world are coextensive, the meaning of "world" must be understood not as the external world in the brute sense of objective surroundings, but as a horizon of meaningfulness or a context of concern—as indicated in something like "the art world" or "He lost his whole world when she died." So when "world" is used in this investigation it pertains to milieus of existential meaning and not simply "objective reality." A world of meaning is phenomenologically prior to objectivity in the strict sense because even objectification must be meaningful (a preferred or proper path to knowledge). The notion of world can be articulated in three ways: the personal-world, the environing-world, and the social-world.[7] It is important to stipulate that these constructions amount to one world with three dimensions, that each dimension is correlative with the others in a reciprocal network, and that no one dimension can be understood apart from the others.

2. THE PERSONAL-WORLD

The personal-world pertains to human selves, not in terms of abstract models of selfhood or identity that are typical in philosophical discussions (consciousness, thinking subject, intentional subject), but rather the personal life that each of us leads, what it is like to live in the world, expressed in first-person language, which is a grammatical indication that experience is *mine*. In this way, the self is not a "what" but a *who*, how one is engaged in life experiences and narratives. The personal-world does not connote something intrinsically selfish or egoistic, and it is not reducible to something purely individual or introspective (as we will see); it involves how the world *matters* to each of us, how everything we do is something we care about, even if what we care about is overcoming the ego, changing the world, or proclaiming the meaninglessness of existence. So statements like "I am a scientist," "I want to help you," or "I am working against injustice" are all expressions of the personal-world.

The personal-world need not have a bearing on objective findings in certain disciplines such as mathematics or natural science, but it cannot be excluded in a comprehensive philosophical examination of any such discipline or any area of life because existential meaningfulness is always animating the area in question—as in the importance of, and commitment to, screening out personal interests in scientific work or the value of, and attraction to, such work. Some disciplines can go wrong if they exclude the personal element and presume to be purely objective (such was the charge against traditional philosophy made by Kierkegaard and Nietzsche). And surely personal concerns are the first and last word for all of us when it comes to human mortality and our fate in the world.

Proto-phenomenology itself begins with attention to first-person orientations that open up the meaningfulness of the lived world, which is suppressed or concealed if the "impersonal" third-person standpoint is assumed to be the starting point and baseline foundation for philosophical investigation.[8] An *indicative* approach to the personal-world must be careful not to slip into a third-person orientation that bypasses the actual experience of the one taking the approach—as is the case right now when I simply offer this conceptual rendition of the personal-world. The *meaningfulness* of the world that proto-phenomenology aims to advance will lack animation if it is merely posed as attention to "what it is like" to experience something in general terms. It is important to add "what it is like *for me*" to experience something. At the same time, it must be stressed that the personal-world is not something merely subjective because it simply initiates a phenomenological method of inquiry and is by no means a restriction to individual selfhood conceived as something distinct from the wider world. Accordingly, the first-person standpoint in phenomenology cannot merely be a matter of introspective mental states, of intentional consciousness, of beliefs and desires related to actions in the world, but rather indicative attention to ecstatic immersion in *fields* of action. That is why each personal-world is inextricably caught up in the environing-world and social-world.[9]

3. THE ENVIRONING-WORLD

The environing-world names the range of natural, social, and cultural milieus in which the self is situated and which present the *affordances* that make human action and practices possible in an *ecological* network.[10] A phenomenological ecology cannot begin with discrete regions of agents and external surroundings, but rather the field-concept of meaning-laden ecstatic immersion.[11] Practical dealings with the environment are a good place to start.[12]

3.1. Immersion and Exposition

I draw a distinction between engaged *immersion* and disengaged *exposition*, the latter term meant to capture occasions when we do experience entities as "objects," as outlying things to be observed and examined rather than put to use in practical tasks.[13] Here the word *exposition* is meant to suggest the "positioning" of a thing "apart" from the self and immersed practice. Immersion, however, does not exhibit such delineations. The phenomenon of usage, in its performative sense, cannot be understood sufficiently by way of exposited descriptions of a user, an instrument, and the activity; we must begin with an *indicative* concept of use, with what it is like *to be using* an instrument in a nonreflective manner. When absorbed in writing, I am not explicitly conscious of my hand as such or my pen as an object bearing properties, or even the larger purpose of my writing; these things are recessed as tacit elements in the immersed practice. Not only is object-language inadequate for the phenomenon of immersion, so too is a model of "exchange" between a subject and an object, between intention, perception of a suitable tool, and application of an aim to its execution with the tool. It seems that conscious analyses and inferences cannot fit the smooth, automatic performance of skilled activity.[14] Such activity is not empty or aimless; it is intelligent in being saturated with meaning and purposefulness, though in a tacit manner. Skilled practices exhibit *circumspection*, or knowing one's way around the practice field and understanding its implications; also *capaciousness*, or knowing how to do something. Normally nothing we do is out of the blue or restricted to the immediate practice at hand. There are wider spheres of circumspection concerning how the activity fits within an extended field of operation and broader narratives. And capacious know-how is a practical intelligence that is not overtly characterized as mental states or propositional forms (knowing-that); it is fully exhibited *in* the practice without having to be articulated. More on this shortly.

3.2. Exposition and Contravention

An explicit awareness of intentions and external conditions usually arises when there is some disturbance in the practice. If my pen runs out of ink or feels uncomfortable after a while, it becomes *exposited* as a thing with properties. The disturbance turns my attention to relevant aspects of the pen (the tip, ink supply, weight, etc.) that are recessed in the activity of writing. I also attend to the purposeful background of the practice in the face of obstacles (I cannot finish writing until I get a refill or another pen). Common reactions to a disturbance (being annoyed or frustrated) *show* the implicitly purposeful character of the practice, so that meaningfulness is intrinsic to the activity in a way that would not be the case for a robotic writing device that broke down, which would simply stop working. Annoyance presupposes that a disturbance has interfered with something that matters, that is infused with existential import. In any case, disturbances to a practice bring its tacit meaning and recessed features to the foreground, usually with a view toward restoring or revising the practice.

What follows is that the meaningfulness of a practice is caught up with an awareness of finitude and limits. As living beings, we are needful of conditions to survive and prosper; yet such conditions can fail or be lacking, which accounts for the natural fragility of life. Practical disturbances specify something that pervades human comportment, namely that meaning is structurally related to some negative condition of privation or deprivation. The meaning in question here is more than simply conceptual or semantic—for instance, when the meaning of the word *success* is understood in contrast to its antonym *failure*—because it has to do with factical meaningfulness, in which the importance, value, and exhilaration of success are *experienced* in terms of both the benefits of success and the looming possibility of failure. If it were not possible to fail at something, performance would not be perceived as success. The same meaning structure is exhibited in any number of existential juxtapositions: sickness and health, loss and gain, death and life. The indicative concept I assign to disturbances and limit conditions is *contravention*, in the sense of something that comes (*venire*) to disrupt (*contra*) meaningful immersion. Contravention can be shown in matters of breakdown, resistance, obstacles, mistakes, absence, lack, danger, surprise, disorder, and unusual or unfamiliar occurrences.[15] More subtly, even phenomena such as wonder, amazement, and curiosity can be considered instances of, or responses to, contravention, in that ordinary familiarity is disrupted by a break with the commonplace and an opening for fresh discovery. In any case, it is contravention that prompts the shift from ecstatic immersion to exposition.

The unfolding of exposition out of immersion helps situate the subject-object distinction in this phenomenological account. The first order of the lived world involves practice-fields that show a confluence of self and environment that is not experienced as a subject-object transaction, as internal cognitive states applied to external things. What functions here is not primarily a propositional knowing-that but a performative knowing-how and a purposeful knowing-for—whose implicit meanings and features become explicit in the face of contraventions. This is not to deny an objective world in the sense of things apart from awareness and use, nor is it to deny subjectivity in the sense of mental beliefs and intentions. It is to say that the modern subject-object binary cannot do justice to engaged practices. With respect to the notions of mental beliefs and external objects, *both* are exposited out of a prior field of ecstatic immersion—when we become conscious of intentions and their settings in the midst of some contravention. This is how proto-phenomenology differs from so-called phenomenological treatments in analytic philosophy, which are grounded in representational relations and expositional distinctions between objective conditions and introspective, subjective mental states—for instance, the examination of "phenomenal qualities" in debates between externalism and internalism, realism and anti-realism, or the relationship between perceptual properties like color and mental experiences *of* such properties.[16]

In a broad sense exposition gives rise to a prevailing tendency in philosophy and other forms of analysis, namely *reification*, a framing of discrete "entities" marked off from other entities and relations. Reification is not restricted to things and objects in the familiar sense. It can involve any demarcation that provides a concentrated focus, such as a concept versus a percept or a mind versus a body. Reification is a natural and important form of comprehension, but the immersion-exposition distinction points to the limits of its scope. The phenomenon of immersed writing can be exposited into a number of focal points: hand, pen, paper, intention, and so on. The practice itself is no less real but it resists reification, even as "writing," which is an exposited focus that is not as such in view normally *when* writing. Proto-phenomenology has less to do with "entities" than with *ways* of acting and living that elude reification and discrete delineations, that are hard to articulate except in an indicative manner. Ecstatic ways of acting in the world allow us to extend philosophical attention beyond familiar categories. For instance, we can say that there is a phenomenon called "making a wooden chair," which can be exposited into subjective and objective elements before, during, and after the process of production (intentions, plans, materials, executions, producer, product). But the immersed activity is better rendered in an ecological way as making-a-chair-out-of-wood, a dynamic field phenomenon that can only be described in an indicative manner. Indicative concepts afford a sense of "being" that is more verb-oriented than noun-based, that can apply to temporal, historical, and social phenomena—which are fully real but not amenable to standards of object-designation, fixed form, individuation, or constant presence. Hence we can legitimately talk of phenomena such as "being educated" or "being a parent." Exposited reification cannot be the first or last word with such phenomena. Even the indicative exposition of, say, a football game is derived from, and cannot fully articulate, what it is like to play or experience the game in a factical sense.

It is important to add that immersion and exposition can be exhibited in varying degrees. So it is not a matter of simply proposing sheer absorption or reflective disengagement alone in mutual exclusion; they can overlap in different proportions (more on this shortly). In addition, immersion and exposition are not restricted to practical dealings with the environment. One can be immersed in thought, in reading, or in conversation. There can even be a kind of reflection *in* an immersed activity (like writing), which is different from exposited reflection *about* an activity. Habitual behaviors like walking, talking, getting dressed, and so on exhibit forms of immersion. Indeed, most patterns and dealings in life can be experienced in an absorbed manner. One can even be immersed in one's culture, job, or social roles in different ways and degrees. The point is that immersion need not suggest a psychological feeling of *fusion* with something, but simply nonreflexive performance without directed attention. Exposition of these kinds of absorption can arise from different types of contravention, at times from outside incursions, at other times from internal malfunction or discomfiture. In any case, a break with expectations or conduciveness can prompt the exposition of any immersed activity and its significance. In the next chapter I will have more to say about the function and scope of exposition.

3.3. Everyday Exposition

Both immersion and exposition are fully real conditions, which are shown and marked in the *shifts* between the two perspectives. From a phenomenological standpoint, however, exposition is derived from immersion by way of contravention, by some interference with the flow of the practice-field. The initial effect of contravention can be understood in a presentational manner, as a direct illumination of exposed significance, rather than some articulated representational inference. Such presentational effects can also be part of ongoing engagement, as in the case of learning through mistakes, which is understood in light of the overall significance of a practice. Particular facets of an activity can emerge through trial and error, and so the familiar notion of learning by doing includes learning by failing.[17] In general terms, most of human experience is an interwoven circulation of immersion, contravention, and exposition, a dynamic that is driven by the existential meaning of practices caught up in variegated environments that can support, thwart, or complicate human efforts.

The meaningful and purposeful background of practices is retained in everyday exposition because attention to environmental conditions stems from caring about the project at hand and how to resolve a disturbance. In ordinary exposition we are still not likely to think in terms of abstract categories like "representations" and "objects." In everyday life we remain involved in particular circumstances, such as my writing project. Modern philosophical models have been wedded to scientific objectivity, which is a sophisticated extension of ordinary exposition that does indeed require drawing back from common sense practices and learning highly abstract conversions of natural things into disengaged "material objects." The everyday exposition of a malfunctioning tool is still embedded in its specific features and role in a meaningful task. Such normal experience is put aside in scientific thinking in order to discover universal and measurable features of entities as such, independent of value or use—in which a broken tool that interrupts my fixing something now becomes an "object" bearing "properties" and subject to natural laws. Scientific disengagement and its modern philosophical legacy can uncover genuine truth about the natural world—for instance, a causal account of how a tool came to break—but not exclusive truth. As a specific *context* of discovery, scientific constructions should not be taken as dispositive of all philosophical questions or the full nature of human action. If a box is "too heavy" to lift, I can respond by looking for someone to help me or perhaps get a dolly. Scientific thematization disregards this existential horizon by way of conversion into measurable elements of mass, weight, and gravitational force, an explanatory order *derived* from factical settings through methods of abstraction and quantification—but no longer *attentive* to the meaning of such settings (too heavy to lift).

Everyday exposition shows a kind of *factical* reflection wherein we think about specific concerns, survey possibilities, or examine elements of our needs and activities. Here the word *exposition* captures the familiar connotation of articulating the aspects and meaning of a practice. Yet this is something different from *philosophical* reflection about knowledge, mental faculties, ontological properties, and so on, although it helps show how philosophical examination is not an alien invader but an extension and modification of ordinary exposition, which will be developed further in the next chapter.

3.4. The Scope of Immersion

Because the relation between ecstatic immersion and exposition is crucial for my analysis, I need to provide more preliminary examination. Surely objective descriptions and talk of mental states are valid, but attention to pre-reflective practices that do not exhibit a transaction between beliefs and external conditions could move standard models of cognition to suggest unconscious representations or inferences that are intrinsic to the practice, an insertion that at least is phenomenologically suspect. Representational and inferential analysis could legitimately be taken as a reconstruction or reverse engineering of a purposeful practice, but the question concerns whether the terms of such analysis are necessary for, or always operational in, the practice as such. In the case of riding a bike, I do not follow a sequence of intentions guiding the execution of movements. I can even daydream while riding or lose sight of my aims and simply enjoy the ride.

Yet what about learning new practices or confronting unfamiliar situations? In cases of, say, learning a new language or how to play the piano, there seems to be a clear sense of reflective distance apart from the practice and a kind of division between mental states and external conditions: that word *Welt* is the German word for my word *world*, that note on the page refers to this key that I must remember to hit with this finger, and so forth. This quite rightly involves distinct spaces of exposited reflection and objectification (because of the contravening effects of having to learn an unfamiliar practice). Yet even here ecstatic immersion is not canceled out because such learning milieus must bank on other skills and familiarities that make the learning possible: I already understand what words and notation are, how to follow instructions, how to converse, how to use relevant devices such as books and pencils, and so on—a background of immersion that is usually neither noticed (unless something gets in the way) nor thematized in the learning environment. Such capacities and many more can be traced all the way back to childhood, when we were first outfitted for engaging the world. In addition, when a new practice has been mastered it becomes a nonreflective and skillful competency, which is to say it becomes the immersion of "second nature" in which one can speak the language or play the piano without rules, reflective distance, bilocation, or analytical dissection. The immersed character of second nature shows that the relationship between immersion and exposition can be *bi-directional*. The reflective posture of learning skills can evolve into new modes of smooth, automatic practice.

Second nature is key to an understanding of dwelling. "First" nature applies to instincts and behaviors that are not learned, such as those possessed by neonates from the start (sucking, crying, grasping). The full range of human capacities, however, must be learned or prompted by the social environment. After initial periods of guidance and training, such capacities become a matter of *habit*, which indicates an acquired skill that no longer needs external direction or self-conscious attention.[18] As *second* nature, habits exhibit an automatic facility that is analogous to first nature. As second *nature*, habits are skills that we have an intrinsic capacity to develop, a potentiality poised to be actualized.[19] Second nature is also exhibited in the manner of expertise, which I would call a special elevated level of ability within an overall range of practical skills and immersed activities. I do not think that there is any fundamental difference between everyday competencies and expert performance, beyond obvious differences in skill levels and the types of training involved.[20] In any case, second nature shows immersed performances that stem from learned behaviors, which involve initial conditions of exposition or rule following. This accounts for the ambiguity in proffering the "rationality" of human behavior. A skilled behavior can be exposited with post hoc explanations and reasons, along with steps followed in acquiring the skill. So there are rational elements implicit in the behavior, yet without it being executed *by way of* rational guidance.[21]

In summation, ecstatic immersion and second nature illustrate the in-habited character of human dwelling that proto-phenomenology is aiming to explicate. In addition to overcoming the subject-object division, such phenomena call into question a longstanding assumption in philosophy that consciousness is at the base of human knowledge and experience, as in Descartes's *cogito ergo sum*, Kant's provision that the "I think" must be able to accompany any representation and is the unified ground of any stable experience and knowledge,[22] or Locke's claim not only that consciousness is "inseparable from thinking," but also that it is "impossible for anyone to perceive, without perceiving, that he does perceive."[23]

3.5. Consciousness

It is important to identify the complex problem of what is meant by the term *consciousness* because my analysis bears on the use of this and related terms. I want to stipulate a distinction between *consciousness* and *self-consciousness*, in which the former denotes wakeful awareness and the latter reflexive awareness and introspection (plus the vaunted *cogito* or "I think" born in modern philosophy). *Unconsciousness* would pertain to nonawareness, as in sleep or biological functions like digestion. Consciousness could therefore apply to wakeful activities that are not reflexively self-conscious. Cases of ecstatic immersion and habitual practice accordingly could be called conscious in being wakeful awareness (and even acutely attentive, as in sophisticated tasks like writing or cooking)—that is to say, they are not unconscious in the strict sense, yet they are not self-conscious or exposited in the full sense.[24] In mixed conditions of engaged practice with exposited moments (that is, neither reflexive self-consciousness nor disengaged exposition, nor sheer immersion), one can talk of *attentive consciousness*.[25] Finally, *sub-consciousness* could pertain to states that are no longer or not yet conscious, as in unretrieved memory, or to influences on thought and behavior that have not come to awareness. The primary distinction in my analysis is between engaged immersion and disengaged exposition, but I note the various terms pertaining to consciousness because they are deployed in different ways in fields such as cognitive science and psychology. This is especially the case with recent research into "unconscious" thought processes and activities, which could apply to my sense of (conscious) immersion and sub-consciousness.[26] From my perspective, elements of human activity that are sometimes described as unconscious or not requiring consciousness would be better deemed activities that are not self-conscious or attentive in an expository manner. I will deploy the primary distinction between immersion and exposition in terms of nonreflective and reflective comportment, but the complications noted here about connotations of consciousness and unconsciousness must be kept in mind and specifically sorted out when appropriate.[27] *Consciousness* has been such a common term in philosophy and psychology that it is hard to avoid. Yet its association with subjectivity and epistemology can hide the ecstatic, ecological character of dwelling emphasized in this study. Although consciousness has indicative sense with respect to wakeful awareness, its philosophical baggage gets in the way of proto-phenomenological description.

3.6. Representation

The notion of representation is a prevailing concept in contemporary philosophy of mind, cognitive science, and linguistics. Representations involve various mental objects (beliefs, concepts, percepts, rules, structures, images) and their referential function, which then brings questions concerning the relation between thoughts, intentions, brain states, or words and corresponding aspects of the world.[28] The primary assignment of representational models is to provide and articulate causal explanations of human thought, experience, and behavior. There is debate over the status of what are called common sense or folk psychology explanations, in which a person's beliefs or desires explain and predict his or her behavior. Some find these explanations salient while others take them as remnants of pre-scientific thinking that should be exchanged for physiological explanations—this latter orientation reflecting a strong trend calling for the "naturalization" of mentality by reference to neurological research and representations in the brain. There is also a debate between internalism and externalism, about whether representational content is caused by intrinsic mental/neurological properties or extrinsic properties of the world and social conventions. Representational theories work with the primary distinctions of reference (denotation), meaning (connotation), and objects of reference. The most basic questions involve how representational relations obtain (how thoughts, words, or brain states match up with their objects), how representations can be assessed, and how representations in one mind can be communicated to another mind.

In proto-phenomenology, ecstatic immersion is not a representational relation but a presentational immediacy. Even accounts drawn from folk psychology (beliefs or desires causing or explaining behavior) stem from an expositional disengagement from lived experience. The very idea of a representation, I submit, is not indicated in most pre-reflective activities, but it has been made possible by the objectification of language in written graphics. In much philosophy of mind, what I call presentational immersion comes to be exposited (or re-presented) as a coordination between mental states and objects and fleshed out in such notions as information processing, brain maps, propositional attitudes, and computational theories of mind.

I suspect that the attraction of representational models arises from 1) the clarity gained from analytical distinctions and 2) the conviction that otherwise human experience and behavior would not be intelligible (my writing this book must be explained by transactions between intentions, plans, and execution) or intelligently responsive (in having some inner modality that can connect with extracranial realities). But proto-phenomenology points to an intelligence in pre-reflective behavior, for which representational explanations are neither necessary nor sufficient conditions. Such explanations are not useless; they can be accounted for as expositional derivations from engaged immersion and they can prepare new occasions of immersion, as indicated earlier in the learning of practices that become second nature, which shows a bi-directional relation between exposition and immersion. Yet immersed practices *in performance* do not exhibit a representational character, and so the only recourse for representational theories would be something like unconscious representation, which is hard to fathom phenomenologically.[29]

The prioritization of representational thinking may be due to the very posture of advanced philosophical thinking, which is a highly reflective departure from factical life and which is then prone to presuming the same for all human comportments, in the manner of mental structures applied to the outside world. Yet this may be called the *philosopher's fallacy*, borrowing from what Dewey named the "psychologist's fallacy," which is the "confusion of experience as it is to the one experiencing [it] with what the psychologist makes out of it with his reflective analysis."[30] My use of indicative concepts is meant to avoid this fallacy and pay heed to factical experience in its pre-expositional, immersed character.

Retrieving the example of learning to play the piano, consider the following: My wife is a trained pianist who can sight-read a new piece of music with relative ease. I am not a trained musician, yet I know enough about music to learn an easy Bach piece, for example, but it takes weeks. I figure out each note and the right fingering. Then I practice each measure until I have it mastered and memorized. Eventually I can play the entire piece by heart, without looking at the score (which I could not read and play at the same time anyway). One day I was playing a piece and got completely stuck at one point and could not remember the next part. I looked for the score to relearn it, but my wife told me to just start the piece over, which I did, and played through the whole piece without getting stuck. She said it was "muscle memory"— an instance of sheer know-how apart from any conscious guidance— which would explain the automatic retrieval without the score and without my "remembering" it. It was strange, in effect, to see myself play through the stuck part, as though another pair of hands were performing something I had forgotten. It seems clear that such an experience could not be explained in representational, intentional, propositional, or inferential terms.[31]

Representational models re-present or "reverse engineer" immersed practices, but *in situ* their presentational character can suffice. Moreover, the model of intentional thought producing action does not fare well with improvising and adjusting behavior when the environment impinges upon activity (there will be more to say on this at the end of the chapter). The notion of representation is certainly not useless. I can imagine a tree or think about a tree in its absence, and many encounters with the world can be depicted in transactional terms, but representational thinking seems out of place in much of engaged dwelling. As Charles Taylor puts it:

> We can draw a neat line between my *picture* of an object and that object, but not between my *dealing* with the object and the object. It may make sense to ask us to focus on what we *believe* about something, say a football, even in the absence of that thing; but when it comes to *playing* football, the corresponding suggestion would be absurd.[32]

A chief advantage here is that the field-character of dwelling dissolves the baseline problem of how mental or neurological representations can "match up" with their objects (immersion simply *is* the coalescence of self and world). With that problem set aside, representational orientations can be allowed to perform whatever legitimate function they might serve—for instance, an articulation of learning environments or causal explanations of human processes in physiological terms. Beyond the mind-world relation, there are any number of representational functions that signify or denote entities, structures, and activities: photographs, gauges, maps, diagrams, road signs, turn signals, and so on. Given all this, especially the fact that representation is a natural consequence of the immersion-exposition dynamic, my analysis cannot be called anti-representational; it simply claims that representational accounts should yield philosophical priority to phenomenological descriptions of the lived world and ecstatic dwelling.

Given the traditional assumption that cognition involves mental states that are "internal" conditions as distinct from the external world (whether such conditions are Cartesian ideas or neurological brain states), there might be some consonance between my approach and what has come to be called "extended cognition."[33] The notion of an extended mind aims to overcome internalist conceptions of cognition by showing how external conditions (especially technological instruments and devices) and practical dealings with these conditions constitute or causally shape cognitive states. External props do not just contribute to cognition; they are essential parts of a cognition *system* that reaches beyond the brain. Yet such a notion remains confined to standard epistemological structures and processes in the nomenclature of cognitive science. The concept of representation is still at work, yet now in terms of complex intersections and feedback loops between external and internal representations.[34] Accordingly, I read extended cognition as still caught up in exposited distinctions derived from the more original phenomenological "extension" of ecstatic immersion.

The "transparency" of immediate presentation in ecstatic practices precedes the subject-object polarity that gave birth to what Hume called the "fundamental principle" of modern philosophy: the distinction between primary and secondary qualities.[35] Here, for instance, extension is a primary quality independent of the mind, while color is a secondary quality dependent on the subject's perception. The field-character of ecstatic immediacy allows for both qualities to be fully real in a phenomenological sense because they are exposed from an immersed environment that implicates them both in an amalgamation, which is neither independent of, nor dependent on, the participating self.

3.7. Know-How

Capacious practical immersion applies to the distinction between knowing-how and knowing-that, between practical ability and propositional knowledge (in cognitive science this distinction is sometimes rendered as procedural knowledge and declarative knowledge). There is an ongoing debate between intellectualism and anti-intellectualism concerning respectively whether know-how is governed by, or separable from, propositional knowledge. My phenomenological account certainly would not side with intellectualism because propositional knowledge pertains to exposition and not ecstatic immersion. Yet my approach is not anti-intellectualist in a strict sense because many forms of cognition can be implicit in, and exposited from, engaged practices, and learning environments can involve an array of propositional, factual, and representational aspects involved in skill acquisition. But when such aspects become recessed in the manner of second-nature habits, an intellectualist reduction to propositional knowledge is incongruous with the phenomenology of immersion.

The so-called anti-intellectualist position can be traced back to Gilbert Ryle, who in 1949 first gathered the notion of knowledge-how as part of an attack on Cartesian dualism and any of its descendants that prioritized mental constructs over behavioral conditions of practical life.[36] In the continental tradition, Merleau-Ponty and Hubert Dreyfus have critiqued intellectualism by emphasizing automatic habits, bodily performance, and skilled practices that are not rule-governed.[37] A recent attempt to defend intellectualism argues that know-how is "guided by" propositional knowledge, owing to a host of factual beliefs about practices that can be assumed or articulated in know-how.[38] A similar defense in cognitive science has even taken "articulation" to include behavioral demonstrations of the nature of a practice and presumes the possibility of "unconscious" declarative knowledge involved in know-how.[39] But such arguments are bound by representational/computational models of knowledge and experience that still rely on constructs drawn from modern philosophy, that are still susceptible to critique from anti-intellectualism, and that are challenged by findings in cognitive neuroscience, which show that know-how can be dissociated from propositional or declarative knowledge.[40] It seems right to distinguish know-how from theoretical reasoning, practical (inferential) reasoning, propositional knowledge, and even conceptual knowledge in a standard sense, in which concepts are context-independent while know-how is context-dependent.[41]

A good example of know-how distinct from propositional knowledge is the automatic performance of skilled athletes, in which the course of activity is a clear case of ecstatic immersion in which conscious analysis (exposition) can even hinder performance.[42] Such dimensions of experience are now receiving due attention in cognitive science and psychological research, described as "flow" or "effortless attention."[43] Here immersed experiences are characterized as a loss of self-consciousness, as a pleasurable display of capacity without strain or deliberation, in which performance can even surpass cases when conscious effort is in play. Within the experience of flow, contraventions or unexpected demands will bring out a sense of conscious effort. Yet even a shift to higher-level skills need not require proportional degrees of deliberate effort when flow is unobstructed. Moreover, there is neurological evidence that automatic practical and social skills do not require a process of conscious willing, indeed that consciousness may not be some primal faculty, but rather emergent in those moments when contraventions call for the preparation and execution of new or revised skills that in time themselves become automatic. Such is what I have called the bi-directionality of immersion and exposition.[44]

A proto-phenomenological account not only supports a clear difference between know-how and propositional knowledge, but also a certain priority of immersed performance over exposed cognition. Going back to the Greeks, we can notice a relevant historical priority in word usage because all terms that philosophers came to associate with "cognition," such as *phronēsis, sophia, gnōsis, eidenai*, and even *epistēmē*, originally denoted nonmentalistic notions of practical skill, acquaintance, and vision. As I will argue in volume 2, the very idea of a "proposition" only came to pass in the context of writing. And the Socratic search for "what" something is in a propositional sense—in terms of some unified, universal essence, as opposed to specific instances and practices—was in many respects a radically new venture. The difficulties experienced by Socrates's interlocutors cannot be attributed to sheer ignorance or evasion. It was more common for Greeks to understand, say, virtue in what I have called an indicative manner, signaling specific ways of being rather than an abstract concept. Yet they certainly knew *how to function* in their world with their language.[45]

Nevertheless, with respect to the debate between intellectualism and anti-intellectualism, we should not separate cognition and action in a binary manner. Proto-phenomenology shows that knowing-how and knowing-that can coalesce in a number of ways, particularly given the shifts from immersion to exposition, which includes the ability to articulate the significance and features of an engaged practice. Also relevant are the analytical and representational aspects of learning a new practice, as discussed earlier. Moreover, in chapter 3 I will argue that most human practices are saturated with linguistic meaning because entry into the human world is accomplished originally by language acquisition in childhood, which first shapes the contours and significance of practices.

Accordingly, the target of critique in this discussion is not the notion of propositional knowledge per se or its role in practical life, but the epistemological fixation on *reducing* knowing-how to knowing-that, the notion that propositional knowledge is somehow always functioning in engaged practices by governing or guiding such actions. I have argued that representational cognition can be utterly recessed in immersed activities and that sophisticated philosophical models of representational structures need not apply at all to everyday practices, in which ordinary language and indicative proto-concepts can suffice for exposition. I have also maintained that at least with developed skills and habits (in performance) propositional knowledge is neither a sufficient nor a necessary condition for such automatic enactments.

The notion of dwelling suggests that reflective exposition, whether in everyday or philosophical terms, is derived from a bedrock of nonreflective immersion in the lived world, which is why an explanatory reduction to "cognitive" states or the assumption that such states are the only provision for genuine intelligibility should be challenged.[46] The limits of cognition in this regard are well indicated in child development, in which much of what is learned arises from direct imitation, as well as trial and error. Yet even with adults we can notice the possibility of learning something, such as a dance move or a cooking technique, simply by physical imitation, without articulation or analytical steps (other than "Watch me and do this"). Here a nonpropositional know-how seems most evident.

3.8. Tacit Knowledge and Habit

Knowing-how and immersion can be gathered in the notion of "tacit knowledge," which was first formulated by Michael Polanyi.[47] Tacit knowledge is a comprehension or capacity that is not exposited, something that is not or need not be explained, articulated, or guided by rules. Tacit knowledge covers a wide range of abilities and understandings: riding a bike, practical skills, daily habits, social customs, facial recognition, working in a lab, speaking a language, reading this book. I would also include what I have called indicative proto-concepts, a kind of lived familiarity that has not been subjected to sophisticated philosophical explication.

Among the most important forms of tacit knowledge are habits, which cover the scope of routine behaviors that function without conscious attention and that form an essential foundation of life because otherwise we would have to deliberately guide and monitor every move we make in the world. Habits are situationally cued by context and operate according to a minimally conscious "procedural memory." Unlike an earlier behaviorist account of habit as a stimulus-response mechanism devoid of "mental" content, psychologists today understand habits as *implicitly* intentional and motivational in character.[48] Tacit knowledge also applies to what is called "automaticity," the immediate processing of one's environment without conscious awareness or intentionality, which issues a host of cognitive, behavioral, and motivational effects. In social psychology, early research on automaticity generally involved the negative effects of bias and stereotyping. But now it is understood how such processes also constitute a background regulative function that contributes to successful self-management and adaptation.[49] I would distinguish two main forms of tacit knowledge: 1) tacit *practical* knowledge, having to do with embodied abilities to perform tasks, and 2) tacit *cultural* knowledge in a broad sense, meant to cover linguistic, social, normative, and cognitive intimations that are recessed in the background of particular performances. As we will see in the next chapter, a tacit background can run very wide and deep, considering the range of comprehensions that normally go unnoticed in any specific attention to things, thoughts, or circumstances.

Something needs to be stressed in discussing tacit knowledge with respect to habit and automaticity. In much of the tradition, habit has been downplayed and even denigrated for purportedly being blind, mechanical, and thoughtless. But the notion of second nature allows us to see habit as spontaneous engagement with the world in a meaningful and intelligent manner.[50] The automatic immersion of habit should not be identified with mindless instinct or involuntary routines because they are meaning-laden and have to be learned. Habits occupy the full range of human capacities, in practical, social, ethical, artistic, and intellectual domains. Though learned and registered by repetition, habits are not bound by past conditions but open for coming occasions.[51] Skilled habits (as in athletics, for example) can be responsive, flexible, and creative. Altogether, habits enable multiple ways of comprehending and navigating the world and they endow the capacity for human self-expression.[52] Finally, habits are not rigidly ingrained because with contraventions they can be modified or changed.

Given the relationship between immersion and exposition established in this chapter, tacit and explicit knowledge should not be separated in a binary sense. Tacit knowledge can involve implicit meanings and characteristics that can be explicated, and some forms of tacit knowledge require elements of explicit knowledge in their acquisition. Moreover, the tacit and the explicit semantically imply each other; indeed the very notion of "tacit knowledge" is something made *explicit* in reflection, which reiterates the indicative character of proto-phenomenological inquiry.[53] In any case, I am emphasizing tacit knowledge that has some relationship with explicit knowledge, rather than something not explicable at all, as in utterly unconscious processes that cannot be brought to awareness or something sub-conscious that can only be brought to attention through a kind of reeducation or therapy.[54]

3.9. Immersion and Conscious Direction

Earlier it was noted that immersion and exposition can be exhibited in different degrees and can overlap in certain ways, as in the case of attentive consciousness. Exposition and conscious attention to practice scenarios not only play a role in developing habits and skilled performance, they also intersect with tacit abilities and automatic behaviors in the course of a sustained practice, especially in the case of skilled activities, with their complex details and need for fine-grained attention. In something like athletics, craft work, or surgery, for example, the course of activity fluctuates with varying levels of automaticity, explicit examination, and considered decisions, even when no significant contravention has occurred. Such performance is neither purely immersed nor purely reflective, but rather an episodic circulation of immersed action and attentive direction. Call this the "controlled" aspect of skilled performance, which is simply meant to characterize the shifting coordinations enacted by the agent and not some kind of systematic governance. Neither intellectualism nor anti-intellectualism can address the complex combination of immersion and conscious direction in skilled control.[55] Nevertheless, immersion and automatic behaviors retain a certain primacy, at least from a developmental standpoint. Skilled control is not a first-order condition of human existence.

3.10. The Scope of Proto-Phenomenology

One advantage of proto-phenomenology is its comprehensiveness because it can incorporate and account for an objective mode of being as a derivative, disengaged exposition out of engaged, purposeful practice. Subject-object frameworks have a difficult task in accounting for pre-reflective practice (if it is treated at all). As indicated before, in using my pen objective properties and self-consciousness are recessed. I normally do not experience writing as the mental formation of an intention that is transferred to bodily actions joined with external conditions judged to fit my intention—I simply pick up the pen and write. Another mark of comprehensiveness is the capacity to articulate engaged elements that usually go unnoticed in highly reflective activities as well. Even advanced domains of scientific knowledge cannot be divorced from the tacit competencies of scientific work (laboratory skills and normal practical habits). Indeed, science has its own environing-world that stands *between* scientific thinking and its results. Institutional settings, experimental scenarios, and various instruments are a kind of "mid-world" that is necessary for scientific findings but that is often recessed and usually not thematized in accounts of science.[56] In addition, a full picture of science cannot be separated from the interest in, and meaningfulness of, the scientific enterprise itself, especially the dispositional drive to find explanations and the satisfaction experienced in solving problems and discovering new facts. Finally, the birth of modern scientific thinking involved many cognitive *disruptions* of customary beliefs that prompted reflection and response, which fits the structure of emergence out of contravention discussed earlier. So science too is a lived world, and here there arises an opportunity to present a richer account of what science *is* in a more complete sense. The *background* of science shows its own personal-social-environing-world, its own range of habits and skills, an immersion-exposition dynamic, and activities saturated with purposes and cognitive/methodological norms.[57] A phenomenology of science need not affect particular scientific findings, but it can address inceptual, motivational, and personal dimensions in the *life* of science, which at the very least are important for attracting people to scientific work, but which I want to say figure in the nature of science as well—because scientific knowledge could not emerge apart from the background of its environing-world. So-called science and technology studies have done much to broaden and articulate the background of scientific work, which must take into account social, material, institutional, textual, normative, cultural, historical, and performative elements.[58]

3.11. Meaning and Value

The environing-world cannot be construed in brute objective terms because its practice-fields are intrinsically purposeful. That is why we can usually give reasons for our actions—an everyday phenomenon that is not the same as a *reductive* rational reconstruction of an action from a theoretical standpoint. Human practices serve aims and needs; they are *for the sake of* meaningful projects large and small. The existential importance of practical projects shapes a network of preferences, requirements, and satisfactions that issue estimations of practical and moral value, of what counts as worth doing or doing well. The *direct* (immersed) meaningfulness of the personal-environing-world shows that values and purposes are not "added on" to external circumstances as some kind of mental injection. Contrary to the fact-value/is-ought divide that took shape in modern science—in which the natural world is value-free, without purpose, and independent of human interests—in factical experience the world is interest-laden, so that from a phenomenological standpoint values and purposes can be said to have a kind of being in the world and not simply in the subject because the subject-object dichotomy is derived from a more original field of enveloping significance.[59] Human beings *dwell* in a meaningful world. When we live out moral values or respond to natural beauty or are excited by scientific investigation, such activities are not experienced as simply subjective projections upon a neutral world. The direction is not taken to be coming solely from us, but also from the setting in which we are engaged. Indeed, the environing-world, as a surrounding *place* of inhabitance, precludes human understanding of the lived world being reduced to any kind of subjectivism, even in sophisticated senses of idealism, constructivism, representationalism, or intentionalism. We dwell *in* the environing-world. We are *thrust* into it from birth and cannot help but engage with it and care about it.

A world of concern is anything but a merely objective domain set apart from its meaningfulness to us. Even nature, understood as an environing-world, is not simply a set of physical entities and forces, but settings of significance in terms of weather, seasons, daylight, nightfall, food, resources, habitation, wilderness, generation, destruction, beauty, fearsomeness, and so on. Finally, as suggested in the previous section, even natural science cannot be understood apart from certain values and purposes that animate scientific thinking, such as the virtues of honest work, open-mindedness, and self-correction, along with the affordances of prediction and control that serve human interests. Consequently, a strict fact-value divide is undermined within the sphere of science itself.[60] The kinds of norms and human character traits that figure in a wider picture of knowledge and its acquisition have been the purview of developments in normative and virtue epistemology.

The classic philosophical question concerning "the meaning of life" has often been cast in broad, universal terms. A more modest formulation would be the question of meaning *in* life. It may be true that an objective, scientific understanding of the natural world undermines traditional conceptions of *global* significance, that there is an ultimate meaning behind or following the emergence of the cosmos, that the finitude of mortality is overcome in some transcendent deliverance or progressive perfection. But a finite sense of meaningful lives in the natural world is not eclipsed by the absence of global meaning. So we want to be careful when a scientist tells us: "The more the universe seems comprehensible, the more it also seems pointless."[61] Nature by itself may disclose no sense of meaning, except when meaning *is* disclosed to natural inhabitants of the planet Earth. The global meaninglessness of the cosmos does indeed render human meaning finite and limited, but no less meaningful in existential terms. In fact, finitude is constitutive of meaning, as something discovered, chosen, and affirmed, rather than being inscribed in reality from the start. Given the presumption of immanence, there is no reason why the question of meaning should be measured by some global or cosmological standard. It is always already in play all the way down in factical life, but not in a uniform or universal manner.

To sum up section 3, the environing-world cannot be understood in purely objective or subjective terms, or even in some kind of intermediation of the two constructs. The lived world is a dimension of dwelling prior to differentiation into subjectivity and objectivity. In fact, the very notions of subject and object are not perennial terms in the history of philosophy; they have a strange history in the course of modern thought that reinforces a sense of their contingency. Surprisingly, in Scholastic philosophy the term *subjectum* referred to a substance existing independent of the mind and *objectum* referred to something mind-dependent.[62] Proto-phenomenology simply shows the blended field-character of dwelling that precedes any delineation of objective or subjective domains.

4. THE SOCIAL-WORLD

The modern conception of the self has mostly been individual-based. The disengagement of reflection divides the self not only from its environment, but also from other selves. The common view has taken social relations as a second-order sphere compared to the original immediacy of self-consciousness. Social arrangements and formats are understood as constituted by, or reducible to, individual conditions and interests. Epistemology has emphasized monological cognition, in which knowledge is analyzed from the standpoint of the individual mind, its faculties and rational procedures. The lived world suggests something different, a "social self," in which correlations with other selves are more original than strict individuation. Nothing in human life is performed in a vacuum; most activities are linked with other people in some way (my writing for readers with a pen and paper made by others, and so on). Very little of knowledge is a sheer individual construction. Given the role of testimony, trust, and corroboration—as well as our having been prepared for mature thinking by early social environments—monological models of knowledge should defer to a "social epistemology."[63]

The experience of social relations is not factically perceived as an inside-out conjunction of erstwhile interior selves. Others are just as much a part of my environing-world as the practical milieus discussed earlier, and there is a similar kind of ecstatic immersion wherein I am absorbed in joint engagements without an explicit division into separate selves. Normally I do not launch myself into social relations from the standpoint of a discrete self-consciousness. I simply dwell with others in innumerable co-concerns and interactions that occupy most of my (nonphilosophical) life. Say I am working with someone showing me how to restore an old piece of furniture, guiding me along in the various skills and handling of materials that mark the practice—pointing, talking, and helping at appropriate times. Phenomenologically this circumstance is a field of joint engagement and comprehension, rather than a matter of internal minds and external stimuli crisscrossing in some complex geometry. And surely the skeptical problem of the existence of other minds would not arise, given the intrinsic social structure of this activity.

Relevant here is the notion of "joint attention," which is the subject of a growing field of research in many different disciplines (philosophy of mind, phenomenology, psychology, cognitive science, neuroscience, child development, and ethology), the findings of which show that human mentality is an intrinsically social phenomenon, beginning in childhood but in maturity as well.[64] Primal capacities such as gaze following, pointing, and communicative looks are interpersonal, reciprocal functions that show a triangular structure of different selves inhabiting a common focus on something in the world. Here a shared experience and embodiment are the *starting point* for coming to understand aspects of the world and their significance. (It is noteworthy that the impairment of autism involves certain barriers to joint attention.) Accordingly, under normal circumstances the first-person and second-person perspectives are co-original in human comprehension.

Some treatments of joint attention remain wedded to representational and transactional models in accounting for a shared network. Other approaches, however, are more faithful to a social-world phenomenology by stressing an immediacy and embeddedness in shared attention, rather than some kind of referential process—so that joint "attention" is better rendered as joint *engagement*. Unlike representational transactions—where the problem of other minds might still find a foothold—joint engagement shows that we always already understand each other *as* minded beings in a common enterprise, as intelligent collaborators in a factical endeavor; so disagreements and disparities are *contraventions* of a default sense of mutual cohabitation. Joint engagement is evident at all levels of social interaction and is most refined in organized activities such as team sports and dance, in which the flow of performance is an irreducible blend of reciprocal comprehension and capacity.[65] In any case, both developmentally and performatively a shared world *precedes* the attribution of perceptual and cognitive states to discrete individual minds. A central feature of this precedence is the degree to which imitation serves human development. Right from birth, newborns display a capacity to imitate sounds, gestures, and behaviors, a fluid and integrated natural endowment that exceeds the capacities of other animals and that launches the full range of human linguistic, cognitive, and practical powers.[66] As will be shown in volume 2, the ecstatic immersion characterizing early imitation shows that the social environment prepares and makes possible the development of an individual child's propensities to engage the world.

The social-world does not entail an utterly uniform set of understandings across the board, in which individual members of the community see the world in the very same way. Individual differences in experience and comprehension persist, but there must be significant overlap in a shared world for human life to develop and function. Even a sense of individual identity—who one is, one's personal-world—cannot be separated from other persons and how one is engaged by them. The writings of Rousseau and Hegel initiated an understanding that *recognition* is essential to self-awareness and self-estimation, such that self-regard is interwoven with how we are regarded and engaged by others in social and practical milieus. Self-development and self-realization cannot be achieved apart from a host of intersubjective processes, affordances, and challenges.[67] This is not to deny individuality, distinctions between one's self and others, or the reality of introspection and self-consciousness; it is only to propose an ecstatic, intersecting social milieu that is more original than the individualized model of a conscious self. The validity of this proposal is strengthened by attention to child development, in which social interaction is essential for the development of all human capacities (which even a hermit will need) and in which individual self-consciousness emerges out of, and is made possible by, a prior social environment. Even an ideal of individual self-determination is socially shaped and encouraged by educational and institutional forces.

The summary point is this: the social-world is not some addendum to the personal-world; the former is only analytically distinct from the latter. Every personal-world is at the same time a social-world. As noted earlier, the first-person standpoint should not be confined to introspective subjectivity, for which intersubjective understanding requires inferential analysis to be intelligible, which therefore continues the reflective isolation of the Cartesian *cogito*—wherein the behavior of other persons is simply base data of the third-person kind that does not exhibit personal characteristics until it is surmised as such by conscious examination. In proto-phenomenology, however, the first-, second-, and third-person standpoints can have specific significance, but they are each expositionally derived from a more original field of ecstatic immersion, in which other human beings are *experienced* as persons like ourselves and *engaged* as co-inhabitants of a concernful world.[68] Only when introspective self-consciousness is presumed to be the starting point for selfhood is understanding other selves taken to be a "mind-reading" project, in which understanding other minds must be constructed in a series of inferences. Yet from early in life, humans become habituated in ways of being that *from the start* are socially charged and expressive of shared existential interest—and thereby originally "co-minded."

Introspective self-awareness certainly has a baseline presence for everyone from a psychological standpoint, but it should not be the absolute foundation for understanding selfhood. So much of what I do in daily life is relationally structured and often instigated by the claims of others upon me or behaviors toward me. Whatever one's own personal nature, a great deal of it is fueled by social environments. Why should introspective individuation be the first and last word with regard to selfhood, even with respect to self-knowledge? Beyond a Freudian perspective, in some ways I might not always know myself as well as others know me. If I have strong doubts about my abilities and feel like a failure, the assessment of others to the contrary could be more accurate.

4.1. Empathy

One avenue to understanding the social structure of selfhood and the ecstatic character of social experience is the phenomenon of empathy.[69] Empathy is a disposition that can be called an ecstatic dwelling with another person's weal and woe, an affective sense of another's circumstance that can involve positive and negative conditions—which thus includes both feeling the misfortune of others (as in sympathy or compassion) and enjoying their good fortune.[70] In any case, empathy is most clearly comprehended in its vicarious character, in which one feels the condition of another person without directly undergoing that condition—so I can feel happiness at someone's success when I myself am not in a successful situation and I can feel sorrow at someone's misfortune when my life is going well. Empathy is therefore an affective response that is more fitting of another person's situation than one's own. This is why the other-regarding character of empathy, though clearly different from self-regarding affects, should not be considered an "identity" with someone's feelings or a "union" of the self and another person; it sustains a distinction between oneself and others, so as to be experienced *as* related to the condition of another person and *as* one's own experience of this relation. An empathic response to someone's pain need not mean a "duplication" of that pain or circumstance, but simply being touched in some way by the person's suffering. Empathic relations can also have an intersubjective reciprocity, in which each person is altered by the other in a feedback loop, which is different from a mere "sharing" of experience. Having and receiving empathy modifies the posture of each person *as* a crossing of normal boundaries of self-regard.

Empathy is certainly not constant or uniformly exhibited because there are limits to empathic regard within and between selves, but some capacity for empathy seems to be normal for human beings (an incapacity for empathy is a central characteristic of so-called sociopaths). The occurrence of empathy appears to be contextual and situational, stemming from an intimation of another person's circumstance. So empathy is not simply affective because it also has cognitive aspects (as in empathic understanding) and is linked with memory, symbolic association, imagination, and role taking. Mature empathy, then, should be understood as a multidimensional blend of affective, cognitive, and participatory elements.[71] Yet affective empathy seems to be developmentally primal and the precondition for acquiring the other elements.[72] Most important, empathy appears to be natural to the human condition, rather than simply a cultural construct that is foisted upon the self.[73] Empathic regard is stronger among intimates and gets its start in that social milieu; it is not merely person-to-person because it also shows itself in group associations. Social identity has an important role in prompting empathy for in-group members, which at the same time can minimize or block empathy for out-group persons. So the initial dynamics of empathic relation can produce problematic divides between "us" and "them."[74] Nevertheless, with experience and exposure, circles of empathy can be expanded.

Empathy is a vivid example of ecstatic immersion in the social-world. Here the relational character of the self is not simply environmental in a situational sense, but a psychological enlargement of the self, a dwelling-with-others that feels their fate with engaged attunement. As a mode of dwelling, empathy should not be explained simply as a form of "transference," which follows the subject-object binary, wherein my feelings for another person are based on my own experience and transported out to an external scenario—so that my sympathy for someone's pain would arise from imagining what it is like or would be like for me to experience pain. The idea of transference certainly has some use in many cases of relating to others, but it seems insufficient for capturing a full phenomenological sense of empathic experience. Consider a face-to-face encounter with someone undergoing pain or misfortune. We can recognize the possibility of spontaneous and automatic affective responses that are immersed in the person's circumstance: We might wince, tears might well up, or sadness might come in immediate response to what is sensed of the person's body, facial expressions, or manner of speech. Analogous to the phenomenology of practical immersion that undermines the notion of representational/inferential processes, empathy shows moments when we simply are joined with another person's fate, a kind of emotional contagion that "comes over" us (which at times can even be an unwanted disturbance). Here we do not take in external data, process them as misfortune, trigger our memory bank, and then transfer them out to the other person—the joint affect simply happens. We are existentially *with* others in cohabitive caring.[75]

Empathy understood as a genuine capacity for shared concern and an enlargement of the self obviously has ethical implications in challenging psychological egoism, wherein self-interest is the full horizon of selfhood and other-regarding dispositions and measures are called into question, or intelligible only if translated into self-regarding benefits. Beyond ethical considerations, empathy can also be seen to play a role in the development of rationality because an attunement to extra-subjective vantage points can generate an open-minded bearing and a capacity for objectivity.[76]

4.2. Persons and Things

It is important to note something specific to the social-world. Although it too is an environing-world, the social milieu is not simply an encounter with "things" in a practical setting, but also engagement with other selves—other personal-worlds, in which the world likewise matters in an existential sense (a pen does not have a world).[77] Other persons are not simply there in my environment; we are co-engaged with a common world of needs, interests, successes, and failures, which saturates the ways in which human beings interact with each other. This is why interpersonal relations are so much more complex and proscribed than thing relations (using a tool does not carry the normative concerns that attach to dealing with persons). We owe something to the interests of other persons, which can modify how we interact with them. Such is the domain of ethics, which can benefit from a proto-phenomenological analysis because empathy and the social-world allow for release from a reductive individualism or egoism that would render the notion of moral obligation to others problematic from the start. The personal-social-world, which exhibits value-laden environments, shows that ethical norms are an intrinsic part of human existence and so moral skepticism can never get off the ground.[78]

4.3. Socialization and Individuation

The personal-world and the social-world are still one world. It is impossible for an individual human being to develop as such apart from a social environment, which is clearly evident with respect to child development. Yet children are from early on recognized as distinct personalities and they are expected to become individual agents to one degree or another. Individuation involves a certain tension between the personal-world and social-world (as every parent well knows). Socialization requires common patterns of behavior, understanding, and valuation. The transmission of cultural meanings and orientations will "incorporate" individuals into wider congregations of significance and purpose. Yet individual differences persist, if only from the standpoint of being distinct biological organisms. The personal-social-world includes the ongoing possibility of divergence and disparity, including the mutual understanding of the meaning of this element of life. The tension between individuation and socialization plays out in the stress between common arrangements and deviation, which can be disruptive but sometimes for the better, as in occasions of productive innovation. In any case, the tensional structure of the personal-social-world shows that human culture is not utterly uniform or static through time (which is one reason why the social-world is not consonant with social determinism). Individuation can be understood within a set of different possibilities: discovering something new, questioning and critiquing one's culture, going one's own way, or coming to "own" one's cultural inheritance as personally meaningful rather than taken for granted. Such possibilities will emerge out of contravening disconnections between individuals and common patterns in a manner analogous to the account of negative conditions interrupting practices. The main point is that individuation is not an utter departure from socialization and shared experience. Yet the force of socialization can tend to suppress individuation or restrict it to commonplace group-think, superficiality, or banality. That is why the social-world cannot and should not be separated from individual deviation, given the importance of innovation, diversity, and critique. What is often called *authenticity* pertains to different ways in which individual persons find their distinctive paths in life that are no longer defined simply by conventional patterns and expectations.[79] At any rate, the personal-social-world is animated by a dialectic of reciprocal contraventions, which 1) regulate individual energies for the sake of common purposes and 2) challenge communal constraints for the sake of novel possibilities.

5. PROJECTION

The ecological character of the social-environing-world includes what I call *projection*, which is meant to capture the sense of being thrown or cast into something, as in a projectile or a film projected upon a screen.[80] Projection involves being caught up in circumstances not of one's own choosing or making. Even circumstances that do involve choice can be a projection when their aspects and norms are already in place before we enter them. Projection specifies something intrinsic to the tripartite world structure we have examined: that selfhood is not a self-constituted phenomenon; the personal-world cannot b fe understood apart from the social-environing-world. Most of the meanings in factical life are a matter of projection, or are already there in natural, social, and cultural environments that shape possibilities in advance of our initiation so that we are projected *into* these milieus.

The original form of projection is birth into a finite natural world, with all its affordances, limitations, vicissitudes, dangers, and trajectory toward death. We simply find ourselves in this world without our consent. Then there are the many cultural patterns, norms, and institutions that take us up from birth and shape us to maturity. As adults we continue to dwell within these cultural parameters that are not of our own making—even if one such parameter calls on us to find our own way. There are passive and active forms of projection, the former excluding any initiating choice and the latter involving choice. Examples of the passive type are being a biological son, daughter, or sibling and the place or country where one is born and raised. Active forms of projection include friendships, occupations, and marriage, which involve the choice of initiation, but *into* milieus that receive us with already constituted domains—into the measures of, say, being a friend, a physician, a husband—which are rarely if ever up for grabs or radically defeasible. The notion of projection in a social-world can supplement what Searle calls "social facts" that are not reducible to physical facts—namely social practices or institutional formats that are anchored by collective agreement and assumed by practitioners, as in the rules of a game that determine outcomes.[81]

Projection shows that many forms of dwelling are not simply environments but spheres of meaning into which we are launched and received—and so not a matter of self-constitution and not in need of reflective justification in order to have warrant or intelligibility. This is not to say that such spheres are beyond interrogation or critique; previous accounts of contravention and discussions to come speak against such conservative closure. This is simply a phenomenological point concerning the default givenness and effectuality intrinsic to domains of projection into which we are cast and sometimes cast ourselves. Yet such domains are not and never have been immune to variation, modification, or transformation.

If we keep in mind that the lived world is one world with a threefold structure, the personal-world is always in play and no less in spheres of projection. Even though individuals are constituted by projected domains, they are also *constituents* in these domains. How individuals experience, engage, and function in projected spheres of meaning makes these domains active forms of *life* rather than essentially fixed structures. Societies vary in the degree to which individual persons are given leeway in these spheres, which nonetheless are void apart from the personal-world, if only from the standpoint of individuals accepting or obeying them. Both passive and active forms of projection require individual (adult) appropriation and enactment, and so they cannot be modes of absolute domination or robotic compliance. Again, allowing for variations across cultures, we can say that being a son, a parent, a professor, or a citizen is neither a strictly active nor passive endeavor but a mix of interests, actions, and decisions *in the midst of* expectations, obligations, and responsibilities. We can borrow from the grammatical form of the middle voice, which was more widely used in ancient Greek than in modern languages. The middle voice would apply to circumstances in which I am actively participating in something not of my own making or control, as in "I am being educated." Projection, therefore, involves middle voice practices and forms of life. The ambiguity of such a construction is well attested in the complicated demands and orchestrations of factical existence, wherein it is often hard to find clear, discrete sites of determination in the self or in outside forces.

The middle voice character of projection helps illuminate the dynamic and generative aspects of the personal-social-environing world, of the ecological forces that not only support but also help develop a human being's capacity to understand and engage the world. In other words, the self's environment is more than simply a surrounding habitat; it is constitutive of how a person comes to *be* a social and practical agent. Here we approach a richer account of affordances, of worldly conditions understood not simply as extant entities but interactive affiliations between an organism and its environment (such as the ground as an affordance for walking and a tool as an affordance for making something). The generative function of human affordances has been called their "scaffolding" effect, how they support, enable, and further human comprehension, behavior, and practical ability. Scaffolding can be found in environmental, technological, and social conditions that show an individual self to be anything but a self-contained entity. The human self must be understood as a dynamically extended and ecological being.[82]

6. TEMPORALITY

The lived world is essentially temporal, which is a primary indication of finitude in the sense that we are stretched between birth and death and experience is never a purely fixed condition. Even if we consider stable constructs like mathematical truths, the engagement with such things arises and passes in time. Here we confront one of the perennial conflicts between philosophical categories and the lived world: how general concepts relate to the changing, variable realm of concrete experience marked by temporal movement. The most prominent example is the concept of "being," which has been counter-posed to time because the former designates something actual and enduring that *is* the case rather than a state of becoming or something past or future. Traditional philosophy has analyzed time as a series of now-points, in which the governing concept is the now-as-present, so that the past is no-longer-now and the future is not-yet-now. Because the course of time therefore seems to involve negation and nonbeing, the question of what time "is" has been an enduring puzzle.[83] But lived temporality can be shown to sidestep this problem. We dwell in a temporal, narrative condition; we experience time as a looping intersection of time dimensions, as a coming to presence out of the future and shaped by the past. The "absences" of the future and past have a *presence* in anticipation and recollection. In this way human experience is *extended* into the future and past; it is presently engaged with future possibilities enabled and prompted by past orientations. Temporal extension can address the question of the self's "identity" through time, though not as some enduring state; the self *is* its ongoing temporal extension gathered by looping interactions of anticipation and recollection.

Factical temporality cannot be captured by a formal conception of time that measures change with quantified units, as in the case of clock time. There are lived senses of time that simply indicate imprecise moments and spans of experience, as in the following: it is time to go; it was a time of peace; I have no time now; daytime; harvest time; having a good time, and so on. Quantified time itself arises out of lived concerns because it serves them in valuable ways by coordinating accounts and activities through a standardized measure, yet it cannot apply universally to all senses of temporality with which human beings live.

There is a certain priority of the future in lived time. We are always presently occupied with the coming forth of life. Even the past comes forth in a way because memories are occurrences that arise and come to us. The meaning-laden character of human experience and activity is usually for the sake of some purpose or aim, some forward-looking bearing that can be implicit and yet brought to attention in the face of contravention. Accordingly, what lies ahead in the future is animating current concerns. Thus life is continually occupied with a not-yet, something yet to come. But the future is not on that account nonexistent or separate from the present and past. Future possibilities are prepared by present capacities and concerns that are shaped in the past. And factical presence is never "the present" or the "now" because it is a movement, a circulation of the future and the past with a looping figure-eight structure; it is both retentive and protentive (as recollection and anticipation), laden with the past and pregnant with the future.[84] The figure-eight structure of temporality can be shown in what seems like the simplest of things, but in fact is quite remarkable: the ability to understand speech as it is coursing along, in which the sounding of each word is coming into being and passing away in rapid succession. Comprehending what is said entails a *flowing* anticipation and retention that is nothing like a piecemeal construction. The immersed character of such a temporal structure can be disturbed by some contravention, such as a long pause in mid-sentence—the experience of which as a state of suspension *shows* the anticipatory nature of normal speech comprehension.[85]

Neuroscience has shown that the function of memory is not primarily to "record" the past but to shape the (present) anticipation of the future, as capacious preparation for action.[86] And memory is triggered by the coming tasks of life. The same kind of circulating figure-eight structure can be found in habits that function as readiness for future action. And this temporal structure can operate in a tacit manner without conscious awareness or explication.[87] In general, then, we never really live in the "now," the past is not gone, and the openness of the future is not wide open. Individual human beings cannot be understood apart from their past cultural inheritance, and current meanings have a temporal shape in being forward-looking concerns and possibilities shaped by traditional bearings. The association of temporality with meaning is essential for distinguishing factical time from abstract conceptions that screen out existential import. The future and the past are a yet-to-be and a no-longer that *matter*, such that the future can be exciting or worrisome and the past can be celebrated or regretted. The factical import of time accounts for how an objective measure like an hour can be experienced as moving faster or slower depending on the degree of interest.

The futurial character of temporality exhibits an intrinsic openness in human existence in that as long as we exist, we are marked by *possibility* rather than full actuality, which from an existential standpoint allows for human freedom. The importance of the future in a conception of freedom can be contrasted with the past-centered approach marking most theories of determinism and freedom. In such theories action is usually examined after the fact, in which determinism tracks the necessary causal chain that preceded the action and libertarianism stipulates an agent that could *have done* otherwise. Yet if we consider the personal-world and a first-person perspective *in the midst of action*, an open future is not only phenomenologically evident, it is experienced *as* possibility, as something pending that could go different ways in actions calling for choices. The stress that can accompany difficult decisions is evidence that human action is constituted by the figure-eight structure of temporality and cannot be adequately understood by a linear picture of time or piecemeal attention to any one dimension of time. In the midst of action, being able to act "otherwise" is intrinsic to the *experience* of deciding what to do, as distinct from some *post factum* condition of causal lines or even self-causation. Analysis after the fact can involve linear exposition that tracks the action in relation to (now) evident preceding factors, but *before* the action is executed, such exposition is antithetical to the experience of setting an action in motion, in which the past and an open future coalesce in a current activation. In this sense, activity *as lived* is "indeterminate" compared to the linear structure of causal thinking, which is one reason why predicting human behavior is difficult.[88] The figure-eight structure of temporality not only undermines a strict determinism, but also the radical freedom of an autonomous self. Engaging the future is always prepared by past bearings and constrained by projected circumstances in the present environment. Yet degrees of freedom are evident because the present-future dimension includes adjustments of inheritance in the light of current contravening conditions, at times to the point of innovation or reformation.

6.1. The Derivation of Objective Time

A lived sense of temporality precedes objective measurements of time according to units of seconds, minutes, hours, days, months, years, and so on. The classic account of objective time was given by Aristotle, who defined time as the measure of motion by way of now-points, which is best understood in the light of clock time.[89] Lived time involves imprecise meaning-laden spans of duration. The question at hand concerns how objective, measured time can be understood as derived from factical temporality. The movement of temporality receives its most original "measure" in terms of day and night, according to the rising and setting of the sun, which can then serve as the basis of calendar time frames. In a factical sense, daytime and nighttime are not simply measures but spans of light and dark infused with existential significance: daytime visibility permitting the course of life concerns and the darkness of night as an occasion for sleep, but also a period of concealed dangers. Accordingly, light and darkness have historically served as real and metaphorical expressions of meaning in human life. Further extensions of durational spans, as in seasonal change, also are marked originally by existential concerns, particularly with respect to weather conditions and agriculture. In addition to these lived temporal meanings, the sun's place in the sky can be a reference for measuring time in a specific manner (sunrise, sunset, and other positions in between), originally serving as designations that can coordinate actions and locate events. In this way, early "primitive" time designations were public and *real* in the sense of literally being in the sky, but also thoroughly meaning-laden and thus not "objective" in the strict modern sense.

A more precise measurement of time was made possible by clock devices, the earliest of which were sundials. The sundial allows a redirected reference of the sun's movement tracked on an artifact with a shadow cast by the style or gnomon. The movement of the sun's shadow can then be marked on the dial plate with a series of lines and numbers. The marks are fixed spots and the shadow moves across them; hence the marks can be seen as "points" of time in relation to previous and subsequent points. A currently shadowed point can then provide an exact "now" reference and other points are then understood as no longer or not yet "now." So time as the measure of motion according to now-points (the *nunc stans*) is clearly discernible through such a device. The imprecise spans and durations of factical temporality—it is now time to leave; I can't talk now; now I see what you mean; I'll see you later; I saw her then—can now be refined into precise, measurable instants. And the "flow" of time can be redescribed as the movement *of* now-points, which creates the philosophical problem of how the past and future (as not-now) can have *being*, which is a present-centered departure from the figure-eight structure of lived temporality.

Mechanical clocks mimicked the circular course of the sun but created more precise movements and designations solely in terms of quantified units and liberated from the contingency of sunlight availability. Digital clocks are even more precise in terms of numerical units coursing along in point-by-point sequence. In these ways, the quantified measurement of now-points is isolated from the natural setting of the sun's movement and can be discerned simply in terms of measured units, which serves the development of the abstract mathematical conception of time. Such a conception directed back to the world can be truly disclosive, especially in scientific terms, but its derivative character suggested in this analysis argues against it being a sufficient account of the meaning of time. Factical senses of time and the environing-world (the sun) remain primary in both historical and existential terms. Indeed, all instances of time measurement remain embedded in the lived world because of their value in serving practical and cognitive interests.

The derivative nature of quantified time can sideline some classic problems in the philosophy of time. A notable instance concerns whether the now can ever be "grasped" because it passes instantaneously into the past even before the time it takes to attend to it. Yet such a problem arises only by way of a punctuated reference that shifts the adverbial sense of *saying* "now" in lived circumstances—which is grasped easily in practical usage—into a nominal designation: *the* now, which could be called a grammatical confusion, at least when posed as a grounding condition concerning the nature of time as such. The confusion can be attributed to expositional reification overriding the immersed character of lived temporality in its figure-eight structure. The concept of now-time is simply a refined objectification process arising out of the original exposition of the sun's place in the sky, which first served as a measure for the flow of temporal experience.

6.2. History

The existential content of temporality is history, which involves the specific narratives, concerns, and projects that animate living endeavors, in other words the course of meaningful cultural events in time. History is not simply given in the past because an interest in the past is not purely antiquarian but rather attention to its value for present life and its future aims. History therefore shares the figure-eight structure of temporality, which should be kept in mind when studying the past to avoid the trap of interpreting a previous age solely in terms of what happened afterward and how it pointed toward future developments.[90] In the past, the future was yet to be determined, and that indeterminacy was part of a past culture's own (then present) concerns.[91] Nevertheless, lines from the past to our own time are extremely important in grasping the rich complexity of current concepts, principles, or ideals. Generational transmission through the ages gives our ideas a historical density that cannot be ignored if their saliency and import are to be well understood. When we study the Greeks, for example, we study ourselves.[92] At the same time, studying the past cannot be construed as a straightforward discovery of a historical period "as it really was" on its own terms, independent of current lenses that affect how historical questions are posed, what the terms of analysis will be, and what aspects will be selected or emphasized.

Given the temporal structure of factical life and its finitude, a sense of history in a culture provides, either implicitly or explicitly, a stabilizing function in the face of temporal contingency. We continually encounter contraventions and chance disruptions of expectations and plans. The future is sheer expectation and possibility, which is engaged as something contingent, open, and thus infused with possible contraventions (whether surmised, anticipated, or unexpected). Such contingency can be afforded degrees of manageability by retaining past patterns to regulate or prepare projects, thus reducing the stress of uncertainty. Memory of the past on a cultural level constitutes tradition, a perdurance that facilitates enduring the contingency of temporal experience. Traditions provide varying degrees of stability, in which the past can be conceived as repeatable continuity (which tends to be conservative), a teleological process of development (more open but guided by presumed ends), or a launch of possibilities with no presumed goal (more open to contingency but still guided by preparation and past cultural formats). Altogether history can be called an inherited openness, with inheritance providing a stabilizing element and futurial openness providing a destabilizing element that undermines foundationalist urges for cultural security. Historicality can support neither a strict conservatism nor a radicalism that moves to sever the present and the future from the past.[93]

6.3. Improvisation and Creativity

The figure-eight structure of temporality opens up another way in which representational models of thought and experience can be interrogated. I begin with the phenomenon of improvisation, which marks a good deal of human life when we spontaneously and smoothly enact new moves in the world that are yet to be and yet readied by acquired capacities and present aims. Here a temporal feedback loop is also placed within an environmental loop of ecstatic engagement with various milieus and affordances. Conversations and practical tasks are made possible by habits of speech and action that have settled into second-nature codes for execution, but *in performance* little is strictly settled as to what will transpire. The plasticity of engagement must likewise be second nature. The prepared openness of temporal movement is also the responsive openness to the environing-world. The course of a conversation or task has a flow that can readily shift in response to variations in the field of operation, even unexpected changes. Think of a problem-solving conversation, driving a car, or playing basketball. The word *improvise* stems from Latin and Italian roots connoting something sudden or unforeseen. If the phenomenology of improvisation shows smooth and ready response, the performance is more immersed in the *field of operation* than in representational structures, intentions, rules, or inferences. There can be exposited accounts after the fact that nevertheless seem alien to the performance *at the time*. Think of the common question asked of athletes: "What was going through your mind when you made the winning play?" Often the most honest answer would be: "Nothing, really. I just reacted." Improvisation is a kind of creativity, but not in the strongest sense because it occurs within various background settings, social structures, habits, and expectations that shape activity, ranging from institutional to informal milieus. Yet improvisation exhibits a spontaneous generation of new ventures within a host of promptings, possibilities, undertakings, problems, and solutions. So improvisation operates within the confluence of individuation and socialization, openness and structure, freedom and constraint.[94]

Creativity in a stronger sense occurs when new settings as such are ventured, which is different from improvisation within a setting. Such is the course of human history, in which challenges to established orders bring about new modes of being in social, intellectual, and artistic spheres, among others. Yet cultural creativity is not a matter of sheer novelty out of the blue. It is never utterly discontinuous with the past, at the very least because of established capacities that make challenge and innovation possible, but also because creative ventures generally arise because of some contravening disturbance or discomfiture within an existing framework. And creativity involves a shift from a current order to the shaping of a new order rather than mere divergence—if novelty is going to mean something in human life and be passed on. The course of history shows an overarching temporal structure of creative movement as a present disturbance to an inherited establishment aiming for future alteration. Such historical structure has a telling continuity because any established setting that is subjected to current creative disruption was itself once a disruption of an established setting. Like improvisation, cultural creativity *in execution* exhibits certain elements that do not lend themselves easily to representational designs. Significant innovations in history usually involve paradigm shifts that call for leaps, risks, and ventures beyond precedent, which from an indicative standpoint are difficult to fathom in causal or inferential terms because they break with established rationales. Again, this is not to deny the possibility of expositional analysis, which however seems to make sense only in retrospect when it comes to immediate creative enactment.

7. EMBODIMENT

The presumption of immanence and proto-phenomenological analysis show that human life is essentially embodied, that every element of dwelling has a somatic base. Not only does this rule out metaphysical dualism, but also a reductive physicalism because a phenomenology of embodied life is analytically distinct from strictly physical descriptions. The *lived body* (identified in the work of Merleau-Ponty) is different from the objectified body, which marks the disciplines of biology and physiology (and even everyday expositional attention to the body). The lived body is an embodied-world that reiterates the personal-social-environing-world and the full array of structures therein, especially ecstatic immersion, engaged practices, habits, and know-how. With my examples of writing with a pen and furniture restoration, I *am* my body in performance, which is thoroughly absorbed in a tangible environment outside my skin. Here embodiment is a *field* of action. As in all cases of immersion, contravention will prompt exposed attention to aspects of the environment and the agent body (a tool can be the wrong size for my hand or cause discomfort). Exposition can range from ordinary attention to refined examination, all the way to physiology. But the lived body must be understood *indicatively* in engaged, pre-expositional terms. It may even be that the phenomenon of practical immersion—in which specific attention to physical properties and states as such is *recessed*—opens space for intimations of "nonphysical" dimensions.[95] The body-in-action, as it were, is "invisible" as an exposed object.

When the body is understood existentially as "flesh and blood" within its temporal arc of birth and death, we attend to the needs and vulnerabilities that give human life its narratives of weal and woe, of desire satisfaction and deprivation, success and failure, gain and loss, security and hazard. The meaningfulness of life is inextricably caught up in the finite limits that mark the fragility of embodiment. We find ourselves continually projected into circumstances of possible threats to well-being, which are of primary importance and concern to human apprehension. In the lived world, even the most objective, exact, and secured constructs of thought diminish in significance when dramas of life and death or safety and harm come to the fore.

A somatic emphasis opens up the importance of touch and the centrality of the hand in specifying human nature.[96] Touch is an underexamined sense, but its importance is receiving more attention, especially in terms of the hand's special role in human practices, perceptions, and capacities. Touch provides a paradigm for understanding ecstatic immediacy. From an ecological standpoint, touch has the least "distance" from its environment because of actual contact and the reciprocal, joint experience of the hand-as-touching and the thing-being-touched. Likewise, the immersed character of practical know-how receives its clearest illustration in tool use and other kinds of manipulation afforded by human hands. Manual touch plays an important role in a child's perceptual development and even mature perception has touch integrated with other senses. Touch also provides a pathway for understanding direct perception without representational mediation. Although the hand is the most prominent locus of touch, the entire body with its skin is a single tactile organ. Skin provides its own ecstatic disclosure of the environment in terms of sensing the elements, temperature, affordances, position, relative location, movement, safety, and pain.

With the ecological field-character of lived embodiment, many philosophical questions can receive a revised orientation. For instance, perception can be understood as ecstatically disclosive and correlated with a meaning-laden environment rather than simply a set of mental states or raw data for cognition.[97] Language can be examined in terms of primal elements of voice, gesture, pointing, and face-to-face engagement. These and other questions will be taken up in coming discussions. But presently we can attend briefly to the concept of space in a manner analogous to the discussion of time.

7.1. Place and Space

As opposed to abstract conceptions such as points, lines, figure, dimension, and mass, a lived sense of space stems from the environing-world and can be better grasped as a sense of *place*, of meaning-laden locations and locales, such as home, field, land, sea, sky, temple, market, neighborhood, city, wilderness, and so on.[98] Many spatial designations arise from the perspective of the human body and positions in the environment: left, right, above, below, here, there, near, far, and so forth. Such designations are originally imprecise indications of location. Space can be measured more precisely by devices with agreed upon units that can track distances and dimensions with shareable information in exact terms (for example, how far or big something is). The first spatial science was geometry (literally "earth measuring"), which measured the shape, size, and position of figures and land areas with devices like the straight edge and compass, primarily for practical purposes of surveying, storage, building, and craftwork. The formalization of geometry was initiated by Euclid and subsequently spatial notions could be abstracted from concrete settings and studied on their own terms. This was far from an idle exercise because advanced mathematical geometry allowed for enormous openings in scientific accounts of nature. But again, I want to argue for the derivative character of abstract spatial concepts and the priority of lived senses of place and location. Rationalist theories of cognition indeed recognized the stark difference between abstract spatial ideas and sense perception, and they aimed to immunize those ideas from the contingencies of experience by grounding them in a priori foundations. From a *contextual* standpoint of scientific investigation, such a differentiation can make sense, but not in the fundamental sense of an exclusive account of the meaning and origin of spatial understanding.

In summation, both spatial and temporal comprehension in the lived world are context-dependent and indicative of specific meanings, while abstract scientific concepts of space and time are context-independent (apart from the context of scientific investigation itself) and meant to apply uniformly to any and all cases. Abstract conceptions of "objective" space and time are perspective-free and cannot give any help in understanding perspectival senses of temporality and place, as in "soon," "later," "earlier," "here," and "there." Lived time and space come first and allow the derivation of abstract time and space by way of expositional disengagement from factical contexts and perspectives. The derivative character of such abstract concepts does not rob them of their descriptive and predictive power, only their exclusivity. Lived senses of time and space are the setting out of which abstract concepts can emerge, and the former exhibit their own intelligibility in being indicative, communicable, and workable in less precise but fully functional ways. Moreover, the ecological character of factical time and space—embedded in worldly circumstances and even the primal measure of the sun—offers relief from the question of whether time and space are "real" or only ideational constructs. Lived time and space are not simply mental frameworks but ways of dwelling in the world.

This chapter has presented a sketch of how a proto-phenomenological analysis attends to the factical background of reflective thinking, the immanent dwelling in a meaningful world that 1) is always already in play and thus precludes justification, 2) precedes the subject-object distinction, 3) makes possible familiar philosophical categories by way of a contravention-exposition dynamic, and 4) unsettles traditional standards in being embodied, environed, enactive, social, projected, inherited, temporal, and finite. This analysis will be applied in kind to the question of language in chapter 3 and will help correct and displace common assumptions in linguistics and philosophy of language. The coming discussion in chapter 2 further prepares such correction and displacement by taking up 1) how the world is disclosed and understood in proto-phenomenological terms, 2) how this account differs from standard models of cognition and bears on the status of naturalism in cognitive science, and 3) how philosophy itself can be understood as a mode of dwelling in the lived world. Chapter 2 will thereby complete the philosophical background for chapter 3 and set up the task of chapter 4, which articulates how a proto-phenomenological analysis of language applies to questions of truth and rationality.

NOTES

1. My use of the term *ecstatic* is limited to the field-structure of normal human experience and thus distinct from more exalted notions of religious or psychological "ecstasy."

2. See Marie Laure-Ryan, *Narrative as Virtual Reality: Immersion and Interactivity in Literature and Electronic Media* (Baltimore, MD: Johns Hopkins University Press, 2003).

3. The internal-external divide in the subject-object distinction accounts for the enduring career of radical skepticism in epistemology. How can any belief, as an internal mental state, ever guarantee knowledge of something external to belief states, something that can never be coextensive with a belief? Hume's representational theory of mind follows this divided structure: the human mind has direct contact only with its own sense impressions and ideas, not the external world.

4. René Descartes, *Meditations on First Philosophy*, in *The Philosophical Writings of Descartes*, Vol. 2, trans. John Cottingham, Robert Stoothoff, and Dugald Murdoch (Cambridge: Cambridge University Press, 1985).

5. David Hume, *An Enquiry Concerning Human Understanding*, ed. Thomas L. Beauchamp (Oxford: Oxford University Press, 1999).

6. Of course I could be a brain in a vat and all my references, though seemingly real, would be illusory. I might ask my wife if she knows anything about this, but that would only extend the problem to her, and to you the reader. We might all be brains in vats, but then all our referential assumptions, whether for or against the proposal, would be put in question. One solution to the puzzle would be that any and all investigations be prefaced with declared commitments to not being brains in vats, pending disconfirmation. Or we could just ignore the problem entirely (pending the actual discovery of laboratories with brains in vats).

7. I use hyphenation in world designations as a graphic reminder of their "field" character. This tripartite world structure matches what Heidegger in an early work called *Selbstwelt*, *Umwelt*, and *Mitwelt*.

8. See Lynn Rudder Baker, *Naturalism and the First-Person Perspective* (Oxford: Oxford University Press, 2013). Yet even the third-person standpoint is not something independent of the first-person standpoint because the former orientation in its constitution and enactment is a meaningful endeavor and an intersubjective perspective with a host of collaborative elements and corroborative practices. See Shaun Gallagher and Dan Zahavi, *The Phenomenological Mind* (New York: Routledge, 2008), 40ff.

9. This section on the personal-world is brief compared to the coming treatments of the environing and social worlds because it is simply the stipulation of existential meaningfulness that animates both of the latter treatments. The discussion of the environing-world is more extensive than that of the social-world, but only to establish a detailed phenomenological orientation that will also apply to social relations. Beyond this chapter, the social-world will be fleshed out further in discussions of language.

10. *Ecology* is a word pertaining to environmental structures and is derived from the Greek word *oikos*, meaning home or dwelling. An "affordance" is an ecological concept referring to a correlated possibility-for-action, which cannot be understood solely in terms of the environment or the action alone. So the ground as an affordance is a possibility for walking. The term was coined by James J. Gibson in "The Theory of Affordances," in *Perceiving, Acting, and Knowing: Toward an Ecological Psychology*, ed. Robert Shaw and John Bransford (Hillsdale, NJ: Erlbaum, 1977), 67–82.

11. George Herbert Mead was an early proponent of a field-concept of the self in the midst of its environment. See "A Behaviorist Account of the Significant Symbol," *Journal of Philosophy* 19 (1922): 157–63.

12. American pragmatism has classically advanced a challenge to subject-object dualities by explicating practical dealings with environments. For a study that correlates pragmatism with Heideggerian phenomenology, see Mark Okrent, *Heidegger's Pragmatism: Understanding, Being, and the Critique of Metaphysics* (Ithaca, NY: Cornell University Press, 1988). A recent neo-pragmatist work is Philip Kitcher, *Preludes to Pragmatism: Toward a Reconstruction of Philosophy* (Oxford: Oxford University Press, 2012).

13. Immersion and exposition designate my account of the underlying dynamic in Heidegger's distinction between *Zuhandenheit* and *Vorhandenheit*. Unlike some interpretations of this dynamic, I go beyond focusing simply on things that are used and then converted to objective attention, in order to capture the *way in which* such things are experienced and the *shift* between immersion and exposition.

14. Immersion can fit what has been called the experience of "flow." See Mihalyi Csikszentmihalyi, *Flow: The Psychology of Optimal Experience* (New York: Harper Perennial, 1991). Hubert Dreyfus calls practical immersion "skillful coping." See *Skill-*

ful Coping: Essays on the Phenomenology of Everyday Perception and Action, ed. Mark A. Wrathall (Oxford: Oxford University Press, 2014).

15. John Dewey's pragmatic theory of knowledge has a comparable account in which some disturbance to the smooth flow of practical familiarity prompts "attention," wherein cognition and truth are not a matter of correspondence between mental states and the external world but the engaged activity of problem solving. See "Does Reality Possess Practical Character?" in *Middle Works, 1899–1924*, Vol. 5, ed. Jo Ann Boydston (Carbondale, IL: Southern Illinois University Press, 1997), 125–42, and "Propositions, Warranted Assertibility, and Truth," in *Later Works, 1925–1953*, Vol. 14, ed. Jo Ann Boydston (Carbondale, IL: Southern Illinois University Press, 1997), 168–88.

16. See, for example, Paul Coates and Sam Coleman, eds., *Phenomenal Qualities: Sense, Perception, and Consciousness* (Oxford: Oxford University Press, 2015), and Walter Ott, "Phenomenal Intentionality and the Problem of Representation," *Journal of the American Philosophical Association* 2, no. 1 (March 2016), 131–45.

17. This will be especially evident in considering child development in volume 2. For an account of how contravention plays an important role in the learning process, see Andrea R. English, *Discontinuity in Learning: Dewey, Herbart, and Education as Transformation* (Cambridge: Cambridge University Press, 2013).

18. Habit as second nature is a central feature of Dewey's pragmatism. See his 1922 text, *Human Nature and Conduct: An Introduction to Social Psychology* (Amherst, NY: Prometheus Books, 2002).

19. An important account of second nature in response to various conundrums of modern philosophy is John McDowell, *Mind and World* (Cambridge, MA: Harvard University Press, 1994).

20. See Harry Collins, "Three Dimensions of Expertise," *Phenomenology and the Cognitive Sciences* 12, no. 2 (June 2013): 253–73. Collins works with the distinction between "esoteric" and "ubiquitous" expertise. In this same journal edition, there is a treatment of immersion in Rodrigo Ribeiro, "Levels of Immersion and Tacit Knowledge," 367–97.

21. For a discussion in the context of ethics, see Hanno Sauer, "Educated Intuitions: Automaticity and Rationality in Moral Judgement," *Philosophical Explorations* 15, no. 3 (September 2012), 255–75. For a collection of essays on the debate between McDowell and Hubert Dreyfus on the status of conceptualization in human practices, see Joseph K. Shear, ed., *Mind, Reason, and Being-in-the-World: The McDowell-Dreyfus Debate* (New York: Routledge, 2013). The bi-directionality of immersion and exposition can strike a balance between McDowell's overemphasis on concepts and Dreyfus's notion of "mindless" coping. More on this in chapter 3.

22. *Critique of Pure Reason* B131-32, B203.

23. John Locke, *An Essay in Human Understanding*, ed. Peter Nidditch (Oxford: Oxford University Press, 1975), II.27.9.

24. In conscious activities we can talk of nonreflective self-awareness that is implicit in the immersed practices and explicable by self-conscious exposition in first-person terms. See Shaun Gallagher, "Defining Consciousness: The Importance of Non-Reflective Self-Awareness," *Pragmatics and Cognition* 18, no. 3 (2010): 561–69.

25. See Carolyn Dicey Jennings, "Consciousness Without Attention," *Journal of the American Philosophical Association* 12 (July 2015): 276–95, and Marvin M. Chun et al., "A Taxonomy of External and Internal Attention," *Annual Review of Psychology* 62 (2011): 73–101.

26. See Ran R. Hassin, James S. Uleman, and John A. Bargh, eds., *The New Unconscious* (Oxford: Oxford University Press, 2005).

27. For a sketch of different ways in which consciousness can be understood, along with neurological factors and the question of animal consciousness, see Jonathan Cole, "The Origin of Consciousness: The Background of the Debate," *Pragmatics and Cogni-*

tion 18, no. 3 (2010): 481–95, which introduces a collection of essays in this edition of the journal.

28. Good surveys of the field include Jaegwon Kim, *Philosophy of Mind*, third edition (Boulder, CO: Westview Press, 2010) and Brian P. McLaughlin and Jonathan Cohen, eds., *Contemporary Debates in Philosophy of Mind* (Malden, MA: Blackwell, 2007).

29. For a review and critique of research in cognitive science purporting to demonstrate unconscious processes affecting conscious operations, see Ben R. Newell and David R. Shanks, "Unconscious Influences in Decision Making: A Critical Review," *Behavioral and Brain Sciences* 37 (2014): 1–61.

30. J. J. McDermott, ed., *The Philosophy of John Dewey* (Chicago: University of Chicago Press, 1981), 165.

31. For a debate between John Searle and Hubert Dreyfus concerning the phenomenology of engaged practice and logical representation, see Mark Wrathall and Jeff Malpas, eds., *Heidegger, Coping, and Cognitive Science* (Cambridge, MA: MIT Press, 2000), 71–92 and 323–37. Searle in fact does allow for a notion of presentation in direct experience that is not representational. See *Intentionality* (Cambridge: Cambridge University Press, 1983), 45–46. Yet the bulk of Searle's work has to do with representation and subject-object relations.

32. Charles Taylor, *Philosophical Arguments* (Cambridge, MA: Harvard University Press, 1995), 12.

33. See, for instance, Andy Clark, *Supersizing the Mind: Embodiment, Action, and Cognitive Extension* (Oxford: Oxford University Press, 2011) and Mark Rowlands, *The New Science of the Mind: From Extended Mind to Embodied Phenomenology* (Cambridge, MA: MIT Press, 2010); also a collection of essays in *Philosophical Explorations* 15, no. 2 (June 2012), with an introductory essay by Andy Clark, "Extended Cognition and Epistemology," 87–90.

34. For a critique of this element in the theory, see Pierre Steiner, "The Bounds of Representation: A Non-Representationalist Use of the Resources of the Model of Extended Cognition," *Pragmatics and Cognition* 18, no. 2 (2010): 235–72; also Lambros Malafouris, *How Things Shape the Mind: A Theory of Material Engagement* (Cambridge, MA: MIT Press, 2013).

35. David Hume, *A Treatise of Human Nature*, eds. David Fate Norton and Mary J. Norton (Oxford: Oxford University Press, 2000), I.IV.4.3.

36. See Gilbert Ryle, *The Concept of Mind*, Introduction by Daniel C. Dennett (Chicago: University of Chicago Press, 2000). For a contemporary collection of essays on Ryle's legacy and its critical reception, see John Bengson and Marc A. Moffet, eds., *Knowing How: Essays on Knowledge, Mind and Action* (Oxford: Oxford University Press, 2011).

37. See Merleau-Ponty's classic work, *Phenomenology of Perception*, trans. Colin Smith (Atlantic Highlands, NJ: Humanities Press, 1962); Hubert L. Dreyfus, "Overcoming the Myth of the Mental," *Proceedings and Addresses of the American Philosophical Association* 79, no. 2 (November 2005): 47–65, and Hubert L. Dreyfus and Stuart E. Dreyfus, "From Socrates to Expert Systems: The Limits of Calculative Rationality," *Technology in Society* 6, no. 3 (1984): 217–33.

38. See Jason Stanley, *Know How* (Oxford: Oxford University Press, 2011).

39. See Jason Stanley and John M. Krakhauer, "Motor Skill Depends on Knowledge of Facts," *Frontiers in Human Neuroscience* 7 (August 2013): 1–11. In *Know How*, Stanley refers to Heidegger's analysis of *Zuhandenheit* as establishing a "practical way of thinking" that can support his account (124). Heidegger's treatment of practical usage was indeed meant to open up an expanded sense of disclosiveness, but not as a manner of "thinking" or propositional knowledge.

40. For a critical assessment of Stanley, see Jessica A. Brown, "Knowing How: Linguistics and Cognitive Science," *Analysis* 73, no. 2 (April 2013): 220–27, and David Wiggins, "Practical Knowledge: Knowing How To and Knowing That," *Mind* 121, no. 481 (January 2012): 97–130. For neurological findings that support know-how set apart from propositional knowledge, see Elena Daprate and Angela Sirigu, "How We Interact with Objects: Learning from Brain Lesions," *Trends in Cognitive Sciences* 10, no. 6 (June 2006): 265–70, and John R. Hodges, Josef Spatt, and Karalyn Patterson, "'What' and 'How': Evidence for the Dissociation of Object Knowledge and Mechanical Problem-Solving Skills in the Human Brain," *Proceedings of the National Academy of Sciences* 96 (August 1999): 9444–48. For a discussion of know-how in the light of neurological findings, see Charles Wallis, "Consciousness, Context, and Know-How," *Synthese* 160 (January 2008): 123–53. I will take up the relationship between phenomenology and cognitive neuroscience in the next chapter.

41. See Ellen Fridland, "Knowing-How: Problems and Considerations," *European Journal of Philosophy* 23, no. 3 (September 2015): 703–24.

42. For a discussion, along with the relevant research, see David Papineau, "In the Zone," *Royal Institute of Philosophy Supplement* 73 (October 2013): 175–96.

43. See Brian Bruya, ed., *Effortless Attention: A New Perspective in the Cognitive Science of Attention and Action* (Cambridge, MA: MIT Press, 2010), on which some of my remarks rely.

44. See John A. Bargh, "Bypassing the Will: Toward Demystifying the Role of Nonconscious Control of Social Behavior," in *The New Unconscious*, chap. 2. Unfortunately, the research here and in the previous note deploys representational processes to explain behavior that surely seems to function without them.

45. Socrates's interlocutors were frustrated not because they were inept at philosophical analysis but because they often did not understand the *point* of Socrates's search for universals. See *Laches* 192 and *Hippias Major* 287d–e.

46. See Daniel Kahneman, *Thinking Fast and Slow* (New York: Farrar, Straus and Giroux, 2011), which takes up psychological research that suggests two systems in human thought and experience: System 1, which is largely nonconscious, automatic, and affect-laden; and System 2, which is conscious, deliberative, and logical. System 1 is the stronger and more basic system.

47. See Michael Polanyi, *The Tacit Dimension* (London: Routledge and Kegan Paul, 1966).

48. See David T. Neal, Wendy Wood, and Jeffrey M. Quinn, "Habits—A Repeat Performance," *Current Directions in Psychological Science* 15, no. 4 (August 2006): 198–202.

49. See John A. Bargh and Erin L. Williams, "The Automaticity of Social Life," *Current Directions in Psychological Science* 15, no. 1 (February 2006): 1–4.

50. For a general discussion, see Tom Sparrow and Adam Hutchinson, *A History of Habit: From Aristotle to Bourdieu* (Lanham, MD: Lexington Books, 2014).

51. For a discussion in terms of Merleau-Ponty's thought, see Maria Talero, "Merleau-Ponty and the Bodily Subject of Learning," *International Philosophical Quarterly* 46, no. 2 (June 2006): 191–203. For Merleau-Ponty on habit, see *Phenomenology of Perception*, 164ff. For Aristotle on ethical virtue as habit and second nature, see *Nicomachean Ethics* 1103a14ff.

52. See James McGuirk, "Phenomenological Considerations of Habit: Reason, Knowing, and Self-Presence in Habitual Action," *Phenomenology and Mind* 6 (2014): 112–21.

53. See Harry Collins, *Tacit and Explicit Knowledge* (Chicago: University of Chicago Press, 2010), 7. This work is a thorough and refined examination of the intricate questions involved in such matters.

54. For an account of subliminal perception and persuasion, which would fit more my conception of the unconscious or subconscious, see Ap Dijksterhuis et al., "The Power of the Subliminal: On Subliminal Persuasion and Other Potential Applications," in *The New Unconscious*, chap. 4.

55. See Ellen Fridland, "They've Lost Control: Reflections on Skill," *Synthese* 191, no. 12 (August 2014): 2729–50; also Wayne Christensen et al., "Cognition in Skilled Action: Meshed Control and the Varieties of Skill Experience," *Mind and Language* 31, no. 1 (February 2016): 37–66.

56. See John William Miller, *The Midworld of Symbols and Functioning Objects* (New York: W. W. Norton, 1982), chap. 10.

57. See Dimitri Ginev, "Two Accounts of the Hermeneutic Fore-Structure of Scientific Research," *International Studies in the Philosophy of Science* 26, no. 4 (December 2012): 423–45. See also Jan Faye, *The Nature of Scientific Thinking: On Interpretation, Explanation, and Understanding* (New York: Palgrave, 2014).

58. See Edward J. Hackett et al., *The Handbook of Science and Technology Studies* (Cambridge, MA: MIT Press, 2007).

59. The classic account of the fact-value divide is provided by Spinoza. See his *Ethics*, appendix to part 1, for example: Human beings falsely project onto nature their own sense of purposefulness. This is a fabrication that has hindered science from concentrating on mechanical causes rather than teleological explanations inherited from Aristotle.

60. For an account of the role of values in science, see Philip Kitcher, *Science in a Democratic Society* (New York: Prometheus Books, 2011). For a study of how meaning, purpose, and ethical values can fit in with Darwinian naturalism, see Bana Bashour and Hans D. Muller, eds., *Contemporary Philosophical Naturalism and Its Implications* (New York: Routledge, 2014).

61. Steven Weinberg, *The First Three Minutes: A Modern View of the Origin of the Universe* (New York: Basic Books, 1993), 154.

62. See William Hamilton's account in *The Works of Thomas Reid*, vol. 2, ed. William Hamilton (New York: Elibron Classics, 2005), 806–9.

63. See Sanford C. Goldberg, *Relying on Others: An Essay in Epistemology* (Oxford: Oxford University Press, 2010). See also Michael Tomasello, *A Natural History of Human Thinking* (Cambridge, MA: Harvard University Press, 2014).

64. See Axel Seemann, ed., *Joint Attention: New Developments in Psychology, Philosophy of Mind, and Social Neuroscience* (Cambridge, MA: MIT Press, 2011), from which some of my remarks are taken.

65. For a discussion of dance in this vein, see Maxine Sheets-Johnstone, "From Movement to Dance," *Phenomenology and the Cognitive Sciences* 11, no. 1 (March 2012): 39–57.

66. See Andrew Meltzoff and Rebecca Williamson, "Imitation: Social, Cognitive, and Theoretical Perspectives," in *Oxford Handbook of Developmental Psychology*, Vol. 1, ed. P. R. Zelazo (Oxford: Oxford University Press, 2013), 651–82.

67. See Axel Honneth, *The Struggle for Recognition: The Moral Grammar of Social Conflicts*, trans. Joel Anderson (Cambridge, MA: MIT Press, 1996).

68. This is why some developments in analytic philosophy that admit the significance of phenomenological attention to the first-person standpoint should be met with caution when they assume that standpoint to be a matter of introspective consciousness. See Dan Zahavi, "Subjectivity and the First-Person Perspective," *Southern Journal of Philosophy* 45, Spindel Supplement (2007): 66–84.

69. Some of what follows derives from my *Ethics and Finitude: Heideggerian Contributions to Moral Philosophy* (Lanham, MD: Rowman & Littlefield, 2000), chap. 6. For an excellent study that blends phenomenological, analytic, and empirical research

well, see Dan Zahavi, *Self and Other: Exploring Subjectivity, Empathy, and Shame* (Oxford: Oxford University Press, 2014).

70. For studies of empathy, see Amy Coplan and Peter Goldie, *Empathy: Philosophical and Psychological Perspectives* (Cambridge: Cambridge University Press, 2011), Mark H. Davis, *Empathy: A Social Psychological Approach* (Boulder, CO: Westview, 1996), Nancy Eisenberg and Janet Strayer, eds., *Empathy and Its Development* (Cambridge: Cambridge University Press, 1987), and Hans Herbert Kögler and Karsten R. Steuber, eds., *Empathy and Agency: The Problem of Understanding in the Human Sciences* (Boulder, CO: Westview, 2000).

71. See Davis, *Empathy*, throughout.

72. Eisenberg and Strayer, *Empathy and Its Development*, 63 and chap. 10.

73. This will be reinforced by a discussion of empathy in volume 2.

74. See Ken Fuchsman, "Empathy and Humanity," *Journal of Psychohistory* 42, no. 3 (Winter 2015): 176–86.

75. See Dan Zahavi, "Empathy and Direct Social Perception: A Phenomenological Proposal," *Review of Philosophy and Psychology* 2, no. 3 (2011): 541–58. An excellent recent survey of the evidence for empathetic responses is Kory Sorrell, "Our Better Angels: Empathy, Sympathetic Reason, and Pragmatic Moral Progress," *The Pluralist* 9, no. 1 (Spring 2014): 66–86. Also covered are the various senses of empathy, all through the lens of pragmatism.

76. See Michael Slote, *From Enlightenment to Receptivity: Rethinking Our Values* (Oxford: Oxford University Press, 2013).

77. The person-thing distinction here does not mean that "things" are only understood as bare objects devoid of meaning. As indicated earlier, entities in the world can be invested with meaning; think of deeply personal things like one's home, mementos, or family artifacts.

78. See my *Ethics and Finitude*, chap. 3. More discussion will follow in chapter 4.

79. For a treatment of individuation and socialization with references to the liberalism-communitarianism debate, see my *Ethics and Finitude*, chap. 7.

80. Projection is my take on what Heidegger called *Geworfenheit*, or thrownness.

81. See John Searle, *The Construction of Social Reality* (New York: Free Press, 1997).

82. For an account from the standpoint of cognitive psychology, see Anna Estany and Segio Martinez, "Scaffolding and Affordance as Integrative Concepts in the Cognitive Sciences," *Philosophical Psychology* 27, no. 1 (February 2014): 98–111.

83. In the background of this problem is the fact that the philosophical concept of "being" is a grammatical derivation from the verb "to be," which is intrinsically temporal in being tensed, like all verbs.

84. Because of the temporal structure of experience, the notion of "presentation" offered in this investigation is not something present-centered, but simply a phenomenological alternative to representation. The "immediacy" of presentation is not something atemporal or fixed in time.

85. The same phenomenon can be exhibited in following a musical melody, in which withholding the final tonal resolution is experienced *as* a privation.

86. See Moshe Bar, "The Proactive Brain: Memory for Predictions," *Philosophical Transactions: Biological Sciences* 364, no. 1521 (May 2009): 1235–43.

87. See Philip Gerrans and David Sander, "Feeling the Future: Prospects for a Theory of Implicit Prospection," *Biology and Philosophy* 29, no. 5 (September 2014): 699–710.

88. See Theodore Schatzki, "Temporality and the Causal Approach to Human Activity," in *Heidegger and Cognitive Science*, eds. Julian Kiverstein and Michael Wheeler (New York: Palgrave Macmillan, 2012), 343–64. Merleau-Ponty provides an important analysis of freedom in *Phenomenology of Perception*, 458–83.

89. See *Physics* IV. 10–13.
90. Heraclitus would not self-identify as a "Presocratic." People in the "medieval" period would not see their time as the "Dark Ages."
91. In studying a period right before, say, the outbreak of a war, the terrible consequences that followed might easily color the way we read that period, as blind or naïve for example. See David Carr, *Experience and History: Phenomenological Perspectives on the Historical World* (Oxford: Oxford University Press, 2014). This is an important study of the narrative character of history.
92. This is what Foucault called "history of the present" in *Discipline and Punish*, trans. Alan Sheridan (New York: Vintage Books, 1995), 30–31.
93. See Jonas Grethlein, *The Greeks and Their Past: Poetry, Oratory, and History in the Fifth Century BCE* (Cambridge: Cambridge University Press, 2010), 1–15.
94. For an account of improvisation and habit that bridges phenomenology and pragmatism, see Wendelin M. Küpers, "Embodied Pheno-Pragma-Practice-Phenomenological and Pragmatic Perspectives on Creative 'Inter-Practice' in Organizations between Habits and Improvisation," *Phenomenology and Practice* 5, no. 1 (2011): 100–139. For Gadamer on the "medial structure" of play, see *Truth and Method*, trans. Joel Weinsheimer and Donald G. Marshall (London: Continuum, 2004), 91–119.
95. See Drew Leder, *The Absent Body* (Chicago: University of Chicago Press, 1990). More on this in chapter 4.
96. See Matthew Fulkerson, *The First Sense: A Philosophical Study of Human Touch* (Cambridge, MA: MIT Press, 2014), and Zdravko Radman, ed., *The Hand: An Organ of the Mind, What the Manual Tells the Mental* (Cambridge, MA: MIT Press, 2013). Some of my remarks are drawn from these studies.
97. See Merleau-Ponty, *Phenomenology of Perception*, 235–83.
98. For a definitive account, see Edward Casey, *The Fate of Place: A Philosophical History* (Berkeley, CA: University of California Press, 1998).

Chapter Two

Disclosure, Interpretation, and Philosophy

1. WORLD DISCLOSURE

Next for consideration is how human beings open up, and are open to, their environments, how the world is disclosed in factical experience. Disclosure names the ways in which we engage and comprehend what the world is like and how it manifests itself. Four basic avenues of disclosure will be examined in this and the next chapter: affective attunement, tacit intimation, interpretation, and language.

1.1. Affective Attunement[1]

Much in the world can be revealed by emotions and moods, which should be distinguished from "feelings" that are more focused in the self (such as pain or hunger). Emotion (fear, for instance) is more focused than the atmospheric character of mood (such as anxiety or boredom), which is often the constitutive setting for an emotion. Affect in this discussion is meant to span the range of moods, emotions, and feelings, especially because each of these can be interwoven with the others. A mood like boredom can influence an emotion like love. An emotion like fear can affect a feeling like pain. A feeling like hunger can influence emotions and moods. In any case, a mood is more diffuse and less intentional than an emotion, and feelings have a more subjective horizon than emotions and moods. Research on affective life often suffers from lack of precision in differentiating mood, emotion, and feeling. Moreover, the first-person perspective so important to phenomenology is often sidestepped in research protocols. Experimental milieus are usually controlled circumstances geared toward inducing a particular affective response in a somewhat artificial manner, which bypasses the contextual, variegated, and haphazard character of factical life. With discrete short-lived episodes of induced responses, the richer temporality and ecology of affective experience can be diminished or lost. Finally, most of the research is geared toward causal questions, which misses the phenomenology and disclosive capacity of affects.[2]

Affect is a matter of existential *disposition* rather than mere cognition. Yet affect need not be the absence of cognition; it can attune us to the world in an illuminating manner.[3] Emotions can be intentional in that they are *about* something in the world, often in informative ways (such as appropriate fear in dangerous circumstances). Different affects can alter how the world is perceived or apprehended and how affordances are disclosed: love and anger will shape different engagements and worry can prompt salutary attention. We are also familiar with "emotional intelligence," the capacity to recognize and assess the affects of others, a kind of emotional radar that can reveal and intimate psychological conditions in the social-world.[4] Empathy can be taken as a significant example of emotional intelligence, of being duly attuned to another person's fortune or misfortune.

Appropriate access to the world is rarely a matter of strict cognition alone. Sometimes sheer reasoning can be inapt. If I ask the doctor why my wife is sick, then how best to take care of her, and finally why I should take care of her, I am (paraphrasing Bernard Williams) asking one question too many. And strict adherence to the letter of the law or utilitarian calculation can supplant mercy or human decency. Of course, emotions can lead us astray, but it would be wrong to think that knowledge is utterly without affect or mood. Consider the role of curiosity in cognition: it involves being struck by a mystery or a problem in such a way that we are interested and drawn to understand it. Even "objectivity" is not without mood; it follows a detachment that is not itself a cognitive state because it stems from an *interest* in being objective, a disposition of drawing back from other interests, and a stilling effect on other affects. Moreover, research in neurobiology has shown that emotion can play a key role in high-order thinking and that rationality cannot function well without emotional input.[5] From an evolutionary standpoint and in general terms, emotion is central to *evaluating* situations as relevant to existential concerns, and without such evaluation, cognition would lack the capacity for a good deal of situational intelligence.[6] The world-disclosive character of affective attunement is more evident when "world" is construed as contexts of meaning—not mere cognition but existential meaningfulness, how and why things matter. Affects do not, and should not, satisfy traditional standards of "objectivity," but this does not entail them being simply subjective, if that means only an individual preference or an internal state separate from environments. As indicated in chapter 1, that objectivity matters to us is not itself an objective matter, nor would we want to call it simply a subjective feeling; it is rather an affective attunement to the world in a specific manner.

It is wrong to separate reason and emotion into two separate spheres because each can have elements of the other in its function.[7] Even scientific thinking is not utterly detached from affective dimensions in its work.[8] Because reason and affect can both have disclosive power and in an interwoven manner, we can posit a continuum along which relative proportions of the two powers can be located. This is an improvement over carving out two separate faculties or domains, which generates a host of difficulties in accounting for their relationship and mixed occasions. Reason and affect can be understood indicatively rather than constatively and stand for a balancing act rather than separate functions. A reason-affect continuum can allow for polar extremes of mutual exclusion. A person might "lose it" in an emotional explosion, but some element of cognition is usually still implicated. As we will see later in this chapter, a computer is a good example of purely cognitive functions. But with human beings, disclosive bearings will involve some blend of comprehension *plus* being "touched" by the world in a felt or sensitive manner, which at the very least indicates that knowledge is something we care about.

1.2. Intimation

Another element of disclosure is *intimation*, and this term is meant to capture the tacit familiarity and background comprehension that mark much of the environing-world discussed in chapter 1.[9] Intimation is a kind of "peripheral" understanding that is different from more focused cognition (ideas and beliefs). It implies the "intimacy" of ecstatic immersion and yet it can be articulated by exposition; so it is not noncognitive in the strict sense. Intimation also involves know-how and the full range of import entailed by an activity or practice (which again is often recessed). With my writing, for example, I not only have capacities and aims, I also intimate the *point* of the practice, as well as an implicit comprehension of how this practice fits in with the rest of my life and its narratives.

Intimation pertains to the (usually tacit) background understanding of the meaning of a project; it also sets up many foreground as-indicators, which pick out those elements that are pertinent to the project. For instance, from an earlier example, the meaning and purpose of restoring furniture is the background that animates the as-indication of certain practices, tools, supplies, and relevant items: disassembling *as* a repair procedure, a piece of metal shaped *as* a brace, a piece of wood *as* a leg, or a swath of cloth used *as* a protective tarp. Most human endeavors exhibit such a background-foreground structure with a wide variety of as-conditions arising from animating scenarios of meaning or purpose. For example, parts of a car are all determined as fitting the purpose of driving, the tacit meaning of which can be exposited in the face of some malfunction in a car's operation. As-conditions can even shift their significance in one and the same thing depending on the context: a pen can be taken as a useful instrument, a beautiful artifact (I collect pens), or a physical object that is kept from sliding off the desk; a hammer can be a tool or a weapon. Background-foreground structures also pertain to general areas of inquiry, such as history and mathematics, whose different projects will call for different ways in which, say, numbers will function. Even natural science—which takes the world *as* a set of objects to be examined independent of involvement and use in order to discover causal explanations—presupposes a background of meaningfulness: an interest in discovery, a preference for measurable accounts, the motivation to expand knowledge. In line with previous discussions, even the most exact disciplines cannot be separated from the lived world because they have to *matter*.

A plurality of as-indicators also pervades the personal-social-world, given the variety of background standpoints and postures that human beings inhabit. There are any number of group associations along the lines of family, race, ethnicity, nation, religion, gender, and language; also social roles pertaining to occupation and profession or to being a parent, friend, spouse, sibling, competitor, and so forth. It is evident that in certain contexts these as-indicators can carry reciprocal tensions or exclusions, for instance when occupational and family obligations conflict. Such disparities account for the complexities and difficulties that persist in the course of factical life.

Intimation brings up an essential feature of the lived world, its *correlational scope*.[10] In various contexts of meaning, there are networks of relationships that figure in the significance of activities, usually in a recessed and tacit manner. Consider my using a marker on a whiteboard in class. The marker is produced by other people and is specifically geared toward the surface of the whiteboard, which is structurally related to the room and building, which was built by other people. The purpose of the marker is to communicate with students in the context of my course, which fits within a curriculum of university education, which students pursue for a wide variety of purposes, and which inherits a long history of intellectual and pedagogical thinking. The correlational scope of the lived world in fact is an immense set of connections that is comprehensive of everything that matters in life, in such a manner that piecemeal analyses can never be the last word.

Intimation can also capture the sense of knowledge by *acquaintance*, an accumulated familiarity with something or someone that is more than a set of propositions or practices, that follows from sustained engagement and includes a rich sense of particularity and nuance. All this is indicated when one says, "He really knows baseball" or "She knows him well." Knowledge by acquaintance, especially regarding persons, combines fine-grained detail, subtle distinctions, and correlational scope in such a way that simple declarative propositions or reductive generalizations will not suffice. This is why it can be harder to answer certain questions about a person one knows very well (What's she like? Was he to blame for the breakup?). Knowledge by acquaintance can be better indicated in engaged dealings than in propositional statements.

Intimation also pertains to the meaning-laden and immersed character of lived experience. When I see my friend, there is a direct recognition of this encounter *as* seeing my friend rather than something along the lines of philosophical models that explain knowledge as the conceptual processing and organization of raw sense data—in which I "organize" sense experience by way of the "form" of "friend." In protophenomenological terms, I do not have a "sense experience" of my friend, I simply recognize my friend directly. Even ordinary experiences of things in the world exhibit a meaning-laden immersion. Hearing my front door open is not a matter of bare sound calling for analysis but an immediate sense of someone entering my home (my wife returning from work). Even hearing an unfamiliar sound is normally received in the meaningful manner of something yet to show its meaning (What was that?).

1.3. Language

The most important mode of disclosure is language. A phenomenology of language cannot begin with an examination of lexical units, verbal meanings, rules, references, structures, and so on. Language is not at first an object of investigation but the background for any investigation. Speech is not originally an exposited domain of representational relations but a personal-social-environing-world that is ecstatically structured as a field of communicative practices, in the midst of which the meaning of things is disclosed. Language, of course, is a central topic of this investigation; it has been implicated in everything explored thus far and will be fleshed out in the next chapter and all coming discussions. The proto-phenomenological analysis in chapters 1 and 2 provides the necessary preparation for a proper focus on language, understood as dwelling in speech.

2. THE SCOPE AND IMPORTANCE OF EXPOSITION

Immersion has a certain phenomenological priority because exposition emerges out of contraventions to ecstatic engagement. Yet exposition is no less real in its world-disclosive function, nor does it carry any deficiency compared to immersion (unless it leads to philosophical alienation from the lived world). Indeed, immersion can involve deficiencies that exposition could repair. As indicated earlier, one can be immersed in one's social and cultural environment in an unreflective manner that can host a range of impediments to improved or advanced understanding. Thoughtless absorption is a precondition for undue biases, prejudice, and blockage of new possibilities at all levels of personal, social, and cultural life; also for superficial and simplistic beliefs that conceal the richness and complexity of natural or cultural phenomena.

So immersion, in addition to being phenomenologically basic, is also problematic when it confines, constrains, or diminishes human understanding. Disturbances to immersion, internal or external, can prompt expositional examination and interrogation, which can improve comprehension, redress biases, or open new horizons. It is surely these problematic elements of immersion that spawned the traditional philosophical preference for reflective thinking. Yet a reflective standpoint also generated epistemological models and methods that proto-phenomenology aims to question and limit. The positive role that exposition plays in opening up what immersion can conceal does not alter the phenomenological priority of factical engagement that much of philosophy has concealed. Moreover, ecstatic immersion is not *by definition* a problematic mode of disclosure; it can be but need not be. There will be more to say about the function and scope of exposition in coming discussions of language and truth.

It should be obvious that proto-phenomenology itself is a kind of exposition, a reflective bearing on the pre-reflective lived world, and presumably an enhancement of understanding that is preferable to an unreflective posture. What distinguishes this kind of exposition is that its indicative concepts constrain the scope of reflection by opening up space "between" engaged immersion and disengaged exposition. Phenomenological concepts aim to intertwine expositional and pre-expositional orientations.

3. INTERPRETATION

The proto-phenomenology of the lived world shows that no inquiry can begin from scratch because it is saturated with prior modes of understanding and engagement that are *already* in place before inquiry. Part of the saturation is the historical inheritance that shapes us from the start in childhood. All of this can go without notice because of its tacit character, but it speaks against the notion that knowledge can proceed from an unadulterated starting point or achieve purely objective results independent of human involvement or historical influences. Such notions amount to a "view from nowhere," which proto-phenomenology rules out. We have noted that phenomenology attends to appearances without alien presuppositions. Yet one presupposition often found in traditional philosophy is that one can engage the question of knowledge from a presuppositionless standpoint. Proto-phenomenology shows that thought is always already contoured by a host of prior conditions.[11]

Contrary to the Cartesian ideal of a transparent, self-grounding starting point in the rational subject, the inquiring self is already shaped by its world and historical inheritance before reflective interrogation. The absence of an unmediated starting point means that understanding the world is a matter of *interpretation*, not in the sense of "mere" interpretation, but rather two baseline hermeneutical provisions: 1) an explication of something implicit and 2) a particular perspective that sets up one mode of access among other possible modes. The first sense of interpretation is what proto-phenomenology is all about, an attempt to articulate the pre-reflective background of disclosure. Hermeneutical explication stands *between* reflective understanding and the lived world in a manner described in the previous section concerning phenomenological exposition.[12] Interpretation therefore is an indicative endeavor that is freighted with the circularity of immanence. What is "already" in place cannot be understood simply as brute practices or bearings because our ways of living are densely infused with historical sources that reach far back in time and that are sustained in child-rearing and education. That said, the tacit character of a cultural background can benefit from reflective articulation, which can sharpen understanding and open up possibilities or problems that may be concealed precisely because a tacit background tends to go unexamined. The second sense of interpretation involves different possible orientations toward the world, which reiterates the previous discussion of as-indicators, of how a particular background sets up the way in which phenomena are engaged. This brings us to the notion of hermeneutical pluralism.

3.1. Pluralism

Contrary to reductive models of knowledge, there are many possible perspectives on the world that can be appropriate *in context*. Consider the example of a tree. If the question concerns what the tree *is*, it can be taken *as* an object of scientific explanation, a material object with physical properties, a source of lumber, a shady spot for a picnic, an obstacle for a builder, something to be preserved or protected, a historical site, or a thing of beauty. We can say that all of these interpretive as-indicators can be appropriate given a certain background context, that none of them presents the "real tree" in an absolute sense, measured against which the others are "mere" interpretations superimposed on the real thing. The *word* "tree" can cut across the different interpretations and thus gather them together, but only in an *indicative* manner that points to the different uses in their recognizable contexts without having to posit some universal or unified meaning that all the uses are grounded in or have in common. The gathering function of the word "tree" therefore has a *focal* meaning.

Interpretive pluralism does not mean that knowledge is without constraints. Each vantage point will involve specific parameters, guidelines, and forms of sense (which will be developed in chapter 4). Moreover, the brute presence of the tree can have a kind of referential priority. But the tree bears a number of possible forms of disclosure depending on the context or animating question. If the question concerns what the tree is made of or how it grows, a scientific account is appropriate for the question at hand in a more responsive manner than other interpretations. But different questions or perspectives issue different approaches fitting the context (for instance, the tree as a resource for lumber). Even the brute presence of the tree may be hard to fathom as such, if that suggests something utterly unmediated; coming across something "brute" for the first time is mediated by an interrogative context ("What is that?"). Indeed, "brute presence" is an abstract philosophical notion that cannot take precedence over factical and meaning-laden orientations that come first phenomenologically, as in the case of a child's first engagement with trees or "our lemon tree in the backyard, which gives us fruit and visual beauty."

As we have seen, the notion that scientific description gives us the real tree or the foundational account for any approach to a tree has to confront the active reconfiguration of natural phenomena in science and its complex preparatory background, which filters out many *real* ways of engaging a tree before the purportedly real tree is given to us. Science itself is a hermeneutical perspective on the world.[13] The supposed primacy of a scientific object may arise from an intellectual preference for the exactitude of deductive-nomological thinking, with its secured inferences and predictive success drawn from mathematical orders. Yet apart from the contextual validity of such thinking for addressing certain kinds of questions, it is difficult to take such an intricately prepared mode of thinking to be reading nature "as it truly is," full stop. A contextual assignment of different orientations seems more reasonable.

Interpretive pluralism can be tracked in terms of 1) *interrogative diversity*, in which different kinds of questions call for different responses shaped by the contours and implications of the respective questions, and 2) *phenomenological diversity*, in which different types of phenomena—living and nonliving things, artifacts and natural objects, physical bodies and activities, actual and possible conditions, social roles, thinking, feeling, speaking, and so on—call for different kinds of analysis. Reductionism amounts to assuming that all questions can be traced to or judged by one form of inquiry and its manner of response or one sphere of being.

An illustration of reductive thinking can be found in atomistic accounts that began with the Greeks. Compositional questions (What are things made of?) render such accounts appropriate, but if given reductive primacy, problems arise. If atoms are given a baseline ontological status, we have to flag collective entities, like a tree, as less real in a sense, as mere configurations of the basic building blocks of matter, as atoms arranged tree-wise (for the Greek atomists, true "being" could only be found in atoms, not their diverse combinations). And if modern physics tells us that the atomic dimension is not a matter of solid extension, the way a tree looks or feels might be flagged as not fully real. But a practical/phenomenological perspective would render such reductive notions useless. And outside of compositional questions, familiar entities may be impossible to fathom from a purely atomistic standpoint. If you did not know what a tree is ahead of time, no atomic or genetic assembly could get you there. Common sense ontology is our first orientation in the world, which is not and cannot be "constructed" from component parts *beforehand*.

A related form of reductive thinking is the model of mechanistic explanation, which can apply appropriately to machines and inanimate physical processes, but the application to living organisms faces significant difficulties of interpretive cogency. Organic life is often described in terms borrowed from engineering and the discrete functions of designed machines, which even in a metaphorical sense does not accord effectively with the holistic and ecological character of life forms. The common practice of reverse engineering an organism does not even fit well with the more haphazard, tentative, and probative character of evolutionary processes.[14]

3.2. Enactive Interpretation

Given the two baseline senses of interpretation—phenomenological explication and perspectival pluralism—there is also an *enactive* sense of interpretation that pertains to the ways in which the world is actively engaged in the different pathways of understanding. Enactive interpretation can be grasped first in the orchestration of various orientations on things, the shifting between perspectives on given phenomena or circumstances—for instance, the shift between factual and evaluative descriptions. Such is the *selective* character of interpretation that focuses attention on a particular perspective according to its relevance, which screens out other perspectives. Second, whatever orientation might be in place, there is the actual engagement of emerging possibilities of analysis set up by that orientation's criteria, methods, and capacities—for instance, the developing *course* of factual or evaluative accounts in the midst of complex scenarios or contending treatments (as in actual scientific research and ethical deliberation). Enactive interpretation thereby executes the looping figure-eight structure of temporality, the present occupation with future possibilities prepared by the past. The ongoing openness of such engagement and its often-improvised performance call for the suppler connotation of the word "interpretation" rather than more foundational conceptions of knowledge. The question of how interpretation can be coordinated with truth will be treated in chapter 4.

A phenomenological sense of interpretation is meant to counteract foundationalism and fixed determinations of meaning. Enactive interpretation operating in the lived world and engaged practices is different from "theoretical" models of interpretation, in which human understanding is the application of theories to experience or the reception of speech, as in the work of Donald Davidson. There comprehension is restricted to a monological spectator-model of processing cognition, wherein the social-practice-world is hidden from view. In many factical activities and conversations there is an immediacy and spontaneity that cannot be reduced to theory construction. When we normally engage the world and each other, we are not usually "interpreting" experience in the sense of fashioning how we should think or construct an assessment of what is happening.[15]

3.3. Reductive Naturalism

A common type of reductionism in contemporary philosophy is the naturalistic assumption that answers to philosophical questions must be based on findings in natural science.[16] The mind-body question, for example, has been dominated by versions of physicalism, especially informed by brain physiology, and the field of cognitive science addresses a wide range of philosophical questions by way of burgeoning developments in neuroscience and brain mapping. In some respects it is wrong to think that cognitive science and proto-phenomenology are mutually exclusive. Brain research and phenomenology can supplement each other in a number of ways (as I will show below). But interpretive pluralism rules out the notion that physiological facts could provide a sufficient account of human thought and experience.

Much of contemporary philosophy is preoccupied with causal accounts of thought, perception, and action. I can accept answering causal questions with scientific facts about human physical systems. But I want to maintain a distinction between causal explanation and phenomenological description, in which the former represents a highly refined form of exposition. If the question concerns, say, the biological cause of an experience of worry, I would be satisfied with a physiological account. But if such an interrogative context assumes an explanatory reduction, such that worry is nothing more than physical processes in the body, that is another matter. What *causes* a feeling in physiological terms cannot suffice for answering the question of what a feeling *is* in the full sense, its meaning and character in lived experience—which is the domain of phenomenology. Here I am confining the notion of causality to standard scientific accounts of physical processes in terms of constant conjunction, regularity, or probability, all gauged by the standard of repeatability and predictability. I therefore do not want to say that "reasons" can be causes. Reasons can explain why I am worried, but this would occupy a dimension phenomenologically distinct from a causal explanation of what produces this feeling in my brain. Reasons satisfy communicative expectations addressing *why* people do what they do, while causes are better reserved for explaining *how* things in the world operate in the way they do. The psychological concept of "motivation" can bear a quasi-causal function, but in a looser sense than scientific causality; a motivation fits in a space of *meanings*, not the objective space of physical processes. Besides motivation, there are a number of quasi-causal notions that generate or bring about certain effects in nonrandom ways with varying degrees of probability: intentions, aims, desires, inducements, influences, and so on. But I reserve the notion of causal explanation for the domain of natural science rather than the sphere of human action and interaction.[17] Neurological causes, for instance, do not count as "actions" in a phenomenological sense, whose quasi-causal antecedents could be called activators or generators in a rough sense. Such antecedents can be exposited from actions but in a manner different from physiological causal explanations. The distinction matters because the contextual-interpretive shift will result in very different vocabularies (why I help my friend versus what is going on in my brain at the time). Reasons stem from a first-person perspective within interrogative and conversational formats in the social-world, whereas causes are better reserved for third-person factual descriptions distinct from dialogical milieus.[18] Third-person scientific accounts are *constituted* by screening out factical contexts like dialogical practices. The former by definition cannot make sense of the latter as lived phenomena. Honoring the latter therefore requires a nonreductionist constraint.

Inspired by Wilfrid Sellars's distinction between "manifest image" and "scientific image"—between the normal given setting of human conceptual experience and the scientific shift to nomological thinking—writers such as John McDowell have worked with a distinction between the space of reasons and the space of natural causes in an effort to avoid reductive naturalism.[19] With the notion of dwelling in view, I prefer the "space of *meaningfulness*," which is more original and inclusive of the full range of factical meanings than are standard models of reasoning and conceptualization. Such inclusiveness can expand the "spaces" of disclosure in line with what I have called interrogative diversity—which is to say, an interpretive pluralism that tracks responses to different kinds of questions: space of descriptions (What is X?), space of causes (What brought about X?), space of reasons (Why did you do X?), space of abilities (How did you do X?), space of purposes (What is X for?), space of desires (Why do you want X?).

In chapter 4 there will be more to say about how interpretive pluralism can be orchestrated by way of interrogative diversity and a pragmatic account of language usage. For now I am simply saying that causal questions should not be the last word in philosophy, that scientific explanations of physiological processes cannot suffice for addressing philosophical questions. From the standpoint of physicalism, anything described as "mental" is really only a brain state (an "idea" or "feeling" is nothing more than a neurological event). Besides the impressive findings in brain science that correlate cognitive and behavioral capacities with neurological processes, one motivation for advancing physicalism may be the worry that the only alternative would be metaphysical dualism or theism—with the assumption that something other than a physical object will involve a different sort of "entity," a mind or a soul (like the Cartesian *res cogitans*). But proto-phenomenology is not primarily about reified "entities" but *ways* of being in the world—such that the word *mind* would not be a designation of a nonphysical substance but a *focal indication* pointing to the various ways in which knowing and feeling manifest themselves in life.

The personal-social-environing-world is a realm of meaningfulness that cannot be captured by physiological or neurological findings, which can indeed suffice for causal explanations but not for lived concerns and interests (which bring us to scientific orientations in the first place). Dwelling in the world eludes purely physical descriptions. If I am "in love," it makes no sense to say that love is "in" my brain or that my brain is in love. My brain cannot love any more than it can walk. Reductive physicalism amounts to a category mistake or the mereological fallacy, in which some horizon of life is reduced to component parts, thereby missing the full horizon of meaning. Being in love pertains to *persons* in a social-*world*, and meanings such as this call for articulation in phenomenological terms rather than a reduction to physical properties.[20] A neurological reduction cannot account for familiar senses of agency that are intrinsic to the personal-world, especially the sense of gathering experience into a coalescing whole ("my" writing project), which then shapes experience along the lines of "planning," "willing," "effort," and so on. Such psychological phenomena perform a narrational and explanatory role in factical life that neurological descriptions cannot supply.[21]

Proto-phenomenology is not a denial of, or a substitution for, causal explanations—I have no doubt that without my brain and its neurological processes I could not be in love—but rather an appeal for descriptive pluralism, in which the mental and the physical indicate different dimensions of *natural life* in the light of what I have called existential naturalism, which therefore is nothing like metaphysical dualism or theism. A plurality of irreducible perspectives on existence simply tracks different ways of attending to and talking about the factical world. Even if every element of my experience were precisely coordinated with my brain states, even if access to brain data could successfully "read" my mind—thus overcoming the "privacy" of introspection—that would not override phenomenological pluralism. Brain state descriptions could not fit what experience of the world is like or even fit the world-disclosive language that would have to transpire between myself and researchers to validate neurological mind reading. Moreover, because such experiences are *world*-disclosive, even a reduction to a "mind" would not suffice for expressing their meaning. In any case, a nonreductionist phenomenology can include physical and neurological accounts in the context of causal explanations. Interpretive pluralism would simply broaden the scope of philosophical investigation to include phenomenological descriptions (also to assume a certain priority of these descriptions over causal accounts). The main question I ask is this: Because physical and causal accounts are not replaced or ignored, what would be lost in adopting the phenomenological pluralism advanced here?[22]

Existential naturalism can include natural science while avoiding any trajectory beyond earthly life and experience. What is natural in this broader sense has to do with immanent emergence, that which manifests itself from its own power rather than being produced by an external agent, for instance trees versus wooden tables (such was Aristotle's distinction between *phusis* and *technē*). Consider again the notion of time. The figure-eight structure of temporality is natural to the human condition, a looping intersection of present, past, and future, which helps science get off the ground in the first place. Causal thinking, however, screens out this temporal background and shifts to a linear scheme with discrete time frames, wherein cause and effect exhibit an irreversible succession, such that the cause "is" prior to the effect. The point is that natural science requires a natural background of practices, intimations, and temporal sense in order to come to its causal findings at all. A reductive naturalism gets things backward and presumes to explain that which made it possible from the start. Science therefore has its own "natural history" in terms of how it emerged and developed and how its practitioners grow into its horizon.[23] Of course, the same natural history is evident in other disciplines as well.

A pluralistic check on reductive naturalism need not mean that natural science is simply left to its own devices without any interrogation of its methodologies. The concession of causal explanation to science in the mind-body question should also pay heed to questions about how neurophysiology can justify some of its own claims and contributions to the matters at hand.[24] It is often not clear how "causes" of behavior can be located precisely in specific neural states because brain activity is enormously complex and multifunctional. Moreover, there are organic and motor functions distinct from the brain that also figure in behavior, which brings intricate and contingent ecological factors into the mix. This is important because oversimplification and uncritical confidence in brain science have brought on questionable applications or proposals concerning neurological causes of complex conditions such as addiction, depression, criminal behavior, and learning processes. Such shortsighted projects can cause undue dismissal of, or suspicion about, longstanding and more circumspect beliefs about human agency in moral, legal, medical, and educational spheres.[25] Neuroscientific accounts of disorders and impairments can shift the analysis from "persons" to physiological causes, which can prompt the idea that disorders are more like a disease than a human tribulation. Even with the importance of physiological findings, we should be careful not to eclipse familiar senses of intention, effort, responsibility, volition, and choice, which seem to be intrinsic to the personal-world—and so presumably applicable to the *scientists* who are "responsible" for "seeking" and "discovering" such findings.

A core element in the personal-world is a sense of freedom. In the first chapter I noted that the phenomenological priority of the future and possibility opens space for human freedom. The first-person *experience* of performing an action or making a decision can surely seem to be free, as something self-initiated and of a different order than the force of compulsion. In the context of natural causality, presuming the so-called causal completeness of physics makes it difficult to defend the notion of human freedom if everything is reduced to physical states. But a contextual pluralism allows the phenomenology of engaged *action*, as distinct from natural *events* and *causes*, even the idea of *self-causation* advanced in some theories of freedom. This would simply involve the recognition of our sense of voluntary action as opposed to involuntary conditions—along with degrees in between, which can be sorted out in the course of enactive interpretation.

If physical causation is the reductive standard for understanding human behavior, we are told that the phenomenology of free action is not valid. We may believe in freedom, but in reality all action is determined by natural causes. Yet contextual pluralism would call for separating causal accounts from the factical experience of action—and asking what is lost by allowing the commonly perceived openness of action to have its appropriate place. If it is not real, we should ask the determinist what is to be *done* in life if our sense of freedom is false. A wide range of psychological, moral, and legal milieus would face a loss of legitimacy if none of our actions could have been otherwise as a matter of choice. Within the sphere of natural causality, even if we accept the fact that physical events are subject to causes, in the case of biological organisms (especially such complex types as ourselves) the *correlations* of intricate systems and subsystems—particularly the feedback loops between organisms and their variegated environments, along with extended figure-eight temporal loops—show that precise causal regularities evident in simple physical systems cannot apply to the circuitous complexities of higher life forms.[26] Some research shows that findings in neuroscience, which challenge the validity of free will, can be a self-fulfilling prophecy in altering how people regard self-control and responsibility in both their beliefs and their brain states in the course of making decisions.[27] As a metaphysical claim, it should be said that determinism is not empirically confirmable or even applicable to complex conditions of actual events, especially the behavior of higher organisms. It is more an ideal construction that fuels certain theories without being realizable or provable in all cases.[28] The distinction between phenomenological and causal descriptions is not strictly speaking a compatibilist model that allows the coexistence of determined events and tropes of free choice, because the domain of causes need not imply a deterministic closure that rules out flexibility and alternative possibilities, especially if causality is understood in a probabilistic manner. Nonetheless, the domain of free choice is more clearly disclosed in phenomenological terms.

Because proto-phenomenology sees the personal self as situated in world-environments rather than some discrete psychic entity or interior consciousness, there is no need for some sort of metaphysical freedom, in which self-causation is the presumed remedy for a deterministic reduction to natural causes. A central feature of the modern subject-object dyad was the notion of an autonomous subject with a different order of being than objective nature. Such differentiation opened space for the free-thinking subject that could stand for radical intellectual and political challenges to traditional constructs; also space for moral freedom as distinct from the mechanistic system of nature described in physics (this was the project of Kant's philosophy). Yet the subject-object divide creates many of the binary debates that have marked philosophy ever since: freedom versus determinism, liberty versus social order, values versus facts, and so on. There is another kind of binary in certain existentialist conceptions of strong subjective freedom (in Kierkegaard and Sartre, for instance), which has ultimate self-determination untethered not only from objective nature, but also from the social-world and inherited traditions.

A pluralistic contextual phenomenology, together with an ecologically situated self, can avoid such binary divides and their subsequent disjunctive debates. Situated freedom would simply describe various indications of open possibility within environments that also issue constraints on human action—in other words, environments that show or allow both voluntary and involuntary conditions, both variance and coherence. In this way, freedom can be understood not as a metaphysical ground or condition *of* the self but a capacity for self-direction *within* environmental constraints—also varying degrees of freedom in the midst of these constraints. Freedom, then, is something situated in contextual circumstances calling for hermeneutic analyses of what kind of freedom is at issue in relation to what kind of constraint and for what end. There are different kinds of freedom (behavioral, personal, economic, political, creative) with respect to different agents and roles (adults, children, workers, employers, students, teachers, leaders, innovators) in relation to different forms of constraint (physical nature, material need, instruction, social coercion, conformity)—and all of these factors vary and fluctuate between and within circumstances and agents. A phenomenology of such situational balancing acts need not be founded in some primal freedom of the self. We should not begin with the concept of freedom *from* constraint, but rather freedom *in* various milieus that help shape and sustain the self. In other words, human freedom can be understood as a *projected middle voice* phenomenon—an ecological sphere that is neither active nor passive in strict terms—that can neither be canceled out nor separated from worldly constraints. A phenomenology of freedom would be based in common sense beliefs about moments of choice as distinct from elements of chance or compulsion. Enactive interpretation would track clear shifts between choice, chance, and compulsion—and also labor over ambiguous cases of overlap, which elicit the many moral and legal distinctions of diminished responsibility.

4. PHENOMENOLOGY AND COGNITIVE SCIENCE

Cognitive science today is a vibrant and extensive discipline that investigates human knowledge and experience from the standpoint of neurological and physiological research programs. The discipline usually disregards or dismisses phenomenological descriptions, assuming them to be merely subjective reports that do not fit the demands of objective scientific explanations. Those in the phenomenological tradition likely return the favor and critique cognitive science as a barrier to genuine philosophical work because of its reductive naturalistic assumptions. Yet in recent years there have been developments that aim for a coordination of phenomenology and cognitive science, especially from the standpoint of Husserlian phenomenology because Husserl was working to provide a foundation for scientific thought with invariant, transcendental structures that are discoverable in the full range of intentional relations between consciousness and the world, which would be missed in a purely naturalistic framework.[29]

A Husserlian approach may indeed be effective in building bridges between phenomenology and cognitive science, but proto-phenomenology involves certain hermeneutical departures from Husserl—which might make it harder to coordinate with scientific research, even when not dismissive of science. Husserl was able to overcome the subject-object division with his correlational model of intentional consciousness, but he performed his own reduction by famously "bracketing" the natural world in order to discover space for necessary cognitive structures and ahistorical starting points. From my perspective, Husserlian phenomenology remains caught up in standard questions of cognition, even when it aims to describe practical and social life—and thus it works more in the mode of reflective exposition, which misses the dimension of ecstatic immersion and an indicative approach to phenomenological concepts.

I think there is ample room for a coordination of phenomenology and cognitive science, if only in terms of a coexistence of mutual recognition and reciprocal delimitation. Yet much work has been done to open up a robust sense of mutual *assistance* as well.[30] Phenomenology can help refine and interpret the concepts that are employed in cognitive science and perhaps resolve enduring debates such as internalism and externalism, intellectualism and anti-intellectualism. Phenomenology can also pose questions that are usually overlooked in empirical research (such as first-person accounts), as well as suggest experimental designs that might test phenomenological findings.[31] At the same time, phenomenology can draw some assistance from scientific research and its empirical findings, especially with regard to physiological causes.

Within my approach, proto-phenomenology and cognitive science need not be at odds, at the very least because of the stipulation that causal explanations occupy a hermeneutical domain distinct from phenomenological description. Yet causal questions are far from irrelevant in my estimation. Even though phenomenological investigation need not involve neurological research, there can be engagement in some respects. Cognitive science can provide supplemental support when neurological findings can correlate with phenomenological insights and thus draw attention to these insights from those who might otherwise be dismissive. Even more, I am comfortable relying on causal findings in the following way: If there were no neurological evidence at all that emotion and cognition are intertwined in brain activity, it would be a serious blow to philosophical claims about the world-disclosive role of affects in human understanding. And new causal discoveries, if duly supported, can and should have a bearing on phenomenological work in terms of whether a certain philosophical claim has any correlate at all in physiological findings. The argument in this investigation is against a reductive and exclusive reliance on causal explanations. Neurological facts cannot suffice for a philosophical account of human thought and experience in their factical character. Moreover, a plurality of interpretive standpoints includes certain "breaks" between them when contextual shifts occur (between, say, "how" questions and "why" questions or matters of fact and value), which marks what I have called enactive interpretation.

It must be emphasized that the "priority" of the lived world does not suggest a grounding framework to which all other orientations must be referred in a systematic manner. As the *first* world, factical life makes science possible and figures in the meaning and execution of scientific work. But modern science does involve significant shifts from factical orientations, especially with its mathematical and methodological features. Such shifting makes for regional conditions of incommensurability that are simply orchestrated by enactive interpretation without the need for a conjoining or unifying framework.[32] Herein lies a significant departure from Husserlian phenomenology, which aimed to ground scientific work in the life-world in such a way that scientific concepts could be based in cognitive structures intrinsic to intentional consciousness. Accordingly, scientific accounts could still be referring to the lifeworld. From a proto-phenomenological standpoint, however, scientific descriptions as such *diverge* from factical experience in decisive ways. Outside of such scientific findings, however, a wider picture of science does overlap with phenomenology when it comes to the meaningfulness and practices of scientific life.

4.1. Mirror Neurons

In discussions thus far, I have noted instances in which cognitive science can supplement phenomenological findings: in matters of immersion, the field-character of pre-reflective experience, know-how, habit, sociality, and affective attunement. I would like to add a brief treatment of how so-called mirror neurons can bear on my account of the social-world and the ecstatic nature of empathy. The notion of mirror neurons comes from the discovery that the same neurological activity occurs when someone is performing an action and simply witnessing the same action by someone else—thus suggesting a physiological basis for an intersubjective bridge between selves.[33] I take mirror neurons as supplemental support for social-world phenomena, especially empathy as an ecstatic shared attunement that is not directly exposited as a transaction between discrete selves or dispatches between mental subjects.[34] Yet a proto-phenomenological account of this shared social-world does not require neurological evidence to be cogent and is indeed lost when turning to such evidence—because of the expositional break between causal accounts and immersed engagement.

The phenomenology of a shared world also differs from typical models of "intersubjectivity" that account for shared experience in transactional terms and that have been invigorated by the discovery of mirror neurons.[35] Such models enlist neurological mirroring on behalf of "mind reading" theories, which aim to explain how we can understand and predict the attitudes and behavior of others. Yet these theories sustain a subject-subject divide that stems from the subject-object split: the "theory of mind" theory, in which I understand others by testing accounts of their behavior in a manner analogous to scientific theorizing; the "intentional stance" theory, in which I assume others to be rational agents like myself and make predictions accordingly; and the "simulation" theory, in which I imagine what I would do in other people's circumstances and predict accordingly. Here intersubjective understanding is not something immediately evident because first-person subjectivity is restricted to an introspective zone, which engages the behavior of others as a third-person event "outside" consciousness, requiring analysis before it can be understood as subjective agency.

In different ways, these theories presume mind reading to be a predictive process and a construction of understanding by testing various belief-desire-action sets, which can be cogent in some circumstances, but which in my terms is an expositional picture that does not fit the ecstatic immediacy and automaticity of immersed social relations or everyday tacit intimations that mark so much of social life. If someone reaches out to shake my hand, I normally do not go through analytical steps to interpret what is going on and prepare my reaction; I simply act in kind. Of course, I could be wrong (it might be a zombie trying to kill me), but there is generally an implicit trust in the meaning of social behaviors—which we immediately *live* through rather than think through. We dwell in ecstatic joint endeavors that presume a reciprocal, co-active, meaning-laden world that as such does not need to be analyzed or tested. If I see that someone is angry, this can be called a direct, noninferential perception. I am not reading the person's mind because the behavior itself is "minded" in a meaning-laden sense.[36]

As has been indicated, immersed practices can be recast in expositional terms, and appropriately so in the face of contraventions. But expositional accounts are neither necessary nor sufficient for ecstatic practices in the lived world. The same concerns apply to mind-reading accounts of empathy, which I have called "transference" models that do not accord well with immediate occasions of empathic contagion. The notion of mirror neurons is a significant development in cognitive science because it can prompt attention to the ecstatic character of the social-world. Yet besides the stipulation of an analytical break between causal explanation and phenomenological description, we should be suspicious of transactional mind-reading theories that likely have been reinforced by an inside-outside picture implied in attention to neurological states "inside" the brain processing data from "outside" the brain.

All philosophical concepts are expository in nature. Proto-phenomenological concepts aim for an indicative relation to pre-exposited experience. Traditional concepts that have accrued historical vestiges of the subject-object divide, that have missed or suppressed an indicative relation, may purport to have a bearing on nondivided dimensions (as in the work of Husserl), but the historical accretion carries a lot of baggage that can get in the way. For example, the notion of intentional consciousness, with its consciousness-of structure, aims for a mind-world correlation but can get bogged down in expositional distinctions and questions pertaining to relational conjunction. Indicative concepts try to avoid this bog.[37]

4.2. Representation Revisited

Cognitive science has generally sustained a representational model of the mind by construing knowledge as a computational process of brain-based representations that serve as causal explanations of beliefs and behavior. The traditional model of representation has operated with notions such as images, ideas, memories, signs, or symbols, which bear a descriptive, functional, or causal relationship with what is represented, in such a way that currency *between* the two sides is presumed and measured by appropriate conditions of satisfaction. Cognitive neuroscience seems to have simply continued this presumption, likely due to the conviction that a representational relation is required for the intelligibility of knowledge and behavior. The problem is that neurological findings as such—in strict physiological nomenclature—bear no evident currency with what is supposed to be represented (in the manner of traditional forms of representation listed above). There surely is a causal relationship between brain states and cognitive functions in physiological terms (as I have allowed), but a representational relation seems to operate in a different way (a cause does not "signify" or "refer" to an effect). It appears that cognitive neuroscience may have slipped uncritically from a mentalistic sense of representation to a physicalistic one. It is appropriate to talk of electrochemical facts in the brain, but it is difficult to know what is meant by a representation "in" the brain. Indeed, cognitive science has faced seemingly intractable problems in trying to deploy representations in a non-question-begging manner.[38]

In proto-phenomenology, representational explanations are neither necessary nor sufficient for indicative attention to engaged enactment, yet they can serve an expositional function. The problem with neural representations is that they appear to serve no cogent function at all; the very notion seems to be a category mistake. The problem is particularly acute when neurological processes are described as a kind of "language."[39] It would be cleaner to restrict neurological research to causal explanations, and whatever significance the research can have for understanding human cognition and behavior would need to be aligned with phenomenological findings to be hermeneutically responsive and robust. One possible avenue in this regard is the turn toward "enactivism" in cognitive science. An enactive approach not only challenges the idea of neural representations as functionally inapt, it also calls for investigating the human mind as fully embodied and embedded in a physical and social environment, so that the brain cannot be properly understood apart from the body's active engagement with its world.[40] This is consonant with the ecological structures described in proto-phenomenology. Moreover, enactivism appeals to empirical research that shows how organisms can respond ably and intelligently to changing stimuli by way of adaptive attunements and habits that do not require mediating mental constructs—which accords with what I have called immersion, improvisation, and enactive interpretation.[41]

4.3. Embodied Cognition

We have indicated previously how embodiment is an essential condition of the lived world. Merleau-Ponty was the progenitor of attention to the lived body and how it shapes world-disclosive comprehension and sets the stage for advanced levels of cognition.[42] In cognitive science the notion of embodied cognition, which aligns with enactivism, pursues research programs that can coordinate with phenomenological findings.[43] Embodied cognition involves the ways in which functions of the body and its dealings with the environment—which are distinct from the brain—contribute to cognitive processing, both causally and constitutively. Such an orientation challenges the reliance of traditional cognitive science on neural representations and the assumption that the brain alone is the site of cognition.[44]

The enormous store of metaphors in human thinking that are drawn from embodied experience—having to do with structures, spatial relations and movements, visual, aural, and tactile images, illumination and concealment, and so on—cannot be taken as merely a set of comparisons or ornaments. From a developmental standpoint at least, but beyond that as well, such metaphors are really the lifeblood of thinking and comprehension.[45] Indeed, research shows that cognition is better understood as a brain-body-world nexus that includes physical abilities and sensorimotor circuits.[46] Thus when we hold a belief, put a thought aside, construct a theory, or get to the bottom of things, and so forth, it may be that such uses are not *merely* metaphors that express mental states because in factical life cognition and bodily engagement go hand in hand. Accordingly, such metaphors would not have to jump some fundamental gap between (physical) doing and (mental) knowing. The biography of thinking begins with and extends from the somatic intelligence of navigating physical environments. Bodily metaphors, then, are inevitable episodes in the story of cognition. There is evidence that if people are first asked to make a hand movement, like reaching out to grasp something, they are more readily able to comprehend a metaphorical meaning, like grasping a concept.[47]

With respect to perception, contrary to a brain-centric theory of vision, a person's sensorimotor engagement with the environment constitutes visual experience in a manner not attributable to neural states.[48] Rather than the notion of "mind reading," an understanding of another person's beliefs and experiences is grounded in a mutual sense of embodiment.[49] Even memory involves bodily capacities and perceptions.[50] Regarding cognition, the traditional assumption has been that concepts are context-independent, which permits clean and secure constructs that are separated from the contingency and variation intrinsic to empirical conditions and natural events. Yet research has suggested that concept formation, in both development and use, is context-dependent in a modality-specific manner shaped by sensorimotor functions.[51] This coordinates with what I have called indicative concept formation and usage.[52]

Research in embodied cognition also helps support the phenomenology of ecstatic immersion in the social-environing-world, the immediate absorption in social relations and practical tasks prior to expositional demarcations. First, we can reiterate the role of mimicry in interpersonal relations. It is well known that humans imitate each other's speech, facial expressions, behavior, and emotions. There is now additional evidence that mimicry can be prompted without conscious awareness or cognitive mediation, thus suggesting a direct and automatic conjunction of perception and behavior without any perusal or deliberate processing.[53] Second, research on what is called haptic and motor incorporation shows that engaged practices allow agents to perform with tools and other objects in a manner that is as immediate and automatic as normal bodily activity, so that they have the experience of acting *there* in the space of the object without exposed attention to the relation of body and object. Such "being out there" is precisely what the phenomenology of ecstatic immersion indicates.[54]

In general, then, many developments in cognitive science from an enactive and embodied standpoint call into question the sufficiency of a subject-object framework and its representational corollaries.[55] Embodied cognition has also been recognized as an intrinsically social phenomenon, so that environmental networks include active participation of other bodies, not in a mind-to-mind relation but a reciprocal distribution between *participants* in a practical environment (think of my furniture-restoring example).[56] What I have called affective attunement has also been studied from an enactive standpoint.[57] Finally, embodied cognition can be enriched by taking the first-person perspective into account to open up a qualitative hermeneutics of the lived body in factical experience.[58]

Despite the great promise in coordinating phenomenology and embodied cognition, certain provisos and cautions should be kept in mind. The outreach to cognitive science can get co-opted by the experimental milieus and expositional vocabulary that mark the research. Controlled protocols emphasize piecemeal, isolated conditions that induce confined and relatively static moments of perception, comprehension, and action—all measured by presumed categories of cognition and experience that retain vestiges of the very mind-body distinction purportedly put in question.[59] Even research that aims to overcome representationalism can be betrayed by representational concepts like intentionality.[60] What is generally missing is the dynamic ecological field enveloping the spontaneous activity of an "animate organism."[61] Indeed, what no scientific research can capture is the proto-phenomenological "experiment" of first-person reflection on lived experience, which opens up the indicative concepts that have marked this investigation: ecstatic immersion, spontaneity, temporality, meaningfulness, and ecological world-structures. The inevitably expositional character of research in cognitive science and its third-person standpoint cannot presume to be the first and last word in the philosophical questions at hand. In general terms, the relationship between embodied cognitive science and proto-phenomenology can be understood as both co-determination and reciprocal constraint, in which phenomenology protects against reductive naturalism and neuroscience keeps the body in play causally, thereby protecting phenomenology from tendencies toward transcendental idealism.[62]

4.4. Proto-Phenomenology and Artificial Intelligence

The project of artificial intelligence (AI) in the strong version claims that computer technology can duplicate and perhaps surpass natural human intelligence. Proto-phenomenology is the most effective avenue for critical interrogation of this project. The meaning of "artificial" is clear in referring to a designed artifice as opposed to natural self-manifesting phenomena. The meaning of "intelligence" is the key factor in unpacking the problems in this question. If intelligence refers to sophisticated data processing, analytical capacities, and logico-computational functions, AI more than meets the test, even outclassing human ability in speed and accuracy.[63] It is safe to say that AI at bottom is a computational domain that banks on representational, analytical, and logical thinking, operating with intricate formal systems of algorithm code. As such, AI gathers the most refined elements of formal and material expositional thinking. From the standpoint of proto-phenomenology, AI operates in a derivative domain that is different from factical elements of the lived world: the meaning-laden immersion shown in know-how, tacit knowledge, intimation, and affective attunement, along with personal and interpersonal concerns. If these elements can be said to exhibit a kind of intelligence in a practical and world-disclosive sense, the replication project of AI faces a significant limit in seeming to lack important forms of intelligence. This limit reflects more than merely a barrier that more research and new techniques might be able to overcome; it suggests an incommensurable divide between computational and factical intelligence.[64]

Embodied cognition, as sketched in the previous section, stands as a significant case constraining the prospects of AI. With regard to the mind-body question, AI is certainly nothing like metaphysical dualism, but in some respects it exhibits a kind of dualism in its supposition that cognition is in principle separable from the *human* body. But embodied cognition as a challenge to AI would have to be understood primarily from a phenomenological standpoint because developments in advanced robotics exhibit remarkable capacities for navigating, manipulating, and even "sensing" physical environments. The comparative difference would turn on the lived character of human embodiment and its nonrepresentational, noncomputational elements. What is decisive here is recognizing the *biological* aspects of human intelligence, which carve out a different sphere compared to the engineered physical systems in AI.[65] This question goes all the way back to Aristotle, who took thinking to be a function of a living organism, unlike Descartes, who moved to separate the mind as a thinking substance from the living body.[66] Embodied cognition should thus be called *bio-intelligence*, in which the needs, experiences, desires, and vulnerabilities of a living body are not separable from cognition. Environmental comprehension, navigation, and manipulation are originally sensorimotor functions that are ecstatically situated in the world and driven by *sensitive* registers of attraction and repulsion, pleasure and pain, benefit and harm—which are not a matter of computation but *felt* perceptions of weal and woe.

Some might take a computer's separation from bio-intelligence to be an advantage because carnal forces can often get in the way of cognition. But if desire, need, pleasure, and pain do figure significantly in human comprehension and achievement, it is hard to see how these elements can be replicated in a lifeless machine. A computer can be programmed to "sense" an obstacle, but the factical experience of an obstacle *as* an obstruction to desire seems to be qualitatively different. Computers are impressive in performing sophisticated *functions* that figure in intelligence, but it is something else to call them "intelligent" in the full existential sense that is ascribed to human beings (and even animals). Science fiction aside, computers do not recognize the situation they are in at the hands of human beings *as* something fully in the service of human interests, which could be perceived *as* exploitation, or at least undesirable, by living, striving beings. We don't consider such matters in using computers and that is the point. We recognize the difference between animate and inanimate objects, in which animate interests entail a wealth of intelligent assessments of how things *matter* in life concerns. As noted in the previous chapter (section 4.2), we intimate the difference between a person-person relation and a person-thing relation, in which our treatment of a thing does not matter *to* the thing in terms of existential meaning. It is hard to see how a computer could comprehend the meaning of its operations in the way that humans can. We might attribute "personal" characteristics to a computer when our own concerns are involved (if something goes wrong with an entry, we might say: "It doesn't like that" or "Why won't it respond?"). But one sign of personhood is spontaneous resistance to mistreatment *as* something undesirable (which is a mode of interpretation). A revolt by human slaves entails that they *can* obey a command but *refuse*. If a computer does not obey a command, it is not refusing to do it; some malfunction has simply disabled a response.

In general terms, an important difference between AI and human intelligence turns on the question of design. Bio-intelligence is not "designed" in the sense of being conceived and produced by a conscious rational agent (*pace* creationism). Bio-intelligence is intrinsic to an organism and self-activated—and, from an evolutionary standpoint, not the product of an intelligent design. This is the difference between "natural" and "artificial" intelligence (going back to Aristotle's distinction between *phusis* and *technē*). What is important here is not a proposed "superiority" of human intelligence, but simply the recognition that bio-intelligence is a self-manifesting capacity that is meaning-laden and intertwined with its natural environment. Ecstatic immersion, intimation, tacit knowledge, and a range of sensitivities amount to an ecological "holism" that cannot be separated into discrete separate spheres. How can AI duplicate bio-intelligence when computers must *originate* in a design domain, which is the mechanical aggregation of piecemeal components and inanimate functions that *lack* a holistic biological structure? AI itself is a result of the disengaged subject-object divide that made mechanical production possible in the first place. Indeed, digital computation is based on the maximum abstraction of binary code (0 and 1), which by itself bears no relation to any knowledge of the world. Natural intelligence includes those dimensions of experience and disclosure that precede the representational and computational functions that have produced the operations of AI. A specific illustration of the difference between artificial and natural intelligence can be gleaned from what I have called enactive interpretation, which involves contextual shifts between different perspectives—factual, normative, practical, personal, interpersonal, cognitive, affective—normally in an automatic manner without the need for transitional steps or explication. This natural capacity to switch orientations, to grasp what is relevant or irrelevant, appropriate or inappropriate, is more a matter of intimation than conscious attention or reckoning—which accounts for the difficulty of replicating it in AI. Such a hurdle has been named the "frame problem."[67] Knowing the differences, for example, in engaging a question from a student, a police officer, a child, or a spouse is not a matter of computation. But the trouble goes beyond contextual shifting per se. Different perspectives are distinct but not always separate because they often overlap and are intertwined in certain contexts—all "gathered" by the intimated *meaning* and *purpose* of a given situation. Think of how the perspectives named above (factual, normative, practical, etc.) can circulate and interact in various contexts: classrooms, trials, sports, weddings, and so on. Expositional factors certainly apply here, especially in coming to learn how to navigate such contexts, but in time enactive interpretation becomes a matter of habit and spontaneous execution. Interpretive focus is *at once* a selection and deselection of what to ignore or suspend. But a withheld sphere is not a case of sheer absence because it simply recedes into the background and the deselection can be explicated or reversed if called for. In general, what is "called for" in enactive interpretation seems to elude computational processing.

Enactive interpretation—the automatic capacity to select/deselect for relevance/irrelevance by way of intimating a background of meaningfulness and correlational scope—is a fancy way of describing "common sense," which has been a sustained problem for AI because it is usually not a function of inference, rule following, or application of a format (and so not amenable to algorithmic coding). Common sense *reasoning* is surely something that can lend itself to computation, especially with respect to ordinary conceptions of time, space, and causality.[68] Yet not everything in common sense falls under the banner of reasoning, especially when it comes to cases of ecstatic engagement or immediate disclosure. This helps explain the irony that AI shows impressive success in the most sophisticated cognitive functions, while the presumably simplest comprehensions (such as face recognition) are the hardest to replicate. If I sense that I am driving too fast, that my class is restless, or that a last-second field goal wins a football game, such disclosures are not a matter of drawing inferences from a set of data facts according to rules of reasoning. As proto-phenomenology has shown, much human intelligence stems from immersed, embodied field-structures that precede the subject-object delineations that have driven much of epistemology and AI programs.

One of the blessings of AI is that the difficulties or limits facing the program can help illuminate, by contrast, distinctive features of natural human intelligence. Performance differences can pertain here, but even if computer programs can match human performance—and there are significant advances in computer "learning," voice recognition, and many environment-sensitive operations—one central fact remains: AI *by design* depends on representational and computational functions that are expositionally disengaged from the immersion-field of factical intelligence. Indeed, the very idea of artificial "design" is of a different order than the self-activating character of natural intelligence. Naturalists such as Daniel Dennett are keen to mark the difference between evolution and "mind-first" cosmologies that depend on divine creation or direction. AI is touted as ammunition in supplanting nonmaterial conceptions of mind by force of the computer's purely physical format.[69] The problem is this: Any way one wants to construe mentality, AI itself requires a *mind-first* design format in the production of computers. Proto-phenomenology is compatible with a biological and evolutionary orientation that rules out *any* conception of "intelligent design" (divine or artificial) being advanced as the guiding framework for understanding the full story of intelligence.[70]

5. PHILOSOPHY AND THE LIVED WORLD

How can philosophy itself be understood in relation to a proto-phenomenological analysis? We can begin with the notion of interpretation. Interpretation undermines the idea that thought can start from scratch, and so it implies an unavoidable circularity that is nonetheless not a vicious circle but a "circulation" between background and foreground, between already functioning modes of understanding and their explication. This helps us understand the phenomenon of philosophy. Philosophy puts the world in question rather than take it for granted, which is an openness that nevertheless emerges out of an already engaged world. Such questioning is therefore an *engaged openness*, a mingling of presence and absence, of having and not having, because we wonder about the meaning of something with which we are already familiar to some extent (What is the good life?). Our inheritance and past involvements give us vague intimations of familiarity, but something has contravened routine understanding and prompted an interest in questioning and discovering something yet to be formed. In this way, present inquiry, past orientations, and future possibilities circulate together in a figure-eight temporal structure.

The lived world examined in this investigation names what is already in place before philosophical reflection and analysis. It should be clear that what is already in the background is not akin to standard philosophical conceptions of the a priori (Platonic Forms, Cartesian innate ideas, Kantian transcendentals), which have been pitched as abstract theoretical structures that provide necessary and ahistorical conditions that govern thinking with a stable foundation. The existential background, as we have seen, is less than stable in being embodied, inhabited, interest-laden, active, social, and temporal, which is why traditional philosophy has typically shown dissatisfaction with the factical world. But philosophy itself emerges out of this first world and can be understood in terms of its own existential elements that fit the proto-phenomenological findings in chapter 1. Let me sketch some of these elements.[71]

5.1. Disposition and Exposition

As a form of reflection, philosophy is essentially a matter of exposition, yet of a much more far-reaching sort than ordinary exposition. And philosophical disengagement from immersed conditions is triggered by its own specific kinds of contravention, which are generally not practical disruptions but dispositional prompts that are precognitive in nature. Aristotle said that philosophy begins in wonder (*thaumazein*), which is not idle imagining but being *struck* by a lack of understanding and *striving* to investigate because of a natural *desire* for knowledge.[72] We are also told that philosophy involves confronting a kind of impasse (*aporia*) to understanding and explanation, a contravention that causes stress and an urge to find a resolution.[73] Such is the dispositional background of philosophical exposition. Let me call it an *interrogative mood*. Most philosophical questions deal with notions that have already been part of familiar understanding (like goodness or truth). And such questions most authentically stem from some contravening disturbance to everyday indicative concepts or established assumptions.[74] This mode of being-in-question, as I have said, involves the temporal structure of a disoriented present inquiry into an inherited notion with an eye toward a coming resolution, and the disorientation is not sheer ignorance but an odd combination of having and not having, an unfamiliar bearing on a familiar idea.

The dispositional background of philosophical investigation is more indicative of the personal-world in terms of how philosophy *matters* and why someone would care about it. Philosophy can never be fully understood in a third-person manner, despite this being the preferred grammatical form in philosophical writing. From an existential standpoint, philosophy emerges from, and points back to, factical life. There is always a personal dimension, if only to satisfy curiosity and the desire to know. Yet one way or another, philosophy is motivated by an interest in how life is to be engaged and understood, perhaps to bring order out of confusion or challenge the prospects of order. In any case, *something* factical is the lifeblood of philosophy.[75]

The personal-world cannot supply a sufficient existential account of philosophical life because philosophy is not sheer monologue, but also a social-world, at least in being stimulated by, or aiming to influence, other persons. Beginning with Plato, we can posit the intrinsically dialogical character of philosophy, a mutual search in conversation or writing that elicits intersubjective effects and discoveries, which would be missing in individual thinking alone. Philosophical dialogue is more than simply a mode of conversation because it involves a reciprocal *search* for a coalescing understanding that is yet to be formed—a possibility, of course, that may not often be actualized. The personal-world shows why philosophy is never sheer coalescence, but ever open and variable in composition and reception. That is why understanding a philosopher cannot omit attention to personal motives, interests, dissatisfactions, histories, and contravening factors.[76]

5.2. Philosophy and History

The figure-eight temporal structure of philosophical inquiry has a material form in its historical structure, in which history names specific *meaningful* temporal movements of cultural significance. Any cultural practice or domain has a historical structure when current aims for the future are prepared and shaped by an inherited past. The extent and complexity of inheritance usually go unnoticed, but any move in the world relies on a vast and wide-ranging network of influences bestowed by generational transmission. Philosophy has the same kind of historical scope, but it is often recessed, especially when current thinking is absorbed in its own projects or when past thinking might be deemed irrelevant. Yet the history of philosophical terms can be essential to careful consideration of intellectual questions. Psychological investigation, for instance, should attend to the historical transmission of the Greek words *psuchē* and *logos* because the original words and their modifications in translation and application can matter significantly in clarifying or guiding inquiry.[77] Another example is the complicated history of the words *subject* and *object*, which actually came to reverse the meanings of the Latin words *subjectum* and *objectum*.[78]

The temporal-historical structure of philosophical inquiry entails an intrinsic openness because it puts in question inherited meanings for the sake of some possible comprehension to come. Unless one commits to the idea of a completed search that resolves all questions, philosophy *is* historical to the core in being an ongoing search informed by the past. This is something different from the history of philosophy conceived as simply a sequence of periods. Any period of philosophy was or is an inherited reach forward. So we cannot separate current work from the complex of past conditions, and any consideration of past periods should avoid seeing them retrospectively as simply precedents for future developments because in *their* time the future was an *open* project that marked how their past would be engaged. In addition, any current tradition that is put in question was itself once a destabilizing interrogation of its tradition. Again, short of imagining philosophy as a path toward a final method or completed search, the historical structure of philosophy is an open project of questioning an inherited present, an openness that is not unhinged or autonomous because it has been shaped by the past and prepared for the future.[79]

The historical openness of philosophy together with its existential inception in a disposition like wonder creates a problem for reductive thinking and any metaphysical proposal of ultimate foundations. If such thinking stems from a question like "What is the ultimate source or explanation of everything?" it cannot answer or even address how it is we come to ask such a question in the first place. This is simply a phenomenological remark in line with the presumption of immanence. Philosophy as a lived endeavor cannot locate its own ground without already being in place as the *seeking* of grounds. Nevertheless, we can provide an indicative account of how philosophy comes forth in life.

5.3. Philosophy and Contravention

Philosophical exposition is stimulated by contravention in two basic ways. First, there are disturbances in the engaged interpretation of philosophical investigation within a particular orientation. This marks the problem-solving and exegetical character of most philosophical work. Then there are more fundamental contraventions that open up *new* orientations, which mark key periods in the history of philosophy. With Socrates and Plato, for example, we see the revolutionary response to traditional religion and poetry, together with a challenge to democratic openness, leveling, and rhetorical excess. In medieval philosophy there is the work of Christian apologetics, comprehending the mysteries of faith, and the ambivalent engagement with pagan thought. Modern philosophy was driven by the clash between new scientific thinking and the traditional complex of common sense, custom, and religious faith. Kant's philosophy can be understood as the attempt to both justify and limit science in the face of its threat to moral freedom. Post-Kantian philosophy confronted various dilemmas and restrictions in modern thought, as advanced by Hegel, Marx, Nietzsche, and twentieth-century developments in existentialism and phenomenology. Analytic philosophy was born in part as a retrieval of scientific thinking and the critique of metaphysical or idealist consequences of post-Kantian thought, especially British Hegelianism and historicism. Proto-phenomenology too is prompted by a basic contravention: dissatisfaction over the gulf between traditional philosophy and factical life.

In general terms, then, the history of philosophy presents various forms of reflective exposition in the face of some contravening disturbance, a mix of interrogation, elucidation, and new modes of disclosure. Too often—because of divisional, counter-positing tendencies in reflective detachment and expositional reification—such developments have operated with binary divisions or exclusive choices: between reason and emotion, realism and idealism, immanence and transcendence, empiricism and rationalism, science and common sense, body and mind, objectivity and subjectivity, determinism and freedom. It is conceivable that from a historical standpoint, such polarities may have been functional in carving out clear space for a given orientation in the face of competing forces. Yet proto-phenomenology involves a number of challenges to such divisional thinking in light of the thick correlational structure of the lived world.

As opposed to deep contraventions that generate new philosophical movements, in normal operations philosophical work will often look for, even imagine, contravening factors, either to help illuminate the work at hand or to heed standards of argumentation by addressing possible objections. Yet often such self-contravening discipline remains within the orbit of a prevailing theory or it serves a standard of indefeasible certainty by not resting until all possible objections have been met, even logically possible scenarios. Although notional contravention can be relevant, illuminating, even dispositive, actual contraventions in the wider world should be given pride of place so that notional doubts about the existence of the external world might be put aside; likewise, the possible secret machinations of an evil scientist who has programmed me to write a phenomenological work that overrides my actual metaphysical convictions.

5.4. The Importance of Philosophy

In everyday life we care about what we do and when some contravention happens, we care about how and why something got in the way or went wrong. Philosophers care about how and why things are the way they are all the way down or as far as such questions can take us. Most people don't care about philosophy, yet they can be drawn to it when deep or far-reaching contraventions occur in life.[80] Perhaps more people would be interested if the lived world were more the terrain of philosophical investigation than much of the discipline tends to allow.[81] In any case, philosophical reflection and exposition can be a great benefit when immersion blocks or conceals insights into important areas of life. When we hear, for example, "America stands for freedom," we should ask: In what sense? In what context? To what degree? For whom? For what? Philosophical exposition can attend to the rich complexity of phenomena that is usually covered up by everyday associations, routine customs, or simple generalizations. In the midst of human dwelling, philosophy can help us dwell *on* things more carefully, attentively, and perspicuously.

An aversion to philosophy is understandable; it is hard work and can challenge or disturb cherished beliefs. Yet there is a kind of historical myopia and contradiction when philosophy is ignored or marginalized. Many current interests that seem to be more important and consequential than philosophical reflection—say, technological achievements or common political protections—were made possible by philosophical interventions into familiar bearings at some point in the past. Much in the lived world and its meanings began with philosophical interrogation and found their way into established settings that (now) mark much of nonphilosophical life. For instance, assumptions about the "inner person" are part of most people's understanding, which is the result of philosophical constructions of subjectivity and objectivity finding resonance in everyday life. Indeed, this is why philosophy from a proto-phenomenological standpoint is not simply a turn to lived experience. Everyday beliefs and activities can easily conceal phenomenological insights and even prepare or carry the effects of traditional philosophical assumptions—such as individualistic tendencies or preferences for stability over change.

A central problem identified in this investigation concerns the lived background of philosophy in relation to an exposited reflective foreground, and whether philosophy takes a corrective or explicative posture toward that background. Some philosophical exposition requires a certain corrective posture—if immersion blocks reflection altogether or when modern philosophy was shaping the departures from common sense and tradition to make room for the new physics. A proto-phenomenological critique targets a more global corrective posture or the assumption that the first world in the background of philosophy must be reformed or reconfigured according to foreground reflective principles and structures. Often philosophical theories presume that the intelligibility of human thought and experience follows the way *philosophers* think, as though normal comprehension is also a theory-driven or reflective construction, and that philosophy will illuminate how we think or should think, even if we do not normally see things that way. Yet such reflective presumptions need to be constrained by attention to factical life on its own terms. Because even philosophy has its own lived conditions, it seems appropriate to begin with an explicative posture toward the first world in a phenomenological and indicative manner. It is not unusual to hear an appeal that philosophy should attend to, and be relevant for, real life. Yet proto-phenomenology goes further because philosophy itself is a living phenomenon and so the appeal has an *internal* warrant. When attending to the lived world, philosophy exposits its own generative environment.

Now that the first two chapters have prepared a phenomenological orientation and its philosophical import, we can turn to the most important component of the lived world and its meaningfulness: language. It is only from an analytical standpoint that we *now* come to the matter of language—which has been implicated in, and constitutive of, everything examined so far. For better or worse, my strategy was to first establish the philosophical background and tools that will render the discussion of language more focused and expressive of what is meant by "dwelling in speech."

NOTES

1. Affective attunement is my take on what Heidegger called *Befindlichkeit*.
2. See Lauren Freeman, "Toward a Phenomenology of Mood," *Southern Journal of Philosophy* 52, no. 4 (December 2014): 445–76.
3. See Martha Nussbaum, *Upheavals of Thought: The Intelligence of Emotions* (Cambridge: Cambridge University Press, 2001).
4. See Daniel Goleman, *Emotional Intelligence: Why It Can Matter More than IQ* (New York: Bantam Books, 2006).
5. See Antonio Damasio, *Descartes' Error: Emotion, Reason, and the Human Brain* (New York: Penguin Books, 2005).
6. See Dylan Evans, *Emotion: The Science of Sentiment* (Oxford: Oxford University Press, 2001).
7. See Christopher Hookway, "Affective States and Epistemic Immediacy," *Metaphilosophy* 34, no. 1–2 (January 2003): 78–96, and Ronald De Sousa, *The Rationality of Emotion* (Cambridge, MA: MIT Press, 1987).
8. See Paul Thagard, "The Passionate Scientist: Emotion in Scientific Cognition," in *The Cognitive Basis of Science*, eds. Paul Carruthers et al. (Cambridge: Cambridge University Press, 2002), 235–50.
9. Intimation is my rendition of Heidegger's notions of *Verstehen* (understanding) and *Umsicht* (circumspection).
10. This is my sense of what Heidegger called "referential totality" (*Verweisungsganzheit*).
11. The error of a "clean slate" assumption has been called a "prejudice against prejudice," against pre-judgments already in operation. See Hans George Gadamer, *Truth and Method*, trans. Joel Weinsheimer and Donald G. Marshall (London: Continuum, 2004), which is renowned for its detailed and comprehensive examination of hermeneutics with respect to language generally and philosophy in particular. For a critique of modern disengaged reason, see Adam Adatto Sandel, *The Place of Prejudice: A Case for Reasoning within the World* (Cambridge, MA: Harvard University Press, 2014).
12. Greek words such as *hermēneia*, *hermēneus*, and *hermēneuō* carry meanings of interpretation, translation, explanation, articulation, mediation, and go-between, which can be gathered from the god *Hermēs*, the messenger of the gods who announces sacred things to humans and who stands between mortals and divinities in this respect. Interpretation of the lived world is analogous to a language interpreter working "between" speakers of different tongues.

13. For a summary discussion that also provides a good bibliography, see Dimitri Ginev, "Perspectives on the Hermeneutic Philosophy of Science," *Hermeneia* 12 (2012): 107–25. See especially Joseph Rouse, *Engaging Science: How to Understand Its Practices Philosophically* (Ithaca, NY: Cornell University Press, 1996) and Robert P. Crease, *The Play of Nature: Experimentation as Performance* (Bloomington, IN: Indiana University Press, 1993).

14. See Maarten Boudry and Massimo Pigliucci, "The Mismeasure of Machine: Synthetic Biology and the Trouble with Engineering Metaphors," *Studies in History and Philosophy and Biological and Biomedical Sciences* 44 (2013): 660–68. See also John Dupré, *Processes of Life: Essays in the Philosophy of Biology* (Oxford: Oxford University Press, 2012).

15. For a critique of Davidson in this regard, see Michael Dummett, "A Nice Derangement of Epitaphs: Comments on Davidson and Hacking," in *Truth and Interpretation: Perspectives on the Philosophy of Donald Davidson*, ed. Ernest LePore (Oxford: Blackwell, 1989), 450–76.

16. For an overview of contemporary scientific naturalism, see Jack Rotchie, *Understanding Naturalism* (Durham, England: Acumen, 2009). A strong version of reductive naturalism is given by Alexander Rosenberg: The answer to the question of what the world really is can only be found in "fermions and bosons and everything that can be made up of them and nothing that can't be made up of them. . . . All the other facts—chemical, biological, psychological, social, economic, political, cultural facts—supervene on the physical facts and are ultimately explained by them." This is from "Disenchanted Naturalism," in *Contemporary Philosophical Naturalism*, 19. See also Francis Crick, *Astonishing Hypothesis: The Scientific Search for the Soul* (New York: Scribner's, 1995): "'You,' your joys and your sorrows, your memories and your ambitions, your sense of personal identity and free will, are in fact no more than the behavior of a vast assembly of nerve cells and their associated molecules" (3).

17. For the treatment of motivation that applies to a wide range of quasi-causal phenomena, including automatic behaviors that are not reasoned out psychologically, see Donnchadh O'Canaill, "The Space of Motivations," *International Journal of Philosophical Studies* 22, no. 3 (2014): 440–55.

18. For the sake of this distinction I want to avoid the language of the so-called causal theory of action. For a helpful account of the theory and an attempt to connect it with immersed activity, see Randolph Clarke, "Skilled Activity and the Causal Theory of Action," *Philosophy and Phenomenological Research* 80, no. 3 (May 2010): 523–50. For a recent collection of debates pertaining to mental causation, see Guiseppina D'Oro and Constantine Sandis, eds., *Reasons and Causes* (New York: Palgrave Macmillan, 2013).

19. See Wilfrid Sellars, *The Space of Reasons* (Cambridge, MA: Harvard University Press, 2007) and John McDowell, *Mind and World* (Cambridge, MA: Harvard University Press, 1994). An excellent discussion of these developments can be found in Joseph Rouse, *Articulating the World: Conceptual Understanding and the Scientific Image* (Chicago: University of Chicago Press, 2015), chap. 1.

20. For a critique of the validity of brain research applied to questions of human nature, see M. R. Bennett and P. M. S. Hacker, *Philosophical Foundations of Neuroscience* (Oxford: Blackwell, 2003).

21. The theory of "strong emergence" has developed to counter a dismissal of such psychological phenomena in neuroscience. See Eric La Rock, "Aristotle and Agent-Directed Neuroplasticity," *International Philosophical Quarterly* 53, no. 4 (December 2013): 385–408.

22. For a well-rounded and balanced collection on the issues surrounding phenomenology and naturalism, see Havi Carel and Darian Meacham, eds., *Phenomenology and*

Naturalism: Examining the Relationship Between Human Experience and Nature (Cambridge: Cambridge University Press, 2013).

23. Rouse, *Articulating the World*, offers an impressive effort to revise "naturalism" in this expansive way, including a background sense of temporality.

24. See Raymond Tallis, *Aping Mankind: Neuromania, Darwinitis and the Misrepresentation of Humanity* (Durham, England: Acumen, 2011).

25. See Sally Satel and Scott Lilienfeld, *Brainwashed: The Seductive Appeal of Mindless Neuroscience* (New York: Basic Books, 2013).

26. See Shaun Gallagher, *How the Body Shapes the Mind* (Oxford: Oxford University Press, 2005), 237–43. Gallagher also analyzes and critiques neurological findings that supposedly subvert free will by recording unconscious brain activity microseconds before conscious decisions to act. Another such critique is Uri Maoz et al., "On Reporting the Onset of the Intention to Move," in *Surrounding Free Will: Philosophy, Psychology, Neuroscience*, ed. Alfred R. Mele (Oxford: Oxford University Press, 2015), chap. 10. For a helpful analysis of Merleau-Ponty's contribution to this question, see Douglas Low, "Merleau-Ponty on Causality," *Human Studies* 38, no. 3 (September 2015): 349–67.

27. See Davide Rigoni and Marcel Brass, "From Intentions to Neurons: Social and Neural Consequences of Disbelieving in Free Will," *Topoi* 33, no. 1 (April 2014): 5–12.

28. See Leslie Stevenson, "Who's Afraid of Determinism?" *Philosophy* 89, no. 3 (July 2014): 431–50.

29. For a good overview, see Dan Zahavi, *Husserl's Phenomenology* (Stanford, CA: Stanford University Press, 2003).

30. See Shaun Gallagher and Dan Zahavi, *The Phenomenological Mind* (New York: Routledge, 2008), from which some of my discussion is drawn (especially from 217–22). See also Shaun Gallagher and Daniel Schmicking, eds., *Handbook of Phenomenology and Cognitive Science* (New York: Springer, 2010) and Susan Gorden, ed., *Neurophenomenology and Its Applications to Psychology* (New York: Springer, 2013). See also Julian Kiverstein and Michael Wheeler, eds., *Heidegger and Cognitive Science* (New York: Palgrave Macmillan, 2012).

31. For a defense of incorporating the first-person perspective in cognitive science, see Stanley B. Klein, "The Self and Its Brain," *Social Cognition* 30, no. 4 (2012): 474–518.

32. For a treatment of the Husserlian approach to science and the life-world, see Thomas Natsoulas, *Consciousness and Perceptual Experience: An Ecological and Phenomenological Approach* (Cambridge: Cambridge University Press, 2013), especially 229–30. It should be said that Husserl gives an astute account of how modern mathematical reason abstracts from the life-world and errs philosophically when it forgets this extension and presumes its constructions to be exclusive accounts of reality. See Edmund Husserl, *The Crisis of European Sciences and Transcendental Phenomenology*, trans. David Carr (Evanston, IL: Northwestern University Press, 1970). Yet the Husserlian life-world remains caught up in subject-object relations and standard questions of cognitive justification, which prompts a grounding in transcendental subjectivity. See David Carr, *Phenomenology and the Problem of History* (Evanston, IL: Northwestern University Press, 1974), 190–211.

33. See Giacomo Rizzolatti and Corrado Sinigaglia, *Mirrors in the Brain: How Our Minds Share Actions and Emotions* (Oxford: Oxford University Press, 2006).

34. See Frederique de Vignemont and Tania Singer, "The Empathic Brain: How, When, and Why?" *Trends in Cognitive Science* 10, no. 10 (October 2006): 435–41.

35. See, for instance, Alvin I. Goldman, *Joint Ventures: Mindreading, Mirroring, and Embodied Cognition* (Oxford: Oxford University Press, 2013), from which some of my remarks are drawn.

36. See Shaun Gallagher, "Inference or Interaction: Social Cognition Without Precursors," *Philosophical Explorations* 11, no. 3 (2008): 163–74, Jane Suilin Lavelle, "Theory-Theory and the Direct Perception of Mental States," *Review of Philosophy and Psychology* 3, no. 2 (2012): 213–30, and William E. S. McNeill, "On Seeing that Someone Is Angry," *European Journal of Philosophy* 20, no. 4 (2012): 575–97.

37. In my view, this is the central difference between Husserlian and Heideggerian phenomenology.

38. See William M. Ramsey, *Representation Reconsidered* (Cambridge: Cambridge University Press, 2007). Because cognitive science seems wedded to representational models in interpreting brain research while not being able to deliver a duly naturalistic account of neural representations, a "fictionalist" account has been suggested in which the notion of neural representations is objectively false but ineliminable because of its utility for explanatory purposes. Yet a fictional model clashes with the causal role that representations are supposed to play in cognitive science. Outside of fictional representations serving merely as labels for neural causality, it may be that the idea of representation loses its force when shifting from traditional to neurological uses. See Mark Sprevak, "Fictionalism about Neural Representations," *The Monist* 96, no. 4 (2013): 539–60.

39. The interaction of synaptic connections could be called an exchange of "information," but only in a metaphorical sense. To call it a language, even metaphorically, seems to violate sense, but that is how some research is being pitched. See, for instance, Morris H. Baslow, "The Language of Neurons: An Analysis of Coding Mechanisms by Which Neurons Communicate, Learn and Store Information," *Entropy* 11, no. 4 (December 2009): 782–97.

40. A seminal text that correlates "ecological psychology" with enactivism is Anthony Chernis, *Radical Embodied Cognitive Science* (Cambridge, MA: MIT Press, 2009). See also Daniel Hutto and Erik Myin, *Radicalizing Enactivism: Basic Minds without Content* (Cambridge, MA: MIT Press, 2013). A pragmatic lens can be brought to bear on both enactivism and the extended mind theory. See Shaun Gallagher, "Pragmatic Interventions into Enactive and Extended Conceptions of Cognition," *Philosophical Issues* 24, no. 1 (2014): 110–26. Such new developments in cognitive science have been gathered in the so-called 4E model: extended, embodied, embedded, and enactive.

41. In addition to *Radicalizing Enactivism*, see Hutto and Myin, "Neural Representations Not Needed: No More Pleas, Please," *Phenomenology and the Cognitive Sciences* 13, no. 2 (June 2014): 241–56. The authors are amenable to phenomenological accounts (Dreyfus, for instance), but they think (wrongly, in my view) that phenomenology is still susceptible to the possibility of unconscious representations.

42. In addition to *Phenomenology of Perception*, see Maurice Merleau-Ponty, *The Primacy of Perception*, ed. James Edie (Evanston, IL: Northwestern University Press, 1964) and *The Visible and the Invisible*, trans. Alphonso Lingus (Evanston, IL: Northwestern University Press, 1968).

43. For an excellent study bringing the two discourses together, see Gallagher, *How the Body Shapes the Mind*. For research on affects in this regard, see Giovanna Colombetti, *The Feeling Body: Science Meets the Enactive Mind* (Cambridge, MA: MIT Press, 2014).

44. A brain in a vat, therefore, could not be a functional organ of knowledge.

45. For classic texts on this matter, see two works by George Lakoff and Mark Johnson: *Metaphors We Live By* (Chicago: University of Chicago Press, 1980) and *Philosophy in the Flesh* (New York: Basic Books, 1999).

46. See Francisco Varela et al., *The Embodied Mind: Cognitive Science and Human Experience* (Cambridge, MA: MIT Press, 1991).

47. See Benjamin K. Bergen, *Louder Than Words: The New Science of How the Mind Makes Meaning* (New York: Basic Books, 2012), chap. 9.

48. See Alva Noë, *Action in Perception* (Cambridge, MA: MIT Press, 2004).
49. See Giacomo Rizzolatti and Laila Craighero, "The Mirror-Neuron System," *Annual Review of Neuroscience* 27 (2004): 168–92.
50. See Margaret Wilson, "The Case for Sensorimotor Coding in Working Memory," *Psychonomic Bulletin and Review* 9 (2001): 49–57.
51. See Vittorio Gallese and George Lakoff, "The Role of the Sensorimotor System in Conceptual Knowledge," *Cognitive Neuropsychology* 21 (2005): 455–79, and Consuelo B. Boronat et al., "Distinction between Manipulation and Function Knowledge of Objects," *Cognitive Brain Research* 23 (2005): 361–73.
52. See the introduction to this book, section 6.
53. See Tanya L. Chartrand et al., "Beyond the Perception-Behavior Link: The Ubiquitous Utility and Motivational Moderators of Nonconscious Mimicry," in *The New Unconscious*, chap. 13.
54. See Filipe Herkenhoff Carijó et al., "On Haptic and Motor Incorporation of Tools and Other Objects," *Phenomenology and the Cognitive Sciences* 12, no. 4 (December 2013): 685–701.
55. See Karim Zahidi, "Non-Representationalist Cognitive Science and Realism," *Phenomenology and the Cognitive Sciences* 13, no. 3 (September 2014): 461–475.
56. See Gün R. Semin and Eliot R. Smith, "Socially Situated Cognition in Perspective," *Social Cognition* 31, no. 2 (2013): 125–46.
57. See Giovanna Colombetti, "Enactive Affectivity, Extended," *Topoi* (2015), DOI: 10.1007/s11245-015-9335-2.
58. See Michael Larkin et al., "Interpretive Phenomenological Analysis and Embodied, Active, Situated Cognition," *Theory and Psychology* 21, no. 3 (2011): 318–37.
59. See Uljana Feest, "Phenomenal Experiences, First-Person Methods, and the Artificiality of Experimental Data," *Philosophy of Science* 81 (December 2014): 927–39.
60. See Jean-Michael Roy, "Anti-Cartesianism and Anti-Brentanism: The Problem of Anti-Representationalist Intentionalism," *Southern Journal of Philosophy* 53, Spindel Supplement (2015): 90–125.
61. Maxine Sheets-Johnstone, "Embodiment on Trial: A Phenomenological Investigation," *Continental Philosophy Review* 48, no. 1 (March 2015): 23–39. Also noted in this article is the omission of ontogenetic learning environments that underlie mature capacities.
62. See Francisco Varela, "Neuro-Phenomenology: A Methodological Remedy for the Hard Problem," *Journal of Consciousness Studies* 3, no. 4 (1996): 330–49.
63. Deep Blue made headlines when it beat a human grand master in chess; also Watson, which defeated champions of Jeopardy, a game that involves a number of surprisingly difficult forms of understanding and inference, which Watson was able to "learn" through trial and error.
64. The most influential analysis in this regard is the work of Hubert Dreyfus, which is inspired by Heideggerian phenomenology. See *What Computers Can't Do: A Critique of Artificial Reason* (New York: Harper and Row, 1972) and *What Computers Still Can't Do* (Cambridge, MA: MIT Press, 1992). See also John Haugeland, *Artificial Intelligence: The Very Idea* (Cambridge, MA: MIT Press, 1989).
65. The biological factor would undermine the functionalist version of AI, in which only intelligent functions matter, not the physical medium (that is, brains and computers).
66. More on this in chapter 4.
67. See Hubert L. Dreyfus, "Why Heideggerian AI Failed and How Fixing It Would Require Making It More Heideggerian," *Philosophical Psychology* 20 (2007): 247–68; also Michael Wheeler, "Cognition in Context: Phenomenology, Situated Robots, and the Frame Problem," *International Journal of Philosophical Studies* 16, no. 3 (2008): 323–49.

68. See Erik T. Mueller, *Commonsense Reasoning* (San Francisco, CA: Morgan Kaufmann Publishing, 2006). Mueller assumes that such reasoning is inferential, representational, computational, and best rendered declaratively rather than procedurally. The format is an "event calculus reasoning program."

69. See Daniel C. Dennett, *Darwin's Dangerous Idea: Evolution and the Meanings of Life* (New York: Penguin Books, 1995).

70. In chapter 3, I will apply this discussion of AI to the question of language.

71. For the Greeks, philosophy was not simply an intellectual endeavor, but also a way of life. Yet sometimes a philosophical life involved a disciplined withdrawal from the lived world for the sake of some higher reality or detached mentality—which departs from the presumption of immanence stipulated in this investigation. Nevertheless, any form of philosophy can be shown to emerge out of the lived world.

72. *Metaphysics* 982b12ff. and 980a21.

73. *Metaphysics* 995a24ff.

74. Often teaching philosophy at the introductory level is best served by finding real contraventions in the lives of students because the interrogations in professional philosophical circles often come across to them as strange. They wonder why any of it matters, which is not exactly the kind of wonder that generates philosophy. Yet I never disparage that reaction. I tell students that some philosophers agree with them, but that spelling it out takes a lot of philosophical work!

75. Such is the virtue of writers in the so-called existentialist tradition.

76. For a classic investigation of philosophy in this regard, see Hans Georg Gadamer, *Dialogue and Dialectic: Eight Hermeneutical Studies on Plato*, trans. P. Christopher Smith (New Haven, CT: Yale University Press, 1980).

77. See my *Myth and Philosophy: A Contest of Truths* (Chicago: Open Court, 1990), chap. 7; also "*Phainomenon* and *Logos* in Aristotle's Ethics," in *Phenomenology and Virtue Ethics*, eds. Kevin Hermberg and Paul Gyllenhammer (London: Bloomsbury, 2013), 9–28.

78. See my "Can We Drop the Subject? Heidegger, Selfhood, and the History of a Modern Word," in *Phenomenology, Existentialism, and Moral Psychology*, eds. Hans Pedersen and Megan Altman (New York: Springer, 2015), 13–30.

79. The figure-eight structure of philosophical temporality and history suggests that past works cannot be seen as antiquarian relics bound to their own time. Every great philosophical text had its own future scope in aiming to affect the course of thinking. In this way our appropriation of these texts is continuous with them, even if we take their meaning in modified ways. The same historical arc holds for currently produced texts and their futures. This is why a philosophical text cannot be construed as a self-contained whole within its own time frame or even its own aims. Such is the dialogical model of textual hermeneutics advanced by Gadamer in *Truth and Method*. Engaging a text involves reciprocal effects on both the reader and the text.

80. The 1960s, for example, generated a lot of interest in philosophy, owing to concerns about war and peace, racial and gender discrimination, and environmental concerns.

81. The phenomenological priority of the lived world suggests that the purpose of philosophy cannot be reduced to its own self-contained disciplinary world. It should have an indicative effect on factical life, which is rare given the professional impulse toward specialized agendas, esoteric nomenclature, and isolated conversations. Graduate programs today are more a kind of monasticism than engagement with public concerns; undergraduate teaching is more often seen as a compulsory burden; and the aim seems to be little more than self-replication, the circular reproduction of professional scholars. For a critique of the professional compression of philosophy into technical skills and specialist conversations removed from everyday life, see John Kekes, *The*

Nature of Philosophical Problems: Their Causes and Implications (Oxford: Oxford University Press, 2014).

Chapter Three

Proto-Phenomenology and Language

1. NATURAL LANGUAGE

Natural language is the language into which we are born, the language we learn as children and come to speak normally, our "mother tongue." A proto-phenomenology of natural language cannot be grounded in signification theories, in which words are signs for things in the world or ideas in the mind. Language should be understood first as a mode of dwelling—indeed as the most important mode—where we inhabit language as the opening up and articulation of meaning in the world. All other elements of dwelling are given voice in language. Examination must begin with factical language, with meaningful speech practices and exchanges in the midst of the personal-social-environing-world. As such, language is not primarily an individual faculty but *public communicative practice*, a shared environment that exhibits an ecstatic condition of engaged immersion, which only derivatively can be exposited into objective conditions such as words, signs, semantic meanings, and grammatical structures. Originally the self is absorbed in a communication network of *talk*, which is a talking *about* the world and its meaning *with* other speakers. Just as we can be absorbed in using an instrument without conscious reflection, we are usually engaged in speech about the world without reflective attention to words, intentions, reference, and so forth.

Factical language must also include embodiment and the full range of ecological factors that go with speech practices: mouth, tongue, voice, sound, intonation, rhythm, gestures, body movements, listening, and responding. Such factors show that words per se are part of the larger phenomenon of communication, which can open up the wider natural setting of language and also the possibility of "language" in nonhuman animals. Nevertheless, central attention should be given to verbal expression for an understanding of language, which I hope will be demonstrated in what follows. It is important to note that my emphasis on communication is different from so-called communicative theories of language, in which natural speech is simply the conveyance of nonlinguistic mental content and cognitive structures to other minds. In my approach, language is constitutive of "thought" (which in my terms is an exposited notion derived from communicative practice). The intricacies of a language-thought correlation will be covered in due course, particularly in section 8 below.

2. THE PHENOMENOLOGICAL PRIORITY OF LANGUAGE

To begin the discussion, my position is that language is at the heart of human dwelling, that language is the opening up of the world and the precondition for thought. Language cannot be grasped simply as object-designation, the representation of things or thoughts, or the conveyance of meaning because any such theory draws from a host of notions already presented in language. To think that the world is a set of nonlinguistic things or events that are designated by words is to overlook the fact that "thing" is a word—as are "event," "world," "is," "a," and so on. The very idea of language as a set of words or signs is exposited from the speech-world in which we dwell before any explanatory or reflective project. It can be said that language *presents* the world before anything (including language) can be re-presented.

What follows is the difficulty in accounting for knowledge by tracing it to the human mind or objects in the world because "mind" and "object" are linguistic presentations (and the consequence of a complex history of usage and theorizing). Any explanatory reduction (to a cause, entity, or faculty) would postdate the operation of language. Even the attempt to explain language must circuitously employ language (for instance, "words" as "expressions" of "ideas"). From this standpoint, there is "nothing" outside of language, at least in the following sense:

What can one *say* about a nonlinguistic foundation of language or something prior to language? Put positively, from a phenomenological standpoint the world is disclosed through language. This is not to countenance something like linguistic idealism. With proto-phenomenology, we *inhabit* a world; it is not produced or even "constructed" by us as language speakers. If I am rummaging around and someone asks what I am doing, I would not answer that I am looking for the phrase "my wallet." There is an extra-linguistic world that must be presumed because speech is first and foremost immersed in practices navigating an environing-world and not simply a set of linguistic signs. Moreover, there are a host of constraints (environmental, practical, and social) that limit and check what can be said. Yet even what is "other" than or "limiting" language has been *expressed* as such and thus rendered comprehensible. Language does not produce the world but it has a certain priority in being the window to the world, without which the meaningfulness of the world would not open up. A dramatic example is the case of Helen Keller, who tells of how the meaning of things was hidden from her until she was finally able to access language and communication through the sense of touch.[1] Accordingly, my approach fits the so-called linguistic turn in philosophy (although perhaps in a more radical manner than some would like), in which philosophical questions must at least begin with an examination of language.[2]

One might object to the priority of language advanced here: Are there not experiences and activities in which language is not operating? Think of silently witnessing a dancer silently performing expressive movements, in which both the reception and the performance function without any words. True, but from a philosophical standpoint, once we are inquiring into the question at hand and bring up this purported counter-example we are caught up in linguistic operations; even an analysis of silence is impossible without language. But what if we are not practicing philosophy and simply witnessing the dancer? First of all, because language is essentially embodied communication, we can talk of the "language" of dance. But more, with the witnessing of the dance, with even the experience of, say, a landscape, there persists a certain priority of verbal expression in the following sense: As language speakers we have already been oriented toward disclosive modes of comprehension that prepare the meaningful engagement of such nonverbal experiences and that allow us to talk about them meaningfully at any time—even if it comes to saying: "Words can't describe how beautiful the dance was" (which is still saying something meaningful).

To have a human "experience" of something presupposes a wealth of prior understandings that go all the way back to childhood and the learning of language. Even an experience of something strange, unmeaningful, or incomprehensible is engaged *as* such because of a default orientation toward meaning shaped by language.

Again, this is not to say that language *creates* meaningful experience. Language unfolds out of its environment in natural life. With the ecological character of the lived world, we are unable to advance binary separations like subject and object or language and world, which rules out any kind of idealism, linguistic or otherwise. Here we also can address the difficult question of how to characterize the lives of animals and infants that do not have speech. Even though mature human practices are informed by language, the phenomenon of nonreflective capacious know-how allows us to recognize the "intelligence" of animal and infant behavior. Yet language will exhibit a qualitatively different character that exponentially alters language-lacking behavior—in such a way that we should not attribute the capable skills of animals and infants to their "concepts," "theories," or any such mentalistic notion, which amount to undue exports from the sphere of spoken (and written) language. Mature language speakers are able to *comprehend* their behavior *as* such, which transforms communication (which animals exhibit) into disclosure of the space of meanings that are otherwise concealed. That is why we can come to the assistance of animals in their circumstances with comprehensions that are not evident to them. But language emerges *in the midst of* an enacted, embodied milieu and retains in many ways its nonreflective modes of habituated life.

3. LANGUAGE AND THE LIVED WORLD

Language exhibits all the elements of the lived world discussed in chapter 1; indeed, it is the articulated disclosure of that world (which is the sphere of interpretation). Language encompasses the full structure of the personal-social-environing-world in that each of us is an *individual* speaker communicating *with* others *about* the world—which is mirrored grammatically in first-, second-, and third-person usage. Moreover, language itself is an environment in which we dwell; it is a meaning-laden activity and capacity that usually goes unnoticed (*as* such an articulated phenomenon) in everyday life. Let me sketch the ways in which language reiterates the phenomenological findings in chapter 1.

3.1. Ecstatic Dwelling

The most basic and original form of language is face-to-face speech in the course of factical life, which primarily concerns engaged dealings with the environing-world and social-world. Normally we dwell in speech in the manner of ecstatic immersion, which is a field of talking-about-the-world, wherein descriptions and meanings are experienced directly without self-conscious reflection about "words" in relation to "things" and "speakers." Speech is an ongoing opening of and to the lived world. Not only does speech concern engaged practices, speech itself is an engaged practice. Not only does speech concern capacious know-how and habituated activities, speech itself is a capacious habit (assuming normal linguistic competency), which *as* such goes unnoticed and recedes in favor of what is being disclosed in speech.

Like all forms of immersion, the ecstatic speech-world can shift into exposition in the face of contravention, which then draws attention to specific facets of this field of speech. Now we can become more conscious of explicit elements of the speech-world, such as the meaning of words or the correlations of words and things—ranging from everyday exposition and interrogation all the way to linguistic theories. Within this field of speech there is also a bi-directional relation between immersion and exposition in a manner equivalent to the discussion in chapter 1 about learning to play the piano. In learning new uses of language or a new language altogether, analytical distinctions and steps initiate a process that can evolve into second-nature capabilities. Still, a background of habituated immersion in native language is the precondition for such developments.

Dwelling in the speech-world is the most telling indication of circular immanence and interpretation, in that no expositional account of language can capture, explain, or override the *already* functioning linguistic environment that makes possible any exposition in the first place. The ecstatic ecology of speech shows that language cannot be sufficiently understood with exposed divisions between words, utterances, propositions, and meanings on one side and the surrounding world on the other side. Within speech immersion there are no such discrete spheres. Indeed, language itself is a kind of environment "outside" us, so to speak, and in which we are absorbed. This is evident when considering the material character of language, namely the sounds we hear and the graphics we read. Language in this respect is *there* in the world as a kind of mid-world between selves and what is disclosed through language.³ This is one reason why language should not be reduced to some "subjective" sphere, even if simply to one side of the language-world relation. Language has a kind of objective aspect in its material presence, and from a phenomenological standpoint immersion in that presence cannot be reduced to subjectivity.

3.2. Existential Meaning

The material presence of language cannot be reduced to an objective sphere either, at least not in the strict sense of being divorced from existential significance. As in the lived world generally, speech practices are meaning-laden, are saturated with the factical concerns, purposes, and possibilities directly indicated in face-to-face conversations. The semantic meaning of words is not the same thing as the factical meaningfulness of words engaged in real-life circumstances. The semantic meaning of the word *love* is not the same as hearing "I don't love you anymore." A comparable abstract distance is shown in all the expositional analyses of linguistics, in formal constructions such as propositions, grammatical functions, signification, and syntax. The same can even be said for proto-phenomenological concepts, although their indicative character is meant to address this expositional problem. In factical speech, existential meaning is the immediate inhabited force of language and not simply a matter of "reference," "expression," or "transmission." In both the production and reception of spoken language, words are not mere conveyors of pre-linguistic meaning and thought; they *present* meaning in a direct manner.⁴ A significant aspect of meaningfulness is affective attunement, how existential import is disclosed by feelings, emotions, and moods. Beyond the function of object designation and description, there is growing understanding of how face-to-face embodied speech communicates a host of affective meanings in direct and indirect ways, which are often intertwined with and influencing so-called descriptive expression.⁵

3.3. The Personal-Social-Environing-World

Language as a personal-world indicates the first-person experience of speaking and listening in a meaningful environment of speech. Yet language readily illustrates the inseparability and reciprocity of the personal and social worlds. Most linguistic theories seem restricted to individual occasions of speech and their meaning, thus following a monological perspective. But the primacy of face-to-face speech means that solitary utterances are derived from the more original dialogical field of speaking-listening-responding—of communicating.[6] The *addressive* character of language shows that linguistic meaning should not be reduced to the intentions of individual speakers. Communication is more than just an exchange of words and their meaning. It is a social-world that is intimated as such by participants. Conversations presume a communicative purpose and shaped meanings in the course of talking; even contraventions of immersed exchanges (like disagreement) are jointly recognized as such, as part of conversational practice.[7]

Language, its acquisition and practice, require a presumption of common usage, yet this does not mean some store of precise and stable meanings to which all individual utterances can be referred. Given different contexts and personal perspectives, speech as a form of address must be flexible, variable, and porous because meaning is rarely fixed and communication is not always isomorphic. To our consternation at times, meaning is not an individual possession or protectorate; it involves intersecting collaborative achievements and movements in a social dynamic of elaboration, sometimes in contravening ways. Perhaps this is why linguistic theories have tended toward monological models; with dialogical address as a baseline phenomenon, language exceeds anyone's control. Even with such excess, communication is the core function of natural language, but in a manner that exceeds another kind of control, namely reflective governance. In line with the immersed character of everyday speech, the conversational capacity to make sense and understand the sense of other speakers is normally a habituated skill, which is enacted in an immediate and spontaneous way and which precedes exposition into conversational components or overt rules. This skill includes enactive interpretation shown in the shifts between diverse settings of speech. The capacity to engage in conversation is more a matter of tacit intimation than conscious direction.[8]

The communicative function of language should be understood as a practice-field that precedes and exceeds a sharp delineation of individual speakers conceived as starting points in the issuance of conversation. Communication is not simply the "result" of transmissions between private agents. From the very beginning in childhood, language is a joint engagement with repeatable meanings, which simply *is* a project of communication, of aiming to be understood and to understand. When we talk, we dwell in a default expectation of communication, which is always already in place as the *point* of speech. This default condition includes an intimation of the possibility of miscommunication and misunderstanding. We find ourselves *projected* into this communicative network, which is an intersubjective phenomenon that challenges individualistic theories of communication grounded in intentional meanings and transmissions.[9] This is not to deny introspective dimensions of speech and thought, which are genuine phenomena. There are certainly monological aspects of language and thinking, yet they are derived from the dialogical structure of face-to-face speech. Even individual self-consciousness emerges out of the more original social-world of language acquisition (more on this to come). Because conversation is joint engagement, the primacy given to "mind-reading" theories should be challenged. Of course, we do not always know what others are thinking and we often need to predict or surmise their thoughts and actions. But such occasions should not take precedence in a philosophical examination of intersubjective discourse and understanding. These occasions stem from contraventions or temporal distance within a bedrock of reciprocal communicative effects that are always already in place and that cannot be in question all the way down.

This is why radical skepticism regarding linguistic meaning and communication is also suspect, because it undermines the very possibility of language, including skeptical communiqués. There is indeed significant variance in linguistic usage, which can be attributed to contextual and practical flexibility. Yet such variance is a problem only for foundationalist theories of language, wherein mutable determination is taken to entail the indeterminacy of meaning. Skepticism in this respect is nothing more than a failed foundationalism. An *openness* to variability and limits avoids radical skepticism by simply tracking the ways in which meaning and communication function in factical life without rigid governance or uniform standards.[10]

Face-to-face communication is not simply a social-world. It includes the environing-world in a triangular structure of addressive talk *about* something or some circumstance in life. Speech in this respect is usually not refined theoretical reflection; it is discourse within engaged joint activity in a given context. Linguistic "usage" is much more than the abstract notion of performing "speech acts" because it is speech in the midst of, and for the sake of, actual practices with other people. This wider perspective does include speech performance, but also the various embodied behaviors that figure in face-to-face conversation (gesture, eye gaze, nodding, pointing, and so on).[11] The language-world in a fuller sense should be understood along the same lines as enactive cognition, as an ecological field of action. Speech itself is a practice, of course, but it is also embedded in, and informed by, active engagements with the world and other people. As with enactive cognition, research has shown that sensorimotor neural activity accompanies the processing of words pertaining to perceptive, motor, and situational factors. Yet experimental conditions themselves isolate subjects from normal involvement and activity, thereby raising questions about impoverished findings. There are interesting developments in using 3-D virtual reality (VR) devices, which can be controlled for research purposes while simulating a domain in between real life occasions and experimentally restricted conditions. Accordingly, VR devices can better capture first-person perspectives and the experience of ecological immersion.[12]

The practical sphere of language as a tripartite personal-social-environing-world can be gathered in the phenomenon of joint attention (a triangular structure experienced and understood as a shared engagement with the world), which seems unique to humans and which from a developmental standpoint precedes and makes possible language acquisition in children. Infants at a certain stage exhibit shared attention and behavior, which can follow the attentive behavior of others (their gaze or pointing; also imitative learning) as well as direct someone's attention (holding something up or pointing). Such social processes are more original than language but they prepare, and seem to be intrinsically geared toward, the triangular structure of language as a joint engagement with the world.[13] It should be noted that the precedence of such processes is another check on linguistic idealism.

The triangular embeddedness of language is directly disclosive of factical circumstances, and such revelatory force is extendable and can have comparable effects in discourse about absent, distant, or possible events and situations, as indicated with the examples that opened the introduction of this book. The social-environing-world can be disclosed in a "virtual" manner by language, yet with an immediacy that can bypass the primacy of representational assumptions in linguistics. The social-world analysis in the previous chapter showed how neurological research on mirror neurons can supplement phenomenological accounts of empathy and other ecstatic intersubjective effects. The same can be said for the disclosive power of language. Mirror neurons fire when simply hearing a linguistic account of something so that the same neurological system can be at work in both an immediate experience and a narration of the same experience.[14] Such research supplements phenomenological evidence that engaging language apart from direct experience can have comparable force.[15]

The personal-social-speech-world exhibits the same dynamic between individuation and socialization that was discussed in chapter 1. The social bedrock of language is never free from individual inflections, from personal variations and idiosyncrasies all the way to creative innovations. Although communication is at the core of language, it is rarely achieved without remainder, excess, or disparity. The shared character of a linguistic world does not entail strictly uniform or identical meanings, but significant overlap must be in place if language is to function at all. Whatever status individual agency in speech may have, it only develops out of the social environment, and even mature self-development and self-awareness continue to grow out of interpersonal conversations, especially with intimates. The dialogical character of language is much more than a crisscrossing of monological content. It is a fluid generative field of emerging effects that continually shape and revise the personal-social-world—by way of sharing, instructing, influencing, challenging, negotiating, and interpreting.

3.4. The Disclosive Field of Language

The field-character of the speech-world is a holistic structure that cannot be properly understood in a piecemeal manner; it therefore blends or correlates specific elements of language that have been emphasized by different linguistic theories—in ways that exclude, diminish, or sidestep other elements. A proto-phenomenological account exhibits a triangulated field in which individual speech acts, social forces, communication, and the environing-world all coalesce in a disclosive network. As noted in the introduction, most theories of language have a representational bias that focuses on particular facets of the linguistic field: reference, having to do with the relation between words or speech acts and reality; meaning, regarding either semantic meaning or the intention of a speaker; communication, in the sense of transactions between individual speakers; and linguistic structures that govern reference, meaning, and communication. The holistic character of language is such that none of these elements can be prioritized or understood apart from the others. Even "analyzing" the field simply in terms of the exposited elements working together misses the immersed character of factical face-to-face speech.

It is understandable that expositional approaches to language would begin with or focus on words and their meaning, but even in linguistics it has been recognized that the meaning of words cannot be adequately understood in isolation from their function in actual sentences.[16] Yet even sentences cannot be isolated from surrounding sentential contexts and the correlational scope of a language system. Attention to dwelling would add that sentences as such need to be understood in the context of their ecological field of usage in factical life and not simply their lexical manifestations, their exposited linguistic characteristics. It is essential to this investigation that the lexical dimension of language not be given priority over a phenomenological account of speech in practice.

Proto-phenomenology also stresses the disclosive element of language in its triangulated field. Questions of reference have typically focused on language and truth, but usually in a representational form and primarily regarding descriptive or declarative functions. A phenomenology of disclosure offers a presentational mode in which language is a primal opening of meaning that precedes referential distinctions. So the disclosive character of language need not be restricted to declarative functions and thus can apply to the kinds of meanings opened up in interrogative, imperative, exclamatory, artistic, and other modes of expression that are often sidelined in descriptive theories. In any case, presentational disclosure will have to be coordinated with the question of truth in chapter 4.

3.5. Temporality

Language and temporality are coextensive and reciprocally correlated. Language itself is temporal as a flowing process of speech, and it is time-structured grammatically in past, present, and future verb tenses, including the looping intersections indicated in complex verb constructions ("Tomorrow we will have been married twenty years").[17] The correlation goes deeper when we consider temporality not simply as a rough sense of time dimensions, which can be evident in animal experience, but as the rich, detailed sense of meaningful time, of past, present, and future dimensions of concrete life, of its concerns and possibilities—in which the virtual worlds of the past and future are intertwined with the lived present. In this respect, temporality is made possible and informed by language, which shapes the narrative character of experience and tells the stories of human existence.

There is also a constitutive sense in which language gives temporality its dimensional scope, by giving presence (in words) to the "absences" of past and future events. This will receive some discussion in section 5 below, but here I focus on memory, the precondition for meaningful temporal experience. In chapter 1 it was noted how memory is not primarily recording the past but coding and preparing future actions, as exemplified in habits. In this way, memory is part of the figure-eight structure of temporality, of forward-looking possibilities enacted with capacities readied by the past. There is evidence from neuroscience and social science that functional memory is made possible by language, which affords virtual reconstructions of past experience that are selective and comprehensive retentions rather than a mere rewind, and that serve as programmatic preparation for present and future actions. Language serves memory with cueing, narrative structure, filtering, shorthand tagging of complex experiences, and macro-level comprehension that sidesteps piecemeal construction.[18] Research comparing normal competency with language impairment shows the role that language plays in working memory.[19] And it is language acquisition that allows children to develop episodic and autobiographical memory, a narrative structure of experience, and generally the sense of finding oneself in time, of being an extended self that is projected in temporal dimensions.[20]

We have previously seen how the comprehension of speech has a temporal figure-eight structure, a flowing anticipation and retention amid the passage of words. The same holds for the dialogical character of speech in its addressive structure. Implicit in every conversation is the sense of reciprocal address, of conversation *as* the intertwining of speaking *to* others and responding *back* in turn. This figure-eight shape of looping temporality is a matter of tacit intimation in conversation and can be sensed explicitly with contravening occasions, as when someone goes silent or breaks with the context of discussion or pattern of reciprocation. The temporal structure of language is also shown when one is searching for what to say or working on a composition. The effort in these cases is more explicitly temporal by being suspended in the present with traces of what has been said cueing the search for words to come. When the right words do come, this is more than a discrete point in time because it *fulfills* what preceded it. The satisfaction at such times and the frustration when words do not come both presuppose the existential significance of this temporal arc of language.

The historical character of language fills out its temporal dimension. Language is ever open in its future possibilities and ongoing improvisations. Yet every language is tethered to its past in the long and complex history of usage that makes any continuing movement possible. Each of us is projected by the history of our native tongue, which makes a serious understanding of one's language a complicated and far-reaching enterprise. The temporal-historical structure of language shows that its "being" cannot be construed as the objective grasp of something extant. Language is not an "entity" because it is the environment for identifying entities in the first place. And the historical projection of language is another angle on its slippage from control. We inherit language in such a way that we are more its product than it is ours.[21]

3.6. Representation Revisited

The distinction between ecstatic immersion and disengaged exposition helps illuminate how certain objective models of language are derived from a more original ecological base. It is common to begin an examination of language with (lexical) entities such as words, utterances, and sentences, which can then be analyzed in terms of meaning, reference, structure, and so forth. In philosophy, truth is commonly associated with "propositions" as truth bearers, which is a formal conception of sentences that sets up the schematic relationship between assertions and states of affairs in the world. Truth does not pertain to things, which are "actual," but to propositions that "correspond" to actualities. Such is the sphere of propositional judgment. The mentality implied in judgment is often called a "propositional attitude," which denotes the mind's relation to a proposition, as in "She believes that the chair is comfortable," in which "believes that" is the propositional attitude. My argument is not that these linguistic, logical, and psychological models are invalid, but that they are not sufficient for understanding language or truth. As in the case of learning a second language, the steps of translation in early stages do show that representational notions of meaning and reference are intelligible in an explicit manner. Yet the learning process requires immersion in an acquired language as the precondition for translation. And developed fluency in a new language reiterates immersion when it comes to second-nature proficiency. Thus representational and propositional models have a derivative status because a focus on dwelling shows that with such models language is exposited out of a prior dimension of ecstatic speech. Moreover, as will be argued in volume 2, the very notion of a "sentence," "proposition," or "representation" is made possible by the freestanding character of written language, which is derived from oral language.

Language (historically and for each of us personally) is originally a matter of face-to-face speech, of communicative practice in the midst of factical concerns. Such proto-speech is a mode of ecstatic immersion in conversations that are not experienced as a transactional exchange of discrete elements between separate agents—of beliefs transported by words out to recipients who process these conveyors into beliefs, the result of which is communication—but rather immediate *presentations* of meanings in the triangular structure of the personal-social-environing-world. In normal everyday conversations among competent speakers there is a smoothly functioning interaction that is absorbed in the disclosive power of speech—most clearly if the conversation concerns directly present circumstances (as in my furniture example), but also in conversations about distant or past and future affairs. In any case, the effects of face-to-face speech can be automatic, vivid, and striking, and therefore world-disclosive in a manner comparable to direct experiences. Some examples: "Your child was in an accident," "The war is over," "Your book has won an award."

As already noted, the ecstatic condition of language can be interrupted and exposited in the face of contraventions. Language itself can also become a re-presented object of reflection and analysis in everything from interrogation of utterances to grammatical formalization and philosophical questions about the nature and function of language. But with the examples given in the paragraph above, it is important to maintain phenomenological discipline and be faithful to such statements *as* experienced in life, rather than as examples of "propositions"—or even as phenomenological examples in my account. "Your child was in an accident" (in real life) is *not* a "proposition," which is the conversion of living utterances into an abstract formal object, of which the statement at hand is now only a disengaged illustration or token stripped of factical meaning. Moreover, if I am the parent of that child, it surely seems out of place to say that my "state of mind" is a propositional attitude, a belief-linkage to a proposition, even to that particular sentence per se. I have argued for the immediacy of language in a case like this, but it is the *disclosive* power of the utterance that counts here, not its propositional form or content as such. My "attitude" is not toward the utterance but what it opens up *in my world*, the fate of my child. With the utterance, I am *projected* into that situation and its significance, in the light of which reflective talk about beliefs and propositions is utterly incongruous.

Familiar propositional models, such as S is P, are made possible by written graphics, in which a letter that by itself has no semantic meaning is meant to stand in for any semantic content and exhibit repeatable structural relations with other parts of speech.[22] Only now can the notion of a "proposition" arise, as an abstract stand-in for any particular utterance or sentence. Such a construction must itself be "meaningless" in the sense of discounting the existential concerns that animate actual speech. The meaning of "This hammer is too heavy"—as an impediment in a purposeful practice—is more than simply an abstract subject-predicate relation. And the impact in 1963 of "The president is dead" was something quite different from the lifeless deployment of "All men are mortal" in logical exercises.

Representational theories of language—including exposited notions of words, meanings, sentences, syntax, and "coding" processes between speakers and listeners—face a number of explanatory difficulties: not only accounting for how representations and codes connect with the world, but also making sense of spontaneous capacities for immediate comprehension and production of language, especially the so-called creative aspect of language usage, in which individual speakers (including children) are not bound by inputs or guidance because they can go on with their own unique occasions of speech, which is a case of enactive interpretation. Also problematic is accounting for implicit intimations of coherence and correlational scope, as well as the interpretive capacity to directly discern what kinds of speech are appropriate for different contexts and circumstances. Research has shown that all such capacities are better construed as functions of ecological, social, and temporal intelligences (all usually in concert)—which is consonant with a proto-phenomenological account. Such macro-level intelligences involve intimations of discrete thing-hood, relative location, and directional movement (ecological intelligence), other persons as minded agents and the difference between the mere utterance of a speaker and what a speaker means (social intelligence), and lastly the temporal differences between spoken utterances and referenced events, along with flexible shifting between temporal perspectives in one's own speech and the speech of others so that the meaning of verb tenses is grasped automatically (temporal intelligence). It is this macro-level functioning that is impaired in certain speech disorders, not the micro-level functions of word and sentence comprehension.[23] From a phenomenological standpoint, such macro-level intelligence is in practice a matter of tacit intimation and therefore the capacities specified above (thing-hood, location, and so on) at first should be understood indicatively rather than theoretically as some categorical capture of how such capacities operate.

4. LANGUAGE AND EMBODIMENT

Language in factical life is originally face-to-face speech, and in this setting embodiment plays an essential role—not in the sense of explaining language by way of physiological, neurological, or organic causes (although such domains can be contextually relevant), but the *lived* body that engages in communicative practices.[24] It is here that a phenomenology of gesture, facial expression, and sound enters the picture. The idea of "body language" is familiar, especially how the body can communicate in a nonverbal manner, sometimes in subtle ways that can belie verbal expression (for instance, tightly folded arms giving away animosity or apprehension). There is even a deeper sense in which corporeal expression is intrinsic to lived speech, which will be developed in coming discussions of language acquisition, orality, and literacy. For now, we can note the importance of gesture, facial expression, and sound *in* verbal communication, in a manner that cannot really be called "nonverbal" but rather *sub*-verbal. Such corporeal elements are often thought to be at best peripheral to language, but they seem to be intertwined with speech in a constitutive manner.[25]

4.1. Gesture

We know well, at least implicitly, how the hands, the eyes, and the mouth play a significant role in face-to-face speech, especially when the meaning of what is said can vary according to how it is said or conveyed facially (think of sarcasm, widened eyes, a smirk, and so forth). It is also evident how gesturing can communicate something without or in place of words. Think of pantomime games or how one tries to communicate when neither party knows the other's language.

Gesturing can display a lot about direction, position, feeling, behavior, practices, and so on. Indeed, gesture was likely a key element in the evolution of language.[26]

What are some of the ways in which gesture figures in face-to-face speech?[27] Pointing is one of the most basic forms of communication and it often accompanies speech in immediate circumstances, as does touching. Nodding and shaking the head are familiar accents in conversation. Multiple hand and arm movements indicate spatial directions, locations, rough mimicry of actions, and degrees of emphasis. So-called beat gestures display nonindicative hand and arm movements coordinated with the temporal patterns and pacing in speech. Gesturing is spontaneous and usually not self-conscious. Its visual role in communication is shown by the fact that people gesture less when not in face-to-face circumstances, such as telephone conversations. Facial gestures are a ubiquitous and vivid component of speech, especially in expressing emotional states: think of a grimace, raised eyebrows, an opened mouth, and particularly smiling, which is a universal indication of pleasure or happiness. Over one thousand facial displays have been detected in human conversations, 75 percent of which are specifically speech related.

In general terms, gesture and speech are naturally synchronous and co-expressive in the sense that a gesture is neither redundant nor merely ornamental to speech. Rather, gesture is functionally correlated with linguistic meaning, often facilitating and enhancing the comprehension of speech. Research has shown that people resist attempts to decouple gesture and speech. Congenitally blind persons use gesture even when talking with other blind persons. Gesture anchors speech in action, embodiment, and sensuous experience, a concretion that can be called a "dialectic of imagery and language."[28] Unlike static conceptions that represent language as an "object," gesture and embodied speech open up a more mobile perspective on language as a dynamic performance.

The sphere of gesture can even be truly linguistic if we consider sign language used by the deaf, for instance American Sign Language (ASL), which allows a fully functioning conversational language and syntax without verbal speech. ASL involves hand shaping, or iconic indications of whole words, ideas, or actions. Finger spelling adds words that are not captured in hand shaping.[29] ASL practice includes nonmanual signals involving movements of the head, eyebrows, and torso. Learning ASL is caught up in factical practice-fields in the same way that speech is learned. Deaf children born to deaf parents who use

ASL acquire sign language naturally, in stages similar to speech acquisition. Such a circumstance accounts for only 10 percent of congenitally deaf children. The majority are usually first exposed to oral environments before ASL is a prospect. Communication skills are rarely well-developed in such children, which shows the importance of gestural sign language for their movement toward linguistic proficiency. In fact, when these children have little exposure to sign language in early years, they produce their own gestures, which exhibit a rudimentary linguistic structure comparable to ordinary speech.[30] With the development of sign language, gesture is transformed into a functioning linguistic world, which illustrates how much embodied signals can be and are implicated in human language. The deaf even come to "think" in such signs apart from their overt usage.[31]

4.2. Sound

In addition to gesture, another embodied feature of speech is its sonic character, usually called intonation.[32] Sound here is not simply the conveyance of spoken words; it is the fusion of sound and words in the manner of *voice*, as distinct from sounds like grunts or moans and the expressive calls and cries made by animals. Human language is at once sound and sense, in which utterances are saturated with meaning in factical speech. Intonation involves a host of sonic elements that figure in the expression of meaning: tone, pitch, tempo, rhythm, emphasis, accent, volume, and even pauses and silences. Intonation is primarily implicated in the expression of emotion and degrees of intensity. Tone, pitch, and volume can express pleasure, excitement, anger, and various resonances linked to different contexts. Consider the difference between a harsh and comforting tone, between giving a speech and giving bad news. Vocal emphasis can have an ostensive effect: Who's *there*? It's *me*. Bring that over and put it *here*. Intonation gives voice to affective attunement. Think of the subtle inflections in sarcasm, which intimates the inverse of what is said, or the different cadences in expressions of boredom and excitement. Silence not only "frames" the sounding of words, it can "speak" in the context of a conversation or question. Pauses, too, can figure in vocal effects. Much is said if someone pauses or is silent after being asked, "Do you love me?"

Intonation cannot be rendered in grammatical terms and yet it is central to oral communication. Written graphics can approximate certain sonic effects, such as punctuated indications of tempo and rhythm or italicized emphasis. But there is a limit to what writing can convey of intonation, and graphics can represent almost nothing regarding manual or facial gestures.[33] If the face-to-face oral character of language is emphasized, such embodied dimensions show that "speech" is much more than simply vocal "utterances" of an aural character; it is a carnal, visual presence in a social environment. Given the immersed and meaning-laden character of speech, an existential understanding of intonation must be distinguished from exposited treatments of sound in language. Such is the case in phonology, which analyzes the ways in which sonic and verbal patterns figure in the delivery and reception of speech: how words are composed of phonemes and syllables (sound units that by themselves have no semantic meaning); rules and variations of pronunciation; the processing, storage, and deployment of sounded words; sonic structures; and the physiology of vocalization.[34] Phonology properly discloses exposited elements of sound in speech, but this is derivative of the ecstatic manner in which sound and sense are immediately *fused*—which is to say, not even "conjoined"—in ordinary speech. I do not hear "sound" that is "processed" as, say, an angry utterance. I *hear an angry voice* (even this is too abstract because I hear anger *about* something).[35] The very notion of a phoneme is an exposited feature of language that by itself has no semantic meaning, especially given the different word sounds across languages that signify a common meaning. In language acquisition, phonetic differentiation is central to the movement from babbling to learning the specific sonic markers of a native tongue. Yet as we will see in volume 2, this learning milieu cannot be understood as simply the processing of abstract phonemes because a child is cued for pronunciation in an ecological field of engagements that are infused with factical meaning.[36] With respect to language and embodiment in general terms, the overall significance of sound and gesture in speech is vividly evident in early language acquisition. One result of considering gesture and sound is that face-to-face speech is *at once* a visual and aural phenomenon. This helps reinforce the ecological character of language as a material presence *there* in one's world, in which one can be ecstatically immersed. The sights and sounds of language together embody this environment.[37]

5. DIFFERENTIAL FITNESS

In line with the analysis thus far, I offer a concept that can gather the nature of language in a way that can inform much of what has been said and what is to come: *differential fitness*. Language is fitness in the manner of nonreflective communicative disclosure as heretofore analyzed. In this sense language and its social-situational environment "fit" each other, not in the sense of representational correspondence but more akin to the way hand and glove fit each other. Think of the bidirectional flow in my furniture-restoring example—in which speech, activity, and things in the environment coalesce as a seamless field of operation. The fitness of language should not be taken as a stable identity or fixture of meaning because speech is shaped by and manifests the temporal movements and contextual shifts of the lived world. Language fitness simply denotes the normal course of life wherein our speaking, behaving, and environing-world are blended as a correlative presentational field and *presumed* to be reciprocally conjoined, in which speech and world fit together.

The differential character of language stems from considering the phonic (and graphic) nature of words as such. Here we notice the general semiotic difference between spoken words and what is spoken about.[38] Even in the fitness of language, a differential element is implicit in both diachronic and synchronic ways. Out of the immediate disclosive power of fitness, the sustained capacity to speak allows the retention of words—*and their existential meaning*—in the *absence* of their referents, a capacity that seems to be unique to humans.[39] In this way the "nonbeing" of the past and future can have a *presence* in speech because of semiotic difference as such, although this is not thematized explicitly in oral language. In any case, the world-disclosive force of language does not need a direct reference in the immediate environment to evince genuine disclosive force ("She said that she hates you"). As discussed earlier, language by itself can have effects comparable to direct experience, for which there is neurological evidence in the "mirror" system.[40] Here the differential character of language retains, and significantly extends, fitting accounts of the world. This includes the disclosive power of fiction and storytelling (the latter playing an important role in child development). With such possibilities, among others, language offers a function of crucial significance: the capacity to extend disclosure beyond firsthand experience, which opens a boundless scope of comprehension for the otherwise constrained access of individuals and groups solely within their own sphere of experience.

It needs to be said that the differential character of language enables the notion of words having a representational function. So one might ask: What else *is* the differential character of language other than a representational relation to the world?—this meant to cast doubt on any nonrepresentational approach. Indeed, speech about an absent phenomenon can be exposited in a representational manner. But the disclosive power of such speech in factical circumstances—when it can have ecstatic immediacy—is more a presentational effect than a representational structure (as a representation-*of* something). Surely the very idea of differential elements in language is itself a matter of exposition, but an *indicative* approach would point to occasions of presentational immediacy, wherein the differential aspect as such is *not* in view.

Semiotic difference makes possible essential features of language: comparison, contrast, alterability, extension of meaning, metaphor, analogy, relation, negation, and the temporality of verbs; also the ubiquitous function of conjunctions such as "and," "or," "but," "as," and "if." It also allows for "semantic shift" of meaning and usage, which makes for inevitable changes in the history of a language, when words can modulate meaning depending on the context of significance or relation with other words.[41] Dictionary entries for many words show multiple meanings that stem from grammatical shift, metaphorical extension, and partial overlap with different contexts (as in the words *clear*, *end*, and *reflection*). In time, even slang meanings can become standard usage with enough reception and sustained use. In any case, the differential capacity for change and variation will always frustrate conservative calls for fixed standards and philosophical theories that presume a unified meaning for linguistic terms. The history of a language shows that "standard" forms are never immune from modification and innovation.[42] At the same time, given the communicative purpose of language, certain degrees of common usage and informal regulation are a precondition for any functioning language. In any case, semantic shift works against the Socratic standard of a universal form governing particular instances of word usage. Metaphorical and contextual expansion, for example, usually involve some kind of overlapping resemblance, but not a universal-particular scheme. Indeed, the meaning of a word like *generous* is continually colored by particular indications, which can then add to the focal sense of the word and subsequent uses. The meaning of *generosity*, then, is an ever-evolving, reciprocal circulation of widening and specifying occasions.

Semiotic difference also makes possible a range of intellectual functions that are the building blocks of knowledge, such as generality spanning a set of particular uses, ranging from indicative concepts to scientific classification.[43] Other capacities include analogical thinking, following inferences, hierarchical classification, describing hypothetical circumstances, learning and using symbolic constructions without direct reference, learning and constructing new terminology, counterfactual thinking, and transmitting cultural codes to the next generation for an extension of possibilities. Most basic in all this is the capacity for relational thinking, which opens up an enormous store of comprehension and extended knowledge, and which appears to be a distinctive mark of human intelligence. Causal thinking is a signature consequence of understanding differential relations because grasping a causal sequence involves traversing temporal dimensions, wherein a present effect is structurally related to past patterns and future repetitions (as distinct from one-off coincidental correlations). Relational thinking also allows for "conceptual blending," which opens new spaces for cognition by juxtaposing different events or lines of thought for the purpose of comparison, contrast, or synthesis.[44]

A significant differential capacity is what has been called *recursion*, which may be unique to human mentality.[45] Language is recursive because it is not bound by the normal constraints of extant spatial and temporal conditions. The differential character of language permits recombinations, insertions, and mixtures that expand understanding in unlimited ways. Time extension and analytical revision are recursive functions that allow for causal explanation, recollection, and prediction. Higher order thinking and formal constructions are recursive because here language is no longer embedded in experience but in its own internal relations and possibilities, freed for its unique set of orders and projections. Recursion also allows understanding other minds by insertion of one's own thinking into their thoughts and vice versa; even self-consciousness is a recursive insertion into one's own thoughts (the classic philosophical recursion is Descartes's "I think, therefore I am").

The differential character of language also generates many linguistic features that frustrate analytical precision: ambiguity, in which a single word can have more than one meaning or application (as in the word *right*); vagueness, in which words can have borderline cases and disparities relative to different cases (as in the word *tall*); and the general polyvalence of linguistic meaning. Yet such features are problematic only for theories that presume governing conditions of precision, rigid designation, and unqualified classification. The contextual tracking of different uses and an admission of imprecision seem to offer a more realistic approach. Such tracking is how the orchestrations of enactive interpretation function in language usage.[46]

In effect, the differential separability of language from immediate experience, together with recursion and the power of imagination, makes possible a virtual-world in which alternative or modified scenarios can be devised in various modes (artistic, practical, moral, scientific), which greatly expands the scope and possibilities of disclosure. Fictional language is virtual in being different from ordinary object designation. But because object designation is not the governing starting point for understanding language from a phenomenological standpoint, the longstanding debate about fictional reference (How can "Hamlet" be assessed in human discourse?) can be resolved in a contextual manner, without restriction to the presumption that words or names are descriptive of (actual) entities. Talk of Hamlet can be disclosive in the context of indicating or coming to understand Shakespeare's play. And the meaning of a fictional work can be fully disclosive of something momentous in life, even in a manner that is more compelling and far-reaching than actual events. The virtual character of fictional language is no less "real" in this expanded phenomenological sense.

The virtual-world is a historically important supplement to the personal-social-environing-world because it marks the engine of productive change that makes history what it is, namely shifts and transformations in how the world is understood, which require differentiation between actuality and alternative possibilities. Moreover, the looping intersections of past, present, and future that constitute human temporality amount to a circulation of virtual worlds. For that reason, any deployment of disclosive language that extends beyond an immediate present setting (like the direct milieu of my furniture-restoring example) can be called a virtual world and is exhibited in both spoken and written forms.

The differential fitness of language is a correlative whole in which difference and fitness cannot be separated, although they can be distinguished in analysis. Yet the fitness of language must have a certain priority. Difference is understood *in* language, and language is first an environment in which we dwell and find ourselves, which is most clear when we take child development into account, in which we first become linguistically outfitted for the world. Without fitness, difference would not emerge as something *other* than immediate reference. Yet without the differential force of language *implicit* in all its moments, the fitness of language would not be capable of extension, responsive flexibility, and innovation.

Language serves to preserve disclosure by handing on and handing down meanings that originally unfold in more direct experiences or new discoveries. The diachronic distance made possible by the differential character of language allows for both the maintenance of a tradition and the tension between normalization and innovation. Inherited traditions generate a second-nature immersion in customs and habits that shape us from birth into functioning members of a cultural community. Yet it is possible for traditions to calcify into regimes of control that can block the advent of modifications or new possibilities.[47] The temporal-historical character of the lived world, however, shows that cultures cannot be immunized from change (what else *is* history but a record of cultural change?), which can be traced to an inherent tension between socialization and individuation, regulation and novelty, immersion and exposition. The differential character of language, in addition to preserving culture in the passage of time, allows modification and innovation to find a voice as well. New paths arise when individuals or groups experience contraventions of normalcy because of disconnection or dissatisfaction with established ways of life. Yet even within a stable tradition, the handing down through time brings a remoteness from originating circumstances, which can result in the diminished animation of a cultural idea and thus a superficial simplification of a complex meaning that has become a familiar discursive commodity (consider the easy talk of Americans about "freedom"). Individuation therefore can emit not only new meanings, but also appropriation of the living force of inherited meanings. In summation, language as a communicative practice marked by differential fitness allows for a continuing and productive tension between socialization and individuation, tradition and innovation.

Differential fitness as here analyzed accounts for the difficulty in trying to theorize about language or identify its "essence," understood as some fixed condition or structure. Language is originally a matter of disclosive fitness and speech *practices* (speaking, listening, conversing). Reflection *on* language (in language) involves a "stepping back" from practical fitness, which can create distortions or omissions.[48] Theorizing about language can easily miss its practical milieu, and essentializing language misses its dynamic, differential character. Differential fitness also undermines anti-essentialist conceptions of language, which carry their own theoretical and reflective biases (even if aiming to avoid the closure of essentialism), as when language is conceived as a human construction, invention, or free play of signifiers. Essentialism misses the unsettled, open, differential character of language, while anti-essentialism misses the stabilizing character of fitness in immediate speech practices.

6. NATURAL LANGUAGE AND CONVENTION

I have referred to natural language in terms of what is native to human speech, the language in which we are born and raised. This borders on another sense of the natural, namely that which is intrinsic to something rather than arbitrary or merely conventional. Ever since the Greeks, questions have been posed about whether language is something natural or superimposed on nature and human life. Such questions have arisen because the word *nature* developed a connotation of something invariant or essential—that is, a thing's *nature* that is fixed and not subject to alteration or conventional differentiation.[49] Given evident differences across human cultures, there followed debates concerning the natural versus the cultural and nature versus nurture—the latter in each pair denoting what is merely conventional or superimposed by human artifice or inculcation.

Such debates have easily been applied to the question of language, especially given its differential character. Not only the difference between words and things, but the presence of different words for the same thing across different languages has encouraged the notion that words are merely "labels" or "signs" for things in the world, tokens that are superimposed upon things as a conventional or even arbitrary construction and then externally transferred to children through social training. Yet the proto-phenomenological approach in this investigation presumes the "natural" character of language, first in the nativist sense, but also in the sense of being intrinsic to human life—though not a matter of mere physical nature or an invariant, fixed essence. I elaborate by distinguishing between the *natural*, the *cultural*, and the *arbitrary*. The natural refers to what is intrinsically self-manifesting (for instance, organic growth); the arbitrary denotes what is merely conventional or externally superimposed (for instance, etiquette); and the cultural can be located in between these polarities rather than on one side or the other. Thus the cultural can exhibit natural *potentialities* that require environmental instigation for their actualization, as in the case of language. Environmental variations will then make for different manifestations of a natural capacity. So the natural and the cultural can be released from the distinction between invariance and arbitrary differences and thus understood as the distinction between an intrinsic capacity and modified enactment.

That is why the nature-nurture binary does not hold up under scrutiny. The consensus in research is that a child's development is neither genetically predetermined nor wholly constructed by the environment, but rather an intersection of genetic endowments, natural propensities, and nurturing stimuli.[50] Moreover, the "second nature" of developed habits and skills stems from a confluence of nature and culture that cannot be reduced to either brute facts or arbitrary superimpositions. The intersection of nature and nurture is not even clearly delineable into two discrete cooperating spheres: the womb is a contributing environment for the biological development of the fetus, and an infant's behavior will influence how caregivers in the social environment respond to the child (and vice versa).[51] Human development therefore is not a predetermined script but a feedback loop between natural and cultural forces.

Language is the most prominent example of the intertwining of nature and culture. It is safe to say that human children are hard-wired to develop language and yet such capacity could not unfold without a prompting linguistic environment. We can conclude that language is natural to human beings, but how language manifests itself can vary, especially across cultures. With respect to the question of grammar, this can strike a balance between so-called nativist and environmentalist theories.[52] As has been noted, the differential character of language is exemplified by the existence of different language systems. But the fitness character of language and the presence of language in all human cultures show that language as such cannot be deemed merely conventional or arbitrary. The different word sounds for the same thing in different languages indeed may be arbitrary, but *that* these speaking cultures access the thing through their words is not arbitrary. We can say that *the fitness of language as a mode of dwelling* is universal across cultures. This is not to say that all human languages understand the world in the same way across the board. There *are* some ways in which the world is understood differently in different languages, but such differences cannot go all the way down (more on this shortly). Language fitness is geared toward the lived world, which has basic common features across cultures (the personal-social-environing-world, practical skills, survival needs, etc.). This is why even the most disparate cultures—think of European explorers first encountering peoples of the New World—can in time come to understand each other's language. This can occur not by way of grammar books or dictionaries (when at least one of the parties is illiterate) but a shared lived world, together with a mutual intimation of *having* language as a mode of dwelling in that world—indeed, the most important mode of dwelling, the bridging of which will be the central pathway to reciprocal understanding between different cultures.[53]

That various languages have different words for the same thing might reinforce the notion that words simply signify extra-linguistic things, which are why they are independent of the way we speak about them—thus undermining the disclosive priority of language advanced at the beginning of this chapter. But we face a conundrum in following through with such a segregation of words and things. We would say that "tree" and "*Baum*" are simply different words for . . . well, what? The tree itself? *Der Baum selbst*? The thing itself? *Das Ding selbst*? It? *Es*? That, there? *Jener, dort*? The best we could do extra-linguistically is simply point, which does indeed speak against linguistic *idealism*. But pointing is a primal mode of communication and a precondition for language acquisition, especially with respect to joint attention. And the question at hand is itself a language-laden move in life. That is the point. Language is not primarily a designation *of* things in life because it animates the way we dwell in the world. When we point to the tree/*Baum* we expect a common "reference," which is not something wholly other than language but how forms of life lie at the heart of what we say; not simply "words" but ways of living (with trees). Language therefore is originally interwoven with active engagements, not "significations." European explorers and Native Americans could come to understand each other's language because of an overlapping lived world (and a lot of pointing and gesturing).[54] Coming to understand a language in this case can indeed involve representational moments, but the primary impetus would involve intimations of language as a way of being in the world.

7. ORDINARY LANGUAGE PHILOSOPHY AND PRAGMATICS

Traditional philosophy has usually seen its task as repairing the contingencies of factical life and thus factical language as well, the native terrain of everyday speech, which in most respects has been judged to be imprecise, vague, variable, and confused. This terrain is marked for reform by way of metaphysical or foundational principles that can bring unity, universality, and necessity to bear on overcoming factical contingencies and governing linguistic usage. Even early analytic philosophy, while eschewing metaphysical speculation, aimed to govern language usage with logical constraints and implicit structures that could provide more accuracy and stability, even to the point of positing an "ideal language." What has been called ordinary language philosophy (OLP) can be traced to the later work of Wittgenstein, particularly his aim to bring words "back from their metaphysical to everyday use."[55] OLP, especially in the writings of J. L. Austin and Stanley Cavell, maintains that philosophical problems stem from forgetting what words mean in normal usage and constructing abstract notions yanked out of everyday contexts. This creates self-generated problems and puzzles (the mind-body problem, skepticism, the nature of truth) that can be "dissolved" by simply tracking how such words function in ordinary use. For example, the perennial question "What is truth?" is exchanged for delineating the various ways in which the word *true* functions in normal speech. OLP thus perceives itself as providing "therapy" for misguided philosophical disorders.[56]

In the latter part of the twentieth century, OLP fell out of favor and was eclipsed by developments in epistemology and philosophy of mind that gravitated toward research in cognitive neuroscience. In large part the eclipse was likely due to a reassertion of typical philosophical aims against OLP's deflation of perennial intellectual questions into a seemingly nonphilosophical sphere. In other words, OLP appeared to be the very antithesis of philosophy. The main objection has been that OLP's correlation of meaning and use conflates two notions that should be kept distinct because the distinction allows space for central philosophical notions of representational inference and conceptual comprehension that purportedly make usage possible. Nevertheless, there has been a recent revival of interest in OLP.[57]

A proto-phenomenological approach to language can overlap with OLP in a number of ways. This is especially true with respect to speech-act theory—notably advanced in the works of Austin and John Searle—and its generation of a shift in linguistics from a semantic to a pragmatic emphasis.[58] Language is not simply related to actions because speech itself *is* action that inhabits a wide range of performances: issuing commands, asking questions, making plans, giving advice, apologizing, promising, solving problems, testing a theory, writing a philosophy book. The pragmatic turn has aimed to unseat a bias in linguistics that confines analysis mostly to object designation and declarative sentences. With pragmatics, abstract models of reference, meaning, and validity geared toward descriptive accuracy and precise definition are exchanged for tracking the myriad ways in which speech acts are situated and assessed, which exhibit less exact measures such as sincerity, appropriateness, and effectiveness.

Such developments are surely more attentive to the lived world than are theoretical models of formal semantics, thus approximating what I have called practical engagement, interpretive pluralism, enactive interpretation, and projection. A performative utterance like "I pronounce you husband and wife" entails real effects and incorporation into a number of social-world phenomena, institutions, and norms. In the words of Wittgenstein, "the speaking of a language . . . is a form of life."[59] Pragmatics also offers a robust alternative to representational models of language.[60]

That said, OLP in some quarters has been generally restricted to empirical investigations of language practices and delineations of correct and incorrect usage. Phenomenology pursues a wider range of issues and is something more than simply a therapeutic deflation of traditional philosophy—wherein the tradition has been misguided and ordinary language is the correction. A phenomenology of the lived world is a genuine attempt to elicit philosophical understanding with indicative reflection, something more than attention to ordinary practices. Moreover, the immersion-contravention-exposition dynamic can help show how and why traditional concepts have gone astray and how they might be revised or replaced. And a hermeneutical pluralism requires a lot of philosophical work, especially regarding perspectival and enactive interpretation. In this respect, some traditional concepts and methods can even find contextual aptness, as in the case of certain philosophical intersections with natural science and the logico-mathematical foundations of computer science. Finally, proto-phenomenology gives explicit attention to the existential meaningfulness of the lived world and factual horizons that animate everyday practices and ordinary language. OLP's attention to meaning-as-use, especially if confined to empirical description, can miss the concrete significance for the *person* speaking a purported example of usage. In other words, it might be little more than an exposited account of usage without indicative attention to circumstances of speech in real life, *as* lived in the personal-social-environing world. Some in the field of pragmatics have attended to this matter of keeping concrete life in view.[61] Indeed, Austin recognized the need to expand beyond analyzing words and their practical meanings to include the "realities" incorporating such usage. He even leaned toward calling OLP "linguistic phenomenology."[62]

8. LANGUAGE AND THOUGHT

Before the linguistic turn, the primary focus of modern philosophy was cognition and thought, notably illustrated in Kant's shift from "reality" to how the rational mind thinks; also in nineteenth-century debates about the nature of logic, particularly the laws governing thought. From this perspective, language is simply a vehicle for expressing thought. Since the early twentieth century, many developments in analytic and continental philosophy have challenged the notion that thought can be understood apart from, or prior to, language.[63] Two main questions arise from these developments, and they have been the focus of much research in cognitive science, linguistics, psychology, and philosophy of mind. The first question concerns whether language is constitutive of thought in the sense that human cognition is fundamentally informed by, and does not precede, linguistic operations. The second question follows from the first. If language to a significant degree is constitutive of thought, does the cross-cultural diversity of language systems mean that the world is understood in different ways? If so, that would imply linguistic relativism (or determinism).

My position on the phenomenological priority of language seems to fit the notion that language is constitutive of thought and that thinking is a kind of internalized speech, or at least is informed by language in a developmental sense. Similarly, my emphasis on pluralism might open the door for linguistic relativism. What I hope to establish, however, is that most research on these questions is driven by representational assumptions and expositional analyses of language and thought.[64] A phenomenology of dwelling and its ecological account of language will allow different pathways that can address these questions without siding with either pole of the research debate: on the one hand that thought is somehow different from, and more original than, language, and on the other hand that different languages imply different forms of thought and different worlds. Although I maintain that language informs an understanding of reality, the lived world allows for much overlap between different linguistic systems. Both sides of the debate emphasize exposited approaches to linguistic formats and cognitive structures, which misses insights drawn from immersion in factical environments. An indicative approach to nonexposited dimensions of speech practices can open space between communicative and constitutive (or cognitive) models of language, in which the latter takes language to be productive of thought and the former takes language to be simply expressive of nonlinguistic cognition.[65]

8.1. Language and Thinking

I begin with a focus on something more narrow than the general sense in which language is constitutive of world-disclosure in the manner advanced in this chapter, a sense that can align with the constitutive model of language noted above—except that "disclosure" is an ecological concept that is not restricted to how language informs "thought," which in most treatments amounts to an expositional demarcation in light of the subject-object split. In this section I narrow the discussion to "thinking" rather than thought because the former term has more phenomenological resonance. Accordingly, I am not separating the "content" or "norms" of thought from the psychological process of human thinking—whereby the heart of cognition can be detached from empirical psychology in a quasi-Platonic/Cartesian manner.[66] I am simply giving indicative attention to the introspective sphere of thinking as distinct from perception of the surrounding world, embodied activity, and especially overt uses of language. So thinking indicates the normal sense of using one's mind in ways such as imagining, remembering, or pondering something—all the way to philosophical reflection. The question concerns how thinking fits in a proto-phenomenological account of factically disclosive language.

My position is that thinking and factical language can be distinguished phenomenologically but not separated in any strong sense. Language, especially in developmental terms, shapes in different ways most of what thinking indicates. Yet because language is embedded in a social-environing-*world*, the ecological structure of speech rules out a reductive linguistic idealism, and whatever thinking is taken to mean, it cannot entail a reductive psychologism or confinement to introspective "mental states." Dwelling in speech presupposes an embodied, enactive, public, tangible practice-field that exceeds, and makes possible, the supposed interior space of thinking.

For this argument to gain any traction, language cannot be restricted to exposited lexical tokens and thought cannot simply entail an exposited sphere of beliefs, concepts, representations, or rules. Both language and thought must be housed in the lived world. That is why something like a "propositional attitude" cannot do justice to the intertwinement of language and thinking in this analysis. The same holds for the "language of thought" theory stemming from the work of Jerry Fodor.[67] Here cognition is understood as computational operations, rational manipulation of symbols, and functional relations of mental representations. Such operations are presumed to be sentences of "mentalese," or formal syntactical structures and semantic properties that are realizable in the brain, but also in artificial intelligence—and thus distinct from natural language, human psychology, and even conscious awareness. This theory adopts a Chomsky-like nativism, in which cognition operates with intrinsic pre-linguistic concepts that underlie their expression and use in human language.[68] A sentence in mentalese is posed as the cognitive meaning of a sentence in natural language. Accordingly, mentalese is not in English or German, say, but it accounts for grasping the meaning of sentences in English or German and for the capacity to translate from one language to another.[69] Yet it is hard to fathom what a "sentence" in mentalese amounts to (akin to the tree/*Baum* problem discussed earlier), unless it is pitched in purely formal terms—and any such formalization, even the very idea of a "sentence," I aim to argue, is a function of written graphics and not language in a more basic sense. A proto-phenomenology of language indicates a pre-reflective disclosive field that precedes formal or structural expositions of thought and that makes such exposition possible. Language in *this* sense precedes thought.

The phenomenological priority of language, like any theory proposing the correlation of language and thought, must attend to the issue of pre-linguistic infants and nonlinguistic animals, which are often described as having thoughts and concepts without linguistic input or output. This question will receive more detailed treatment in coming discussions, but for now I reiterate that language does not *create* thought or disclosure from its own discrete sphere of verbalization. Speech emerges *out of* natural ecological milieus and embodied practices so that language is always originally *in a world*. Infants and animals do exhibit the practical aptitude of capacious know-how that is different from language per se. But it is wrong to say that the capacities of infants and animals are a function of "thought" or some rudimentary form of "concepts." Infants and animals surely have "psychological awareness" (loosely construed) in the context of capacious engagement with the world, but this is different from having a "concept" in any recognizable form—aside from being a dispensable synonym for a capability. Language in children emerges out of and in the midst of an earlier capacity-field (which at the same time is influenced in significant ways by the linguistic practices of caregivers enveloping a child's early world). Pre-linguistic capacious aptitude *is* prior to language in a developmental sense, but any talk of "mind" or "thinking" or "concepts" postdates the emergence of language in the life of those who deploy such terms (indeed in some respects it postdates the effects of *written* language). Language acquisition allows the existential *meaning* of things and practices to open up, which eventually can generate expositional attributions of "thought" to these meanings.

Theories that want to separate thought from language in some fashion understandably emphasize aspects of intelligence that do not involve overt uses of language. I have argued that not every form of intelligence is aptly described as "thought" in a strict sense—for instance, know-how and tacit knowledge. Even though in many respects mature know-how is informed and shaped by language (as are meaningful "experiences" generally), at the same time immersion and habituation allow the *recession* of language understood as overt lexical expression or usage. Yet such ecstatic engagements are not well rendered with the exposited notion of nonlinguistic "thought." Nevertheless, the ecological, engaged, and social model of language that follows a proto-phenomenological analysis does not mean that a monological sense of thought has no purchase. An internalized notion of thinking as opposed to acting or speaking is a genuine phenomenon in the personal-world, as in silently pondering one's own ideas or introspectively withholding from saying what one thinks. Such phenomena can naturally give rise to picturing language as the verbalized "expression" or "signification" of thought.[70] But that picture stems from a myopic disregard of developmental questions, which will be taken up in volume 2. There I hope to show how thinking can be understood as an internalization of speech.[71] We will consider research inspired by Lev Vygotsky, wherein a child's mentality and even self-consciousness are formed by an internalization of the erstwhile social network of language practices.[72] Even with adults the ecstatic social-environing-world shows that whatever is meant by mentality and thought, it cannot be reductively defined in a monological manner. Yet in terms of the personal-world, it can be internalized organically and psychologically. Such internalization of speech allows space for surmising a "nonphysical" mind.[73] Nevertheless, what is internalized originates in a fully embodied realm of speech practices.

There are a number of ways in which natural language can be implicated in specific occasions of thinking.[74] There is evidence from introspection, in which experiments have tracked reports of subjects showing thought processes as internalized images of natural language. Second language learners report the turning point in their comprehension as being able to think, even dream, in the new language. Sometimes we "think aloud" or on paper. Conversations can draw out or shape thoughts. The "tip of the tongue" phenomenon indicates a verbal path of thinking. All such linguistic occasions are themselves modes of thinking rather than mere conduits for thought.[75] Finally, there is evidence of sub-vocal speech activation in nonverbalized cognitive processes.[76]

Although thinking and speaking, thought and language, are correlative in this investigation, that does not entail their *identity*, especially when considered expositionally. We can certainly distinguish ideas and words or beliefs and speech. But the lived world shows occasions of practical intelligence that exhibit neither overt uses of language nor abstract cognitive processes. Moreover, not everything in the human mind is specifically linguistic—and "mind" here is used in an indicative manner to simply point out familiar nondiscursive mental phenomena, such as imagination, recollection, and anticipation. Such phenomena can be called "pictures" in the loose sense of introspective attention to virtual experiences, events, or circumstances. We can add affective and reflective occasions to fill out a recognizable sense of internal mental states that are distinct from cases of acting and speaking.

Accordingly, not everything in human understanding is a matter of language in the exposited sense of *verbal tokens*. This sidesteps a common (and loaded) way of depicting the constitutive theory of language in a strictly lexical and representational manner, so that "a thought about electrons can only be actively entertained by activating a representation of the *word* 'electron' (or some equivalent)."[77] The factical relationship of language and disclosive understanding cannot be reduced to mere verbalization. To move from nonverbalized occasions to a cognitive domain of thought apart from language bypasses crucial developmental factors in the history of every human person. The same could be said for the proposal of psychological domains apart from language. The fact that we can articulate occasions in such domains does not support the notion that language simply gives expression to these occasions. From early in life, human beings are incorporated into a world of meanings and abilities that take shape in the triangular dynamic of joint dwelling in speech. A basic question that looms in the background of this discussion is this: What could be said of someone's mind or thought or even selfhood who was not exposed to language as a child? Some testimony to the depth of this question is given by Helen Keller, who was deaf, blind, and mute until she was able to access language through the sense of touch:

> Before my teacher came to me, I did not know that I am. I lived in a world that was no-world. I cannot hope to describe adequately that unconscious, yet conscious time of nothingness. I did not know that I knew aught, or that I lived or acted or desired. I had neither will nor intellect. I was carried along to objects and acts by a certain blind natural impetus. . . . When I learned the meaning of "I" and "me" and found that I was something, I began to think. Then consciousness first existed for me.[78]

The ecological practice-field of language acquisition, along with mature immersion in speech practices, shows that even overt occasions of language cannot be adequately described by way of exposited verbal tokens, namely "words." This is why nonverbal occasions do not necessarily stand apart from language in a fuller sense. In the next section I consider various forms of research that have addressed the language-thought relation. A significant limitation in this research is that language and thought are almost always understood in expositional and representational terms, which colors the questions, experimental procedures, and findings in such studies. Much can be learned from these investigations, but many implied philosophical questions would be better served by the indicative character of phenomenological concepts.

8.2. Language, World, and Relativism

A good deal of research has been done on the language-thought relation, especially in confrontation with constitutive theories, which claim that different verbal and semantic meanings across cultures generate different understandings of the world, resulting in a kind of linguistic/cultural relativism. Communicative and nativist theories have challenged this framework by testing the performance of different language speakers and showing certain nonlinguistic commonalities that suggest universal modes of cognition behind linguistic variations. Research has not settled the fundamental questions, although radical relativism does not have a strong following. Findings from both constitutive and communicative perspectives have made important contributions, but one reason why settlement is difficult is that both approaches assume a representational model of language and cognition, which misses what the phenomenology of factical language can contribute to understanding the variations and commonalities across linguistic cultures. In the research, thought and language seem to be held apart in an exposited manner so that language is restricted to verbalization and thought is presumed to cover nonverbalized performance and comprehension. Accordingly, the studies begin with lexical differences in descriptions, nominalization, and grammar, then nonverbal tasks are devised (like memory tests) to see if different language speakers "think" in different or similar ways.

I reiterate that representational and expositional assumptions about the nature of language and thought inform the very terms of discussion in this research, which affects what questions are asked and how they are posed, how experimental settings and protocols are devised, and how results are interpreted. Too often a *lexical* model of language creates an expositional divide that misses what a *factical* model can illuminate. In many respects the very domain of experimental research disengages subjects from how their language functions in the lived world, with its contexts, meanings, immediacy, spontaneity, purposes, and temporal structure. A factical approach to language at least can point out such limitations in research, and it may be able to articulate in a more effective way some of the important results that might supplement and approximate phenomenological findings.

Relativistic conclusions following the constitutive theory of language usually stem from the Sapir-Whorf hypothesis (Whorfian for short), based on the work of Edward Sapir and Benjamin Whorf. If language shapes an understanding of the world, significant semantic differences across languages would generate different ways in which the world is comprehended and even perceived.[79] The Whorfian hypothesis should not be taken to omit certain nonlinguistic forms of experience or to entail a strict one-to-one correspondence between verbal expressions and thought, but rather a constitutive or shaping relation.[80] Much of cognitive psychology has been skeptical of linguistic relativism because of an allegiance to a communicative/nativist model, wherein linguistic variation would not affect common forms of human thought—so that even if we lacked a natural language, certain basic forms of cognition would still be operable.[81] Some research has challenged the Whorfian hypothesis by showing how language variations do not affect presumably nonlinguistic forms of spatial cognition.[82] Dutch, Korean, and English exhibit different uses of "on," "in," and "out." For instance, in Dutch one can say "take your coat out" for "take your coat off" in English. Yet despite these differences, there is a common comprehension of joining versus separating. The number of color words across languages can vary from two to twelve. But memory tests show certain common capacities in recognizing a range of colors. There are comparable perceptions of containment despite different ways of describing a container. There also seem to be similar forms of object naming and a common comprehension of motion events. The tests for identifying thought apart from language involve problem-solving and memory tasks that do not involve verbalization. But this seems to beg the question that thought without speaking is thought without language effects. At the very least, memory has been shown to be informed by language, as we have seen. Moreover, second nature and habituation can involve simply the *recession* of overt language effects in skill acquisition. In general terms, the factical speech-world does not allow for discrete, separate domains of language, behavior, and comprehension.

Studies of significant semantic differences (involving object relations, color, and space), as well as developmental studies, have posed problems for the communicative/nativist approach.[83] In language production, language reception, and cognition, linguistic variations seem to affect perception, behavior, and comprehension, as in path and manner of motion; also in different personas and forms of engagement taken up when bilinguals switch languages. It appears that more Whorfian effects are shown when language is not confined to monological production or experimental tasks, but rather presumed to be embedded in a linguistic-social-cultural nexus.[84]

There seems to be room for a middle ground between strong versions of the constitutive and communicative models, especially if key terms in the debate can be clarified.[85] One way to strike a balance is to distinguish between two inheritance systems, the biological and the cultural.[86] With certain biological factors in common, cultural differences would not go all the way down. Human infants are predisposed to pick up all possible language sounds, but once native sounds are acquired, the capacity to register other sounds is blocked. Such original sonic coding is therefore an intrinsic perceptive capacity that precedes language acquisition. The same pattern has been found in spatial perception. English and Korean differ in spatial formats, yet early on, infants can function with either one. After native speech registers, however, the nonnative format is tuned out.

If strong nativism were valid, common linguistic expression would be expected, but there is enough variation in grammatical forms and structure, inflection, tense, and word order to call the strong version into question. For instance, verbs for coming and going are not expressed in a uniform way across languages. Spatial expressions for contact, containment, on, in, and near exhibit significant semantic differences.[87] Such linguistic disparity can make a difference in experimental scenarios because different language speakers vary in their performance depending on what frame of spatial reference is involved in the task at hand. Accordingly, some research supports a degree of validity for the constitutive theory of language. While there are certain biological constants in human nature, linguistic variation can shape different modes of thought. The structure of such variation is usually described in terms of mental and semantic representations.[88] This mode of explanation, however, can stand in the way of other perspectives that might show more than biological commonalities. A phenomenological ecology can turn attention to factical performances that can be comparable despite lexical differences.[89]

Another way to strike a balance between constitutive/relativist and communicative/nativist models would begin with the notion of "core knowledge."[90] Core knowledge refers to intrinsic sensory-motor capacities that are comparable in animals and human infants: having to do with object mechanics, motion, contact, continuity, and spatial relations (know-how would be the preferable term rather than "knowledge"). Such capacities have limits in being domain specific, task specific, and encapsulated (self-contained and separated from other capacities). The acquisition of natural language allows for extension and expansion beyond such limits: combining and relating capacities, as well as novel deployments. Animals and pre-linguistic infants can comprehend object position, color, and spatial location as distinct spheres, but not something like "left of the blue wall." Likewise with respect to numeration, in which children learn numbers with the aid of language references (two dogs, three apples, etc.). Such extensions are made possible by what I have called the differential element in language, which shows 1) how language can be constitutive of thought beyond core knowledge and 2) how linguistic variation across languages might issue different disclosive effects.

A further way to balance relativist and nativist thinking is to consider joint attention.[91] Human infants are biologically predisposed to engage in joint engagement, which precedes the acquisition of language (although, again, the linguistic behavior of caregivers is influential even before the advent of speech) and which makes language possible. The triangular structure of joint attention shows that language is a form of "social cognition" or what I would call a disclosive social-world. Language cannot be understood merely as a kind of representational reference. Animals and pre-verbal infants can understand many utterances of direct reference: A dog will readily understand words like *outside* and *eat*. An infant can respond to "Where's the doggie?" Language in its full sense is a matter of *shared* attention, understood *as* such, and functioning by way of reciprocal effects. The triangular structure of shared effects introduces the child to a long history of cultural usage that is super-added to immediate cases of joint attention and primed for further usage—thus following the threefold figure-eight structure of temporality. Added to this are the varying perspectives of symbol usage. Now actual perceptions can be modified because immediate experiences become "layered" with cultural, social, and symbolic meanings.[92] One consequence of perspectival layering is that language allows for complex compounds, as when a child comes to understand a piece of candy as both something good to eat and a forbidden temptation. Animals and infants can understand one thing in different ways—as, say, benign or hurtful in different circumstances—but not one thing as a compound *of* different meanings.

What is evident in some of this research is that thought and language should not be segregated from each other because that colors experimental projects and tempts the search for a grounding function on either side of the ledger. There are many basic biological factors that precede and make possible linguistic ability and that continue to play a role after the ability is acquired. But language does not simply arise out of basic biological conditions; it exponentially expands and extends those conditions in ways that exceed and transform them into world-disclosive powers. I would call this development a "nesting" effect that builds from the core out in an assimilating manner, but even here the metaphor misleads because the layers in question are only evident as such *because* of the disclosive function of language. In any case, however the research in question is interpreted, a proto-phenomenological account of immersion and second nature is needed to provide the counterweight of a holistic field to correct for representational assumptions that continue to guide most of the research and its interpretive conclusions.[93] Language should not be confined to the representational notion of "words," nor should thought be restricted to cognition apart from verbalization. Both should be incorporated into their "world," their ecological field of enactment. Indeed, it is helpful that some research points in this direction, albeit without the appropriate phenomenological concepts.[94]

As indicated earlier, the reason why research into the language-thought relation has had difficulty answering its questions is precisely because of its representational biases. The basic problem of how representations can link up with the world is compressed by this research into an interrepresentational problem: how cognitive and linguistic representations relate to or affect each other. Experiments configured along these lines then toss back and forth between such exposed domains, seeking to find how they affect each other and which domain might be more basic. From a phenomenological perspective, the research itself has manufactured the problems that have been difficult to solve.

The notion that language development and pre-linguistic capacities come to shape human "intelligence"—in a way that precedes refined conceptions of "thought"—can help address conflicting positions even among those who want to overcome representational biases in philosophy. A case in point is the debate between Hubert Dreyfus and John McDowell.[95] Both want to emphasize practical engagements with the world. Dreyfus offers "mindless" coping, which fits my notion of ecstatic immersion. McDowell insists that practices can be articulated and must be governed by normative concepts. I have suggested the bidirectional relation between immersion and exposition, in which reflective attention can prepare new habits of immersion. The *recession* of exposition and language effects shows that "mindless" is misleading. But with actual performance, Dreyfus is right that automatic skills do not need "governance." My notion of indicative proto-concepts might work in McDowell's favor, but his approach seems wedded to a model of concepts that retains traditional blockage of what proto-phenomenology can offer.

8.3. Language Deprivation

There are many examples and ranges of language deprivation that suggest the significant role that speech plays in human development and cognition. Most notable are so-called feral children, who have been discovered living in the wild and presumably in that condition since very early in their lives. Perhaps the most famous case is Victor of Aveyron, who was discovered in 1800. The summary assessment of Victor and similar cases is as follows: None of the children could speak; they did not respond attentively to human speech; they had much difficulty learning language and could not develop beyond rudimentary forms; they were at first socially unresponsive to other humans; they seemed to lack memory, self-awareness, and temporal dimensions beyond the immediate present; in many respects the children were more animal than human. There have been debates about how to interpret these cases (some surmise mental disabilities apart from the sphere of language), but the consensus seems to be that the absence of a linguistic environment is a crucial impediment to human development. These cases also lend support to the critical period hypothesis, in which optimal language acquisition is restricted to a span between ages two and twelve. This poses certain biological constraints on when language readiness is available.[96] In general terms, studies of feral children have challenged many traditional assumptions about human nature: strong nativism, individualism, and the romantic notion of the noble savage living in idyllic freedom from the constraints of civilization. The latter conception was advanced by some at the time of Victor's discovery, but other interpretations held that his existence in the "state of nature" was not an estimable condition of freedom but a deprivation of human powers that require socialization—thus calling into question the modern ideal of individual autonomy and self-sufficiency.[97]

Conditions of severe deliberate deprivation show effects comparable to feral children, as in the case of Genie, a teenage girl from

California discovered in 1970.[98] She had been physically abused, restrained, and denied practically all human contact. At age thirteen Genie exhibited a mental age of one or two. She could not speak and after rescue was able to learn language at only the most rudimentary level; she could use up to three words together but lacked any grammatical structure or the capacity for novel uses. Obviously, her condition could be attributed to the acute abuse she suffered, but the language deficit seems telling along the lines of feral children. Even with care and nurturing, Genie could not develop a fully functional language.[99]

It is well established that conditions of language impairment—diminished linguistic processing, performance, and development—involve deficits in nonverbal cognition and memory capacity. Yet conditions such as the Williams syndrome—in which language capacity is normal but certain cognitive skills are impaired—have been taken by the communicative/nativist approach as evidence for the dissociation of language and thought. But some research shows that the Williams syndrome is better understood in terms of the interdependence of language and cognition.[100] A number of studies suggest that impairment conditions on either side of the language-cognition spectrum call into question strong versions of both the constitutive and communicative theories.[101]

Communicative/nativist theories might respond to cases of feral children and other conditions of language deficit or deprivation in the following way: Language could be a necessary condition for developing or actualizing cognitive powers (especially more refined forms) and function as a kind of conduit or channel, which thereby could preserve a sense of nonlinguistic thought that is simply blocked by language impairment.[102] But this amounts to a nonfalsifiable thesis that begs the question of thought apart from language. The effects of language impairment seem to be better explained by some degree of the constitutive theory. Yet this should not omit certain pre-linguistic biological capacities (especially joint attention) that prepare and make possible language acquisition—but such capacities are better explained as a pre-reflective ecstatic aptitude rather than a domain of "thought" that seems to be smuggled in from reflective exposition.

9. LANGUAGE AND ARTIFICIAL INTELLIGENCE

A proto-phenomenological account of language can help us expand the discussion of artificial intelligence in chapter 2 by accentuating the difference between factical language and representational formats. In strong AI the provision is that computer programs can replicate human language usage. A measure for success has been advanced with the "Turing test," devised by the computer scientist Alan Turing. The idea is this: If a human being is having an online exchange with another human being and with a computer and cannot tell the difference, the computer program passes the test and is functionally equivalent to a human language speaker—in which the performance is decisive regardless of the material medium (brain and computer).

A classic challenge to AI in this regard is the so-called Chinese room thought experiment proposed by John Searle, which has become one of the most widely discussed philosophical problems since its appearance in 1980.[103] The scenario involves a person who speaks English and has no understanding of Chinese, who is alone in a room in which a language string of Chinese characters is slipped under the door. The person follows a set of instructions in English for manipulating and arranging Chinese characters, which would result in a coherent response to the initial string of characters. Other people outside the room who know Chinese and receive the person's response would think there is a speaker of Chinese in the room. The person has functionally passed the language test, but without understanding Chinese.

The Chinese room is meant to mimic a computer program performing linguistic functions, and to highlight something missing that would seem to be essential in language use, "understanding" language. Searle's point is that even if a program could pass the Turing test, there would be something central that is lacking, thus refuting the claims of strong AI. Computational processes can mimic human language use without its full character of comprehension, which Searle says is a matter of biological processes in a human brain—thus rejecting functionalism because the material medium does matter. Formal and syntactical computation of symbols (represented by the instruction manual for Chinese characters) cannot get us to semantic meaning because the symbols and syntactical rules *by themselves* have no semantic meaning, which for Searle requires mental content and conscious intentionality emitted in the human brain. A representation or symbolic manipulation of the word *tree* is not the same as understanding what the word *means* in relevant settings.

Searle's argument is impressive, but I want to expand its scope beyond semantic meaning and the brain to include the full range of factors indicated in proto-phenomenology—how language is originally a mode of dwelling in the world. So "understanding" language involves all those elements that precede and exceed representation and computation—ecstatic immersion, existential meaning, communicative practice, the social-world, intimation, know-how, tacit knowledge, embodiment—which are of a different order than computer functions, regardless of proficiency. There are indeed remarkable developments in computer voice recognition and language translation. Translation programs originally aimed to mimic human learning processes and linguistic rules. Today, "machine learning" bypasses all this in favor of data processing millions of translation possibilities, in which patterns of success and failure are calibrated until proficiency is possible even beyond specific inputs. But this is not the way humans think. And even where exposition is needed in learning a new language, the immersed character of second-nature proficiency shows a manner of understanding that is neither representational nor computational. My suspicion is that subtle aspects of human language, especially regarding gesture, tone, and accentuation (among other things), may never be fully transferable to computer programs; likewise the "indefinite extensibility" of natural language, which is incompatible with the model-theoretic standard for formal, computational languages.[104] But again, it would not be decisive if such things *were* transferable because language would not *matter* to a nonliving machine in the way that it does for a human being.

Language matters because it serves and discloses factical concerns in the world. Adding the ecologically immersed character of language brings out a feature of human language that an inanimate computer, I submit, could not exhibit. I call this feature *embodied jointure*. Here language is *experienced* as a reciprocal "reach" between self and world, an intersecting structure that "blends" the living body with its environment in a mode of *felt awareness*, which reiterates the "sensitive registers" of attraction and repulsion/weal and woe recounted in chapter 2 (4.4). Embodied jointure is a reiteration of ecstatic immersion, which makes possible exposited relations that representational models are tracking, but that are *derived* from a pre-expositional (immersed) jointure. It is representational exposition that generates the formal structures of grammar, logic, and computational systems based in binary code—which, when housed in an inanimate computer program, are now completely *severed* from factical language, including the normal and refined language enacted by designers of computers and AI researchers. Even scientific language—in human usage—retains its connection with factical language and embodied jointure, from which scientific language is derived and in which scientists continue to dwell in the midst of their professional work. The linguistic functions, inputs, and outputs of a computer are nothing more than formalized extractions *devoid* of embodied jointure, lacking even the *derived* character of exposited language deployed by human scientists—a derivational structure that allows the smooth shifts of enactive interpretation between natural and disciplinary language in the course of scientific practice. No matter the proficient performance of even the most advanced robotic humanoid imaginable, no matter the attempted arguments that computers can be "conscious," without the *biological* dimension of embodied jointure there would seem to be no room for the reciprocal "reach" of a speech-world, in which language and world are joined and experienced *as* joined. Such is the sphere of bio-intelligence discussed in chapter 2.[105]

The felt awareness of embodied jointure is the organic source of the existential *meaning* of a practice, which is illuminated in the face of contravention. As noted in chapter 1, if a robotic writing device encountered an obstacle that impaired the inscription, this would not be experienced *as* an obstacle, which would elicit something like frustration or annoyance, an affective response that presupposes and reveals the forward-looking aim of the practice blocked by a present obstruction. This level of meaningfulness precedes even the exposited notion of "semantic meaning" operating in Searle's account. In general terms what is lacking in AI is that there seems to be no possibility of a proto-phenomenology of computers, no exhibition of existential significance in a computer's performance—in a word, no *world* inhabited by artificial intelligence.[106] If a computer were to count as a world-dwelling phenomenon, it would have to *care* about what it was doing, or perhaps object to its assignments, or issue spontaneous interrogation of what it means to be a computer, whether the world outside the computer really exists, or whether human beings can match computer intelligence.

10. EVOLUTION AND LANGUAGE

The notion of bio-intelligence dictates a discussion of evolution theory, which is at the core of modern biology and which offers an alternative to supernatural or transcendent explanations in accounting for life, its variations, and the emergence of human beings. With evolution, humans are continuous with, and arise from, a natural process of developing forms, a process explained by natural selection, in which a combination of random mutations and varying environmental conditions produce new adaptations over vast stretches of time, succeeding in complexity up to higher mammals and finally to humans. To be precise, evolution is not a theory; the fossil record, which exhibits an invariant order in the development of simple to complex organisms, shows that evolution has in fact happened. For Darwin, natural selection was the theory that explains evolution; and today, the so-called modern synthesis has joined genetics to Darwin's theory to account for evolution. Scientific debates and controversies concerning evolution (which creationists have tried to exploit) are not about whether evolution happened but how. It seems clear that evolution theory stands as the abductive best explanation for the natural facts at our disposal.[107]

The trouble starts when we recognize that if evolution is assumed, then somehow human "culture" emerged out of "nature," and one does not have to be a religious fundamentalist to see stresses between these two domains. I believe that proto-phenomenology can be brought to bear on this question in productive ways because its presumption of immanence and ecological structures can be compatible with, and even assist, the findings of evolutionary biology in trying to make sense out of organic life forms.[108] Yet phenomenology can also show how culture "exceeds" brute nature (narrowly construed) but without transcending the earth (broadly construed). By this I mean that cultural phenomena are not directly translatable from physical and biological conditions and yet this "transcending" aspect of culture is nothing transcendent; it is "natural" in the sense of emerging *in* and *out of* nature and being *intrinsic* to human existence. In other words, proto-phenomenology can show what is wrong with reductive naturalism without appealing to what Dennett calls "skyhooks," namely transcendent, dualistic, religious, or ad hoc explanations.[109]

Phenomenology and evolution can complement each other in a number of ways. Both can be called fully worldly and earth-bound orientations. We might see evolution as pertaining to the immersed character of animal life in the natural-world, and we can understand humanity's biological/animal inheritance as its primal "projection," which shapes its corporeal life from the start as an involuntary endowment. Proto-phenomenology and evolution each advance dynamic models of the world constituted by time, change, movement, tension, and finitude; in these respects, both speak against metaphysical essentialism. I believe that evolution theory should find more affinity with phenomenological concepts than with the discrete, reified, mechanical categories inherited from natural science. The environmental structures of ecstatic immersion, projection, know-how, affective attunement, and intimation are more appropriate for understanding biological adaptation and development than are the more crudely delineated causal, stimulus-response, and mechanistic models common to scientific theories.[110] Evolution presupposes that organisms be conceived as "dwellers," as predisposed to respond to their milieu and adaptive to the practical needs and problems of navigating a complex, variegated environment. The phenomenological notion of immersed pre-reflective practices can easily be extended to the rest of animal life, with the advantage of not having to rely on mentalistic metaphors that confuse more than they illuminate. Evolutionary "capacities" and "adaptations" can be construed as modes of know-how that in their way are intelligent and thus not utterly blind.[111] At the same time, such capacities need not be analogized to conscious intentions and cognitive formats inherited from epistemological tenets in the subject-object binary; so we can be suspicious when we hear of evolution "creating" this or that, organisms "aiming" for this or that, genes "directing" their organisms, an ape's "concept" of this or that, and even Dennett's presumed alternative to strict cognition of "engineering."[112]

An ecological, organic holism can avoid crude reductions that can constrain evolutionary biology. It is not that atomic explanations are false, but that they are insufficient in accounting for organisms as self-organizing wholes.[113] As I indicated in another context, if you did not know what a tree is ahead of time, no genetic assembly could get you there. This matter applies particularly to genetic reductions, as in the infamous notion of the "selfish gene."[114] Here the exclusive unit of natural selection is the gene, so that an organism's behavior is simply in the service of genetic reproduction. Because life began at the level of DNA, it is supposed that all subsequent manifestations of life, including cultural constructs, at bottom must be nothing more than epiphenomena in the mindless process of gene replication. Such a model can be apt in analyzing statistical tendencies and long-term population patterns. It also seems intuitive that whatever life form presently exists must have been made possible by reproductive fitness patterns in the past. But reducing the behavior of an organism to the dictates of the gene pool misses the complex nature of organisms in relation to their environment. Some genetic traits are stable, but others are flexible in being modifiable by environmental variations. The plasticity of a phenotype organism in fact contributes to the furthering of the organism and hence to the long-term development of the genotype. So the behavior of a life form and its evolutionary trajectory must be understood in terms of the complex intersection of genetic and environmental factors, as well as new factors that emerge by way of the interaction of genetic and environmental factors, particularly when the organism modifies its environment in such a way as to further its fitness.[115]

Even if behavior were rigidly determined by genetic traits, we would want to correct conceptual mistakes or bad metaphors that often prevail in genetic reductionism: that genes are "using" their organisms for their own "interests," that behavior "serves" reproduction "in order to" further the genetic line. It would be more accurate to say that an organism's present behavior is following genetic traits that *happen to have been selective* in the past. If there were a radical change in the present environment so that the traits were now unsuitable, we can see the mistake in talking of the primal "interest" of the genes "on behalf of which" the organism is acting. What we would have now are "stupid" genes or "suicidal" genes. The point is not to deny the role and force of gene replication; such explanations can have value as extensive statistical surveys of long-term populations. Rather, the issue is that such accounts bypass the actual behavior of the organism as such, as well as its plasticity. What is gained by saying of an organism that this maneuver, that desire, this function, and that activity are "really" only surface strategies for the underlying need of its genes to replicate? What would be lost by saying that the behavior is in part a function of traits that happen to have been successful in the past and leave it at that, giving attention now to the complex interactions of the organism's inherited capacities, behaviors, ventures, and environment, with all these features taken together as a more appropriate account of the nature of this life form? Because such an account would not ignore genetic factors, objections would seem to stem from an analytical fetish for atomic explanations.[116]

10.1. Nature and Culture

A crucial legacy of modern science has been, in Weber's phrase, the "disenchantment" of nature. Whereas Aristotle held that cultural meanings, purposes, and values are intrinsic to the natural world, modern science with its mathematical base and disengaged objectivity stripped the world bare of such meanings and demoted them to mere subjective occasions.[117] Surely such thinking is magnified with sociobiology and the selfish gene. The reduction of life and culture to the blind process of genetic replication surging forth simply for its own sake leaves us with an implicit nihilism that only a Schopenhauerian pessimism could address with any authenticity.[118]

Dennett has tried to mollify this pressing problem while keeping in line with the basic orientation of evolutionary biology. I agree with Dennett that evolutionary naturalism rules out essentialism, global teleology, and "mind-first" cosmologies.[119] And Dennett wants to make room for cultural meanings within an evolutionary viewpoint. But he does not persuade in posing the following (false) choice: either we account for culture in a manner consistent with evolutionary science or we have to resort to some *deus ex machina* skyhook.[120] Dennett calls for a reductionism that is not "greedy" in canceling out culture in favor of blind forces.[121] Yet it is still reductive in remaining consistent with the basic "algorithm" of natural selection that is "substrate neutral" in being applicable to all phenomena, from nature to culture.[122] Following Dawkins, Dennett accounts for culture as an array of "memes," cultural constructs such as ethical norms that emerge through language out of biological processes and then "evolve" in a way analogous to genetic dynamics in natural selection. So memes compete for adaptive fitness and their organisms (humans) serve as carriers for their replicative strategies.[123] In this way we can have both nature and culture on a continuum without the need for skyhooks.

Dennett's position runs into a number of problems. Even though a memetic theory might have some interesting correlations with structuralism, nevertheless the insistence on a close analogy with genetic natural selection is suspect.[124] First of all, the cultural transmission of memes requires no connection with genetic transmission. And memes are "directed mutations" that emerge out of the interests of human organisms, thus disrupting the analogy with blind genetic mutation and replication. Finally, memes pass along acquired traits, and so they commit the Lamarckian fallacy so anathema to Darwinism.[125] But the most vexing problem, I think, is this. Dennett understands that to avoid greedy reductionism one must give cultural constructs their due in their own terms in some way. Ethical memes, for instance, cannot be explained simply in terms of gene replication. Although genetics would be the *ultimate* historical source of present moral values, that does not mean that gene replication is the *proximate* source or *beneficiary* of ethical practices.[126] Dennett grants that the emergence of memes in humans allows us to "transcend," "overpower," and "escape" biological constraints in important ways.[127] In other words, culture allows us to *exceed* nature in some manner, and yet it seems that Dennett simply stipulates this as an emergence out of a biological base, without much attention to *how* it is so and without thematizing the "excess" as such.

This is where proto-phenomenology can make an important contribution. An account of the factical lived world is able to show that so-called cultural constructs come first, before the uncovering of so-called objective conditions in nature. Given ecstatic immersion in meaning-laden practice-fields, the human world is saturated with existential significance, and so we can say that cultural meanings are *there* in the world (rather than being mere subjective states) and projected in immanent, concrete ways (rather than coming from transcendent sources). Moreover, the temporality of the lived world and the differential fitness of language show how human existence is an openness beyond extant conditions. Proto-phenomenology can articulate certain capacities that some philosophical approaches uncritically assume or take for granted: such as Dennett's stipulation that culture "exceeds" nature or the common notion that human rationality involves deliberation that requires recollections of the past and anticipations of the future—in other words, giving presence to absences and exceeding the present. A phenomenology of the lived world is able to offer a concrete viable account of what Dennett wants out of culture without a reduction to extant conditions of nature and without an ascension to transcendent sources.

From a physical and biological standpoint, I have no doubt that the human species emerged out of an evolutionary continuum, more precisely that the human *animal* evolved from other animals. Yet if we consider humans as cultural animals, there are conceptual problems haunting an evolutionary "continuum" of nature and culture, which presupposes empirically discernible causal connections. Given the distinction between phenomenological and causal descriptions, the disclosive *openness* of the human world displays a kind of "break" that eludes empirical or causal explanations.

Culture is what (apparently) distinguishes humans from other animals and is indicated in such phenomena as art, religion, morality, technology, science, and especially language. I take cultural phenomena and mere natural descriptions to be incommensurable at certain levels. So although a biological continuum is evident and makes sense, when considering the emergence or presence of culture, the notion of a continuum runs into trouble. Here I am not referring to specific products of culture but to the background meanings and intimations of cultural phenomena. Religion speaks of alternative dimensions beyond ordinary experience. Philosophy arises out of wonder, perplexity, and questions. Art fashions new or altered images beyond brute encounters with given things. Morality involves the modification of instinctive brute behaviors. Technology transforms physical nature. And abstract thinking, one consequence of which is science, involves concepts and structures that reach beyond immediate experience and perception.

It is evident that the atmosphere of such cultural phenomena (questioning, evaluating, creating, explaining) presupposes an openness beyond the brute given or the immediate present, and an openness *to* such open possibilities. Culture as such exceeds extant conditions. But then explaining the emergence of culture by means of extant conditions (for instance, as a special organization of material, biological, environmental, or behavioral states) makes no sense (phenomenologically). Put it this way: Culture cannot ultimately be accounted for because "giving an account" is a cultural phenomenon. Science, too, is a cultural phenomenon that exceeds the brute given. Seeing the world *as* a set of empirical conditions calling for causal explanation cannot itself be derived from empirical or causal conditions. The notion of interpretation shows that there are pre-reflective dimensions of meaning that make possible various orientations toward the world. This domain of meaningfulness is already in place before any expositional results and so it cannot itself be an "object" of discovery. Such hermeneutic circularity forever blocks attempts to advance strictly objective explanations of human life. The existential background of knowing cannot strictly speaking be put in the foreground because expositional foregrounding as such is a background operation. The background can be *shown* indicatively but it cannot be "explained" in the sense of a causal or logical trace to extant conditions or concepts.

There certainly are evolutionary and biological links between humans and other animals, especially our primate cousins. I think we can make sense out of certain quasi-cultural links as well, for instance concerning certain social patterns and behaviors. It is easy to picture a clear continuum of ape and human posture, of ape and human locomotion, of ape and human manual dexterity, with the requisite approximations of end results. But it is difficult to understand how, for example, perceiving or remembering something can approximate or "lead to" painting it on a cave wall, or how witnessing the expiration of life can approximate or lead to burial customs, with their implicit sense of a "beyond."

The notion of a "culture gap" between humans and primates is not beyond dispute, of course. When we see a gorilla deftly trimming and using a twig to draw out insects from inside a log, we can surely imagine a continuum in the direction of human tool making and use. But there is still a difference, I think, between such an example (which could have begun with a fortuitous accident followed by repeating, learning, and remembering the use) and tool *making* as a cultural phenomenon, a creative orientation beyond extant conditions, which sees the world *as* "transformable." In phenomenological terms the human world is marked by a radical openness and differentiated otherness that does not seem to be evident in the animal realm. Human culture is more than life, it is living-for, coming-from, heading-toward, living in the midst of death, limits, and possibilities, all of which is a surpassing of actuality. This surpassing element seems to distinguish the human world from the more immediate (and immersed) domain of animal life. Practical immersion to a certain extent is something shared by humans and animals. On the other hand, expositional "distance" from immersed conditions and cultural "openness" seem unique to the human species. Such distance and openness are made possible by language, which prepares cultural capacities and habits that themselves become (now unique) forms of immersion.

10.2. Language and Evolution

The most important topic in this discussion is the question of language. It is common to see language as the distinguishing mark of the human species. In fact, without language there would be no human culture at all. Language is the inhabited environment in which the world opens up for human beings, and it too exhibits a circularity that eludes explication, as we have seen. Any attempt to "explain" language or connect it with pre-linguistic elements must employ language to do so. Even "nonverbal" comprehensions or experiences bank on having been oriented into a language-laden environment from the first moments of life. So language is the very shaping of the human world from the start. And this investigation has argued that in everyday linguistic practices and exchanges we find language to be spontaneously disclosive of the world. In direct conversations, I simply understand immediately the disclosive effects of what is said without marking a difference between speech and reference. If someone is verbally helping me learn a practical task, I am immersed in this field without noticing "words" as distinct from "referents" or puzzling about how words relate to their referents. In this respect, there is a *fit* between language and world. And yet the *differential* character of language makes possible the expansive openness of disclosure, particularly in terms of temporality, in which the presencing of absence makes possible the stretches of temporal understanding that far exceed any primitive time sense that animals might possess. With words, one can retain the past and project the future in vivid detail, one can be released from the actual by envisioning the possible, one can scan temporal dimensions to compare present experience with past experience and uncover alternative futures based on the comparison. All of this is made possible by the differential fitness of language. Without fitness, speech about the past or future would not register. Without difference, speech would be trapped in actuality.

Differential space is what opens up language (and the world) and makes possible the dynamic openness of human language that does not seem evident in animal calls and their functions. In addition to temporal extension, we have noted examples of openness such as metaphor, comparisons, distinctions, negations, new or extended uses, misuses, deceit, and asking questions. All of this indicates that the human linguistic environment is animated by traversals of otherness exceeding immediate states, which strictly empirical descriptions cannot convey. Interestingly, linguistic research shows that one of the few universals across different human languages is the capacity for negation, and that expressing negation is essential to language.[128] In light of the phenomenological "alterity" of language, from an evolutionary standpoint it is difficult to conceive how animal sounds and calls approximated or inched their way toward this surpassing dimension of language. In terms of differential fitness, it is puzzling to envision how mere sounds "evolved" to the point where language *as* fitting and *as* different emerged in some contiguous sense. The puzzle can be aggravated by noticing that my posing this question *as* a problem presupposes my already having been outfitted *by* language *as* a differential dynamic. And what about the *as* as such? What "is" the "as"? Can we take the "as" as, well, what? At this point one appreciates the aptness of Wittgenstein's appeal for silence, or more positively, Heidegger's talk of the self-showing marvel of being that is simply bounded by concealment and thereby not susceptible to explication. In whatever way human life has emerged out of nature, the very powers that let us explore this question cannot themselves be tracked in extant natural facts.

The discussion thus far has been driven by the phenomenological recognition of hermeneutical circularity. Putting this aside, I think that research in evolutionary biology, psychology, and linguistics can accord with several aspects of language discussed in this chapter; it can also lessen somewhat the difficulty in conceiving an evolutionary link between the behavior of animals and the cultural phenomenon of language.[129] In questioning the idea of human language "evolving" from pre-linguistic animal capacities, one is faced with controversies surrounding intriguing animal research. Apes have been taught sign language and other nonvocal functions, and researchers point to an ape's capacity for innovative use and the complex grammatical structure implicit in various performances. Critics concede that apes are clever, bright, and communicative, but they are skeptical that apes *understand* language use beyond mimicry and experimental prompts. Chimps can be taught naming, but they seem to lack an *interest* in naming for its own sake, which is clearly evident in human children.[130]

There surely is animal communication, but human *linguistic* communication seems to be unique in the animal kingdom.[131] Beyond how proto-phenomenology is able to articulate the distinct nature of developed human language, the importance of embodied gesture can show both an evolutionary link with animal communication and the unique aspects of human gesture in its relation to verbal language.[132] There is mounting evidence that language originated with gesture before or at least along with vocalization. Research on nonhuman primate communication and human child development suggests that human gesturing exhibits joint attention, which appears to be lacking in primate gesturing, including their use of sign language. With respect to pointing, for example, joint attention involves a triangular structure of pointing *to* something *for* the regard of someone else, including the tacit sense of *shared* regard and an *interest* in enacting this relational disclosure—infants will point to things simply for the sake of sharing the experience, beyond any desire, say, to get things. Primate gesturing and signing seem to be limited to requesting, while human infants also gesture to inform and share. Because the triangular reciprocity of joint attention appears to be lacking in primates, this suggests a uniquely human capacity for collaborative practices, understood *as* joint endeavors. Primates and other animals do exhibit relational activities, but what seems to be missing is an extra-individual *sense* of togetherness—which marks what I have called the social-world.[133] The same distinct social sense is indicated in human imitation: beyond merely imitating a certain behavior, human infants also intimate the *purpose* of the behavior; thus they have an awareness of shared meanings and interests.[134]

It is not clear how gestural joint attention itself evolved beyond animal relationality, but a likely scenario is advanced forms of hunting, made possible by the development of an upright stance and dexterous manual powers. With hunting, collaboration was highly adaptive and the import of feeding could engender a sense of shared purpose.[135] In any case, a key question concerns how gesture evolved into speech, into sound and vocalization. We can surmise a proto-language that involved the concurrence of gesture and vocal sound, which was relatively simple and biologically based, followed by gradual emphasis on vocalization, which opened up the expansive disclosive capacity of language, especially owing to a richer differential aspect. Vocalization then engendered the cultural power of language beyond more immediate biological needs. At any rate, joint vocalization seems to be the unique capacity that marked human linguistic evolution. What might account for the switch from gesture to vocal sounds? The role of facial gesturing in communication and vocal abilities could blend together. And sound could supply distinctive adaptive advantages: it can communicate from longer distances; it need not be face-to-face; it can function in the dark; and it can free the hands for other tasks while retaining communication.[136] Such a scenario provides some explanatory purchase regarding the evolution of language, but the problem of hermeneutical circularity, wherein any explanatory aim postdates the presence of language, persists. The world-disclosive power of language itself is ultimately a mystery because it cannot be grasped as something disclosed without already being at work.

In general terms, I think that evolutionary science and proto-phenomenology can coexist, at least with the former being restricted to causal explanations of how human capacities came to pass in natural history. Yet the ecological structures, embodied practices, and natural immanence entailed by evolution can imply significant overlap with proto-phenomenological descriptions. With such confluence, a reductive naturalism can be exchanged for a richer sense of animal life and its human extension in such a way that existential meaningfulness need not be bracketed or eclipsed in thinking about what natural science can tell us about life. The fact-value divide can be overcome in philosophical reflection, which would be good news for evolution science too, if it is to be taken as a meaningful endeavor. Evolution is often taken to have a deflationary effect on cultural constructs, in which human love, for example, finds its ultimate explanation in the blind impetus of genetic reproduction—thus flagging the phenomenology of love as failing to capture its "real" agenda. So what we take love to mean in human terms simply has an adaptive function in biological terms. Presumably any cultural construct would be susceptible to the same deflation. But knowledge and science are cultural constructs too. How are we to understand evolutionary science itself? Would it also find its ultimate explanation in blind genetic forces? Would it be "simply" a function of adaptive contingency and thus bereft of any truth in its own terms?[137]

This chapter has only begun an account of how language can be understood in proto-phenomenological terms. The next chapter explores how the disclosive power of language figures in the question of truth, which develops further the way in which factical language can help address a number of core philosophical questions. Volume 2 will round out this venture in the context of language acquisition and the distinction between oral and written language.

NOTES

1. See Helen Keller, *The Story of My Life* (New York: Bantam, 1990), chaps. 5–7.
2. The linguistic turn is a multifaceted philosophical movement that began in the early twentieth century, especially with the work of Wittgenstein and ordinary language philosophy, in continental thought with Heidegger, the structuralism of Saussure, and post-structuralist developments in Foucault and Derrida. A common theme is the critique of traditional metaphysics and objective realism on behalf of the notion that language constitutes human experience and knowledge. Within the linguistic turn there are different positions on how language constitutes experience and how philosophical questions are addressed, but overall there is agreement that philosophical questions are questions about language. For a classic collection, see Richard M. Rorty, ed., *The*

Linguistic Turn: Essays in Philosophical Methodology (Chicago: University of Chicago Press, 1992).

3. See John William Miller, *The Midworld of Symbols and Functioning Objects* (New York: W. W. Norton, 1982), for specific attention to language in this regard.

4. As Maurice Merleau-Ponty says: "The meaning of words . . . is immanent in speech." Thus "speech . . . does not translate ready-made thought, but accomplishes it" (*Phenomenology of Perception*, trans. Colin Smith [Atlantic Highlands, NJ: Humanities Press, 1962], 178–79).

5. See Guillaume Dezechache et al., "An Evolutionary Approach to Emotional Communication," *Journal of Pragmatics* 59 (2013): 221–33.

6. Again, the focus here is different from communicative theories that take language to be simply the public expression of mental states that are distinct from linguistic conveyance.

7. See Harvey Sacks, *Lectures on Conversation* (Oxford: Blackwell, 1992). For language as social sense making, see Elena Clare Cuffari et al., "From Participatory Sense-Making to Language: There and Back Again," *Phenomenology and the Cognitive Sciences* 14, no. 4 (December 2015): 1089–125.

8. The work of Paul Grice is important in articulating "conversational implicature," wherein one understands the tacit but undeclared meaning of an utterance, which can be given by context, convention, or manner of delivery—as in sarcasm, hyperbole, or abridgment ("Can you come to the game?" "I have to work"). Grice lays out a set of maxims and principles that govern the various settings of conversation and that underwrite implicature by locating conforming or deviating instances. See *Studies in the Way of Words* (Cambridge, MA: Harvard University Press, 1991). But such formal analyses of linguistic implicature should be seen as expositionally derived from the more informal and pre-reflective intimations of the sense and patterns of conversations. The Gricean idea of conversational implicature has been taken up and furthered by pragmatics. See Stephen C. Levinson, *Presumptive Meanings: The Theory of Generalized Conversational Implicature* (Cambridge, MA: MIT Press, 2000).

9. For a critique of Gricean models along these lines, see Carelton B. Cristensen, "Meaning Things and Meaning Others," *Philosophy and Phenomenological Research* 57, no. 3 (September 1997): 495–522.

10. For an examination of skepticism from a Wittgensteinian perspective, see José Medina, *Language: Key Concepts in Philosophy* (New York: Continuum, 2005), chap. 3.

11. For a detailed exposition of joint action in face-to-face speech, see Herbert H. Clark, *Using Language* (Cambridge: Cambridge University Press, 1996).

12. See Claudia Repetto et al., "The Link between Action and Language: Recent Findings and Future Perspectives," *Biolinguistics* 6, no. 3–4 (2012): 462–74.

13. See Malinda Carpenter et al., "Social Cognition, Joint Attention, and Communicative Competence from 9 to 15 Months of Age," *Monographs of the Society for Research in Child Development* 255 (1998): 1–74; also Michael Tomasello, *The Cultural Origins of Human Cognition* (Cambridge, MA: Harvard University Press, 1999), particularly chaps. 3–4.

14. See Vittorio Gallese, "Mirror Neurons and the Social Nature of Language," *Social Neuroscience* 8 (2008): 317–33.

15. Greek tragedy did not depict violent scenes on stage; they were reported by eyewitnesses. Yet the dramatic effect was no less powerful.

16. Such was Frege's principle of contextuality. See Michael Dummett, *Frege's Philosophy of Language* (London: Duckworth, 1973), 192–96.

17. In general terms, I maintain that elements of the world and grammatical forms reciprocally shape each other (nouns and things, verbs and actions). But the explication of grammar *as* a set of formal rules, structures, and functions is only possible with the

advent of writing. Natural language has an implicit grammar in terms of how speech and world engagement are mutually shaped in practical forms of life. For a treatment of natural language in relation to philosophical theories that run astray from this factical setting, see William Charlton, *Metaphysics and Grammar* (New York: Bloomsbury, 2014).

18. See Andy Clark, "Magic Words: How Language Augments Human Computation," in *Language and Thought*, eds. Peter Carruthers and Jill Boucher (Cambridge: Cambridge University Press, 1998), 162–83; also Stephen C. Levinson, "Language and Mind: Let's Get the Issues Straight!" and Daniel I. Slobin, "Language and Thought Online: Cognitive Consequences of Linguistic Relativity," in *Language in Mind*, eds. Susan Goldin-Meadow and Dedre Gentner (Cambridge, MA: MIT Press, 2003), 25–46 and 157–91 respectively.

19. See Alan Baddeley, "Working Memory and Language: An Overview," *Journal of Communication Disorders* 36 (2003): 189–208, and Jarrad A. G. Lum et al., "Procedural and Declarative Memory in Children with and without Specific Language Impairment," *International Journal of Language and Communication Disorders* 45, no. 1 (2010): 96–107.

20. See Katherine Nelson, *Young Minds in Social Worlds: Experience, Meaning, and Memory* (Cambridge, MA: Harvard University Press, 2007), especially chap. 7, Janette B. Benson and Marshall H. Haith, eds., *Language, Memory, and Cognition in Infancy and Early Childhood* (New York: Academic Press, 2009), and Erica Consentino, "Self in Time and Language," *Consciousness and Cognition* 20, no. 3 (2011): 777–83.

21. An important source for the temporal/historical character of language, its ecological structure, and the centrality of interpretation in disclosure is the work of Paul Ricoeur. See *Time and Narrative*, 3 vols., trans. Kathleen Blamey and David Pellauer (Chicago: University of Chicago Press, 1984, 1985, 1988) and *Memory, History, and Forgetting*, trans. Kathleen Blamey and David Pellauer (Chicago: University of Chicago Press, 2004).

22. Aristotle was the first to deploy such a lettering technique in the *Prior Analytics*, in which the distinction between form and content was decisively represented in (written) language.

23. See Francesco Ferretti and Erica Cosentino, "Time, Language, and Flexibility in the Mind: The Role of Mental Time Travel in Linguistic Comprehension and Production," *Philosophical Psychology* 26, no. 1 (February 2013): 24–46. The discussion in this analysis remains in the orbit of representational assumptions and computational systems. Phenomenological findings would better capture the extended macro-level dimensions articulated in this research.

24. See Maurice Merleau-Ponty, *Consciousness and the Acquisition of Language*, trans. Hugh J. Silverman (Evanston, IL: Northwestern University Press, 1973); also *The Phenomenology of Perception* I.6: The Body as Expression and Speech.

25. Clark, *Using Language*, 155–56.

26. See David McNeill, *Gesture and Thought* (Chicago: University of Chicago Press, 2005), chap. 8.

27. In what follows I rely on McNeill, *Gesture and Thought*, chaps. 1–2, and Clark, *Using Language*, chap. 6. For neurological findings on the correlation of gesture and language, see Petra Wagner et al., "Gesture, Brain, and Language," *Brain and Language* 101 (2007): 181–84; also in the same volume, Roel M. Willems and Peter Hagoort, "Neural Evidence for the Interplay Between Language, Gesture, and Action: A Review," 278–89.

28. McNeill, *Gesture and Thought*, 4.

29. Finger spelling therefore depends on alphabetic script.

30. See Susan Goldin-Meadow, "Thought Before Language," in *Language in Mind*, 493–522.

31. See Oliver Sacks, *Seeing Voices: A Journey into the World of the Deaf* (Berkeley, CA: University of California Press, 1989). For a discussion of sign language in terms of Merleau-Ponty's thought, see Jerry H. Gill, "Language as Gesture: Merleau-Ponty and American Sign Language," *International Philosophical Quarterly* 50, no. 1 (March 2010): 25–37.

32. See Clark, *Using Language*, 182ff.

33. Emoticons, such as ☺, can communicate facial gestures, but not in sentences per se.

34. A helpful sketch is given by Jean Aitchison, *Words in Mind: An Introduction to the Mental Lexicon* (Malden, MA: Wiley-Blackwell, 2012), chap. 14.

35. As Merleau-Ponty says with respect to an angry gesture (which functions in the same way as angry speech): "I do not see anger . . . as a psychic fact behind the gesture, I read anger in it. The gesture *does not make me think* of anger, it is anger itself" (*Phenomenology of Perception*, 184).

36. See Merleau-Ponty, *Consciousness and the Acquisition of Language*, 21–31.

37. For research on the reciprocal effects of seeing and hearing in face-to-face speech, see Patrick van der Zande et al., "Hearing Words Helps Seeing Words: A Cross-Modal Word Repetition Effect," *Speech Communication* 59 (2014), 31–43.

38. There are also the differential relations *within* language, in which phonic differences play out in pronunciation, where conceptual differences correlate meanings (for example, up and down) and functional differences orchestrate usage. This makes language systematically dynamic and unsettled. The differential character of language animated the work of Derrida (which was inspired by Saussure). See *Of Grammatology*, trans. Gayatri Chakravorty Spivak (Baltimore, MD: Johns Hopkins University Press, 1998), especially 27–73.

39. In linguistics this is sometimes called displacement. See Valentina Cuccio and Marco Carapezza, "Is Displacement Possible Without Language?" *Philosophical Psychology* 28, no. 3 (April 2015): 369–86, and Jana Uher, "What Is Behavior? And (When) Is Language Behavior?" *Journal for the Theory of Social Behavior* (February 2016): DOI:10.1111/jtsb.12104.

40. See Denis Bouchard, *The Nature and Origin of Language* (Oxford: Oxford University Press, 2014), chaps. 4–5.

41. Consider words like *cool* and *gay*. The word *broadcast* originally referred to casting out seeds. A shift can even amount to a reversal of meaning, as when the word *bad* came to mean (subversively) *good* in slang usage.

42. The very notion of a standard form that unifies and governs the wide range of dialects and speech practices is something that can only arise with the advent of writing.

43. In what follows I draw from Dedre Gentner, "Why We're So Smart," in *Language in Mind*, chap. 8.

44. See Gilles Fauconnier and Mark Turner, *The Way We Think: Conceptual Blending and the Mind's Hidden Complexities* (New York: Basic Books, 2002).

45. See Michael C. Corbalis, *The Recursive Mind: The Origins of Human Language, Thought, and Civilization* (Princeton, NJ: Princeton University Press, 2011).

46. Gadamer claims that philosophical conceptualization allows for clarity and insight about the nature of language, but with a cost of suppressing the "inexhaustible ambiguity" of words in a living language: *Plato's Dialectical Ethics*, trans. Robert M. Wallace (New Haven, CT: Yale University Press, 1991), 8–9.

47. Tracking the political and cultural power of linguistic traditions in shaping identity has marked the work of Pierre Bourdieu, who has critiqued abstract and formal models of language for missing, and thereby being complicit with, such forces. See *Language and Symbolic Power*, trans. Gino Raymond (Cambridge, MA: Harvard University Press, 1999).

48. The indicative character of proto-phenomenology amounts to a stepping back that tries to intimate a step back *into* practical fitness.

49. See Aristotle, *Nicomachean Ethics*, 1134b18–35.

50. See James Tabery, *Beyond Versus: The Struggle to Understand the Interaction of Nature and Nurture* (Cambridge, MA: MIT Press, 2014); also Michael Rutter, *Genes and Behavior: Nature-Nurture Interplay Explained* (Malden, MA: Blackwell, 2006).

51. See Daniel N. Stern, *The First Relationship: Infant and Mother* (Cambridge, MA: Harvard University Press, 2004). From the standpoint of moral development, see Elliot Turiel, Melanie Killen, and Charles C. Helwig, "Morality: Its Structure, Function, and Vagaries," in *The Emergence of Morality in Young Children*, ed. Jerome Kagan and Sharon Lamb (Chicago: University of Chicago Press, 1987), chap. 4.

52. Nativist theories are especially influenced by the work of Noam Chomsky, whose research advances an innate "universal grammar," which is a neo-Cartesian model wherein representational and structural forms are already built in the brain and are simply cued by the social environment. This would give secondary status to ecological structures developed in my study. For a critical analysis of Chomsky from the standpoint of social and environmental factors, see Timothy J. Gallagher, "A Mead-Chomsky Comparison Reveals a Set of Key Questions on the Nature of Language and Mind," *Journal for the Theory of Social Behavior* 44, no. 2 (June 2014): 148–67. Innate structures seem hard to validate, even in neurological terms. There are architectural and developmental constraints on how language manifests itself, but brain plasticity and empirical research seem to support an "emergentist" theory, which accords with an ecological, interactive approach. See Elizabeth Bates et al., "Innateness and Emergentism," in *A Companion to Cognitive Science*, eds. William Bechtel and George Graham (Oxford: Blackwell, 1998), 590–601.

53. Davidson argues against gaps of untranslatability between different languages in his seminal essay "On the Very Idea of a Conceptual Scheme," in *Inquiries into Truth and Interpretation* (Oxford: Clarendon Press, 1984). But the emphasis is on standard senses of cognition, which can miss significant differences in forms of life within languages. Yet forms of life understood as dwelling can show the way for bridging language differences at a more basic level than mere cognition. For a good analysis and critique of Davidson's agenda, see José Medina, "On Being 'Other-Minded': Wittgenstein, Davidson, and Logical Aliens," *International Philosophical Quarterly* 43, no. 4 (2003): 463–75.

54. See John D. Bonnvillian et al., "Observations on the Use of Manual Signs and Gestures in the Communicative Interactions between Native Americans and Spanish Explorers of North America," *Sign Language Studies* 9, no. 2 (Winter 2009): 132–65.

55. Ludwig Wittgenstein, *Philosophical Investigations*, trans. G. E. M. Anscombe (Oxford: Blackwell, 1953), section 116.

56. For a classic text, see Stanley Cavell, *In Quest of the Ordinary: Lines of Skepticism and Romanticism* (Chicago: University of Chicago Press, 1988).

57. See Avner Baz, *When Words Are Called For: A Defense of Ordinary Language Philosophy* (Cambridge, MA: Harvard University Press, 2012), which addresses the common objections to OLP in chapters 1–2. See also Sandra Laugier, *Why We Need Ordinary Language Philosophy*, trans. Daniela Ginsburg (Chicago: University of Chicago Press, 2013).

58. An effective summary can be found in Medina, *Language*, chaps. 1–2.

59. Wittgenstein, *Philosophical Investigations*, section 23.

60. See Huw Price, *Expressivism, Pragmatism, and Representationalism* (Cambridge: Cambridge University Press, 2013).

61. See Raymond W. Gibbs Jr., "A Dynamical Self-Organized View of the Context for Linguistic Performance," *International Review of Pragmatics* 5 (2013): 70–86, and

Mark Johnson, "Experiencing Language: What's Missing in Linguistic Pragmatism," *European Journal of Pragmatism and American Philosophy* 6, no. 2 (2014): 14–27.

62. J. L. Austin, *Philosophical Papers* (Oxford: Clarendon Press, 1961), 182. He includes attention to the history of word usage, its generational inheritance (185).

63. For a good survey of this question, see Hans Johann Glock, "Philosophy, Thought, and Language," *Royal Institute of Philosophy Supplement* 42 (March 1997): 151–69.

64. Two volumes that navigate such research are *Language and Thought* and *Language in Mind*, which are referenced in note 18; also Barbara C. Malt and Phillip Wolff, eds., *Words and Mind: How Words Capture Human Experience* (Oxford: Oxford University Press, 2010). I will be drawing on these volumes in coming discussions.

65. For a discussion of these models, see Peter Carruthers and Jill Boucher, "Opening the Issues," in *Language and Thought*, chap. 1.

66. This why Frege and Husserl both worked against psychologism.

67. Jerry Fodor's classic articulation of this theory is *The Language of Thought* (Cambridge, MA: Harvard University Press, 1980); also *The Language of Thought Revisited* (Oxford: Oxford University Press, 2008).

68. For critical engagements with nativism and the language of thought hypothesis, see two essays in the journal cited in note 63: Donald Davidson, "Seeing Through Language" (15–27) and John Searle, "The Explanation of Cognition" (103–26).

69. See Mark Cain, *Fodor: Language, Mind, and Philosophy* (New York: Polity, 2002), chap. 3.

70. The classic formulation of the signification theory is given by Aristotle in *On Interpretation* 16a1ff.

71. Plato seems to say as much when he defines thinking as the soul silently talking with itself (*Theaetetus* 189e ff.).

72. See Lev Vygotsky, *Thought and Language*, trans. Alex Kozulin (Cambridge, MA: MIT Press, 1986).

73. See Drew Leder, *The Absent Body* (Chicago: University of Chicago Press, 1990), 123–25.

74. Here I draw from Peter Carruthers, *Language, Thought, and Consciousness: An Essay in Philosophical Psychology* (Cambridge: Cambridge University Press, 1996), particularly chap. 2. See also Carruthers, "The Cognitive Function of Language," *Behavioral and Brain Sciences* 26, no. 6 (December 2002): 657–726.

75. Carruthers does not advance the strong version of the constitutive theory; he restricts linguistic constitution to *conscious* occasions of thought. Like most investigators, he construes thought in the typical philosophical mode of mental states having "propositional objects," taking the form of that-clauses (*Language, Thought, and Consciousness*, 53). This amounts to an expositional account of thought that sidelines occasions of immersion and habituation. At any rate, Carruthers departs from the language of thought hypothesis and responds to Fodor's approach on 67–72.

76. See Alexander N. Sokolov, *Inner Speech and Thought*, trans. George T. Onischenko (New York: Plenum, 1972).

77. Carruthers and Boucher, "Opening the Issues," in *Language and Thought*, 2.

78. Helen Keller, *The World I Live In* (New York: NYRB Classics, 2004), 113 and 117.

79. See Susanne Niemeier and René Driven, *Evidence for Linguistic Relativism* (Amsterdam: John Benjamins Co., 2000).

80. See Peter Gordon, "Worlds Without Words," in *Words and the Mind*, chap. 10.

81. Carruthers and Boucher, "Opening Up Options," in *Language and Thought*, 11.

82. Here I rely on Edward Munnich and Barbara Landau, "The Effects of Spatial Language on Spatial Representation: Setting Some Boundaries," in *Language in Mind*, chap. 6.

83. I rely on Dan I. Slobin, "Language and Thought Online: Cognitive Consequences of Linguistic Relativity," in *Language in Mind*, chap. 7.

84. With studies of color language as an example, current research seems to be shifting from a universalism-relativism debate to an acceptance of Whorfian effects that are distinguished as deep or shallow. See Elisabetta Lalumera, "Whorfian Effects in Color Perception: Deep or Shallow?" *The Baltic International Yearbook of Cognition, Logic, and Communication* 9 (December 2014): 1–13. For neo-Whorfian research generally, see Vyvyan Evans, *The Language Myth: Why Language Is Not an Instinct* (Cambridge: Cambridge University Press, 2014), chap. 7.

85. See Dedre Gentner and Susan Goldin-Meadow, "Whither Whorf," in *Language in Mind*, 3–14.

86. See Stephen C. Levinson, "Language and Mind: Let's Get the Issues Straight!" in *Language in Mind*, chap. 2, on which I rely in what follows.

87. A statement like "the ball is behind the tree" in some languages can mean that the ball is between the viewer and the tree. Front and back can be reversed. Location relations can be described according to relative position (left and right), absolute position (north and south), or single object position. So someone can say, "Pass the northern cup."

88. Levinson, "Language and Mind," 33–35.

89. In whatever way the ball-tree relation is described, any language presumably can elicit similar practical effects, as in "Bring me the ball." Indeed, Levinson remarks that with different expressions for coming and going verbs, they are uniformly contrasted *pragmatically* (30). Another remark concedes the importance of language-learning *environments*. Such remarks seem to be no more than parenthetical observations, unlike the substantive role that proto-phenomenology would assign to such factors.

90. Here I draw from Elizabeth S. Spelke, "What Makes Us Smart? Core Knowledge and Natural Language," in *Language in Mind*, chap. 10.

91. I draw from Michael Tomasello, "The Key Is Social Cognition," in *Language in Mind*, chap. 3. See also Tomasello, *The Cultural Origins of Human Cognition*, chap. 3.

92. Some research in neuro-imaging shows an overlap in verbal and visual functions. See David Kemmerer, "How Words Capture Visual Experience: The Perspective from Cognitive Neuroscience," in *Words and the Mind*, chap. 14.

93. For instance, joint attention is often deployed to bolster or clarify the (exposited) assumptions animating the "theory of mind." See on this score Juan-Carlos Gómez, "Some Thoughts about the Evolution of LADS, with Special Reference to TOM and SAM," in *Language and Thought*, chap. 4.

94. Neuro-imaging has shown that the thought-language correlation cannot adequately be understood by relating their domains of "representation" but by how both are processed to generate *behavioral* output (Debi Roberson and J. Richard Hanley, "Relatively Speaking: An Account of the Relationship Between Language and Thought in the Color Domain," in *Words and the Mind*, chap. 9); also that the meaning of words should not be restricted to verbal tokens because what must be included are historical inheritances as well as cultural needs, goals, and experiences (Barbara C. Malt et al., "Lexicalization Patterns and the World-to-Words Mapping," in *Words and the Mind*, chap. 2).

95. See Joseph Rouse's helpful discussion in *Articulating the World: Conceptual Understanding and the Scientific Image* (Chicago: University of Chicago Press, 2015), chap. 2.

96. The hypothesis was first posed by Eric H. Lennenberg, *Biological Foundations of Language* (New York: Wiley, 1967).

97. See Adriana S. Benzaquén, *Encounters with Wild Children: Temptation and Disappointment in the Study of Human Nature* (Montreal: McGill-Queen's University Press, 2006), John McCrone, *The Myth of Irrationality: The Science of Mind from Plato to Star Trek* (New York: Carroll and Graf, 1994), chap. 5, and Nancy Yousef, "Savage

or Solitary: The Wild Child and Rousseau's Man of Nature," *Journal of the History of Ideas* 62, no. 2 (April 2001): 245–63.

98. See Susan Curtis, *Genie: A Psycholinguistic Study of a Modern-Day "Wild Child"* (New York: Academic Press, 1977).

99. Less severe deprivation can be examined in cases of institutionalized children who were generally neglected and given minimal human interaction. Such children had linguistic deficits that nevertheless were improved if they were placed in a normal home environment. See Jennifer Windsor et al., "Language Acquisition with Limited Input: Romanian Institution and Foster Care," *Journal of Speech, Language, and Hearing Research* 50, no. 5 (October 2007): 1365–86.

100. See Carolyn B. Mervis and Angela M. Becerra, "Language and Communicative Development in Williams Syndrome," *Mental Retardation and Development Disabilities Research Review* 13 (2007): 3–15.

101. See Jill Boucher, "The Pre-Requisites for Language Acquisition: Evidence from Cases of Anomalous Language Development," in *Language and Thought*, chap. 3. In particular, Boucher challenges Chomsky and nativism.

102. See Carruthers, *Language, Thought, and Consciousness*, 18–20.

103. For a collection surveying the debate, see John Preston and Mark Bishop, eds., *Views into the Chinese Room: New Essays on Searle and Artificial Intelligence* (Oxford: Oxford University Press, 2002).

104. See Laureano Luna, "Indefinite Extensibility in Natural Language," *The Monist* 96, no. 2 (2013): 295–308.

105. The jointure of biological life can be traced back to Aristotle's *De Anima* (II.2), in which the soul (*psuchē*) indicates life and is delineated in three ascending life forms: the nutritive soul (plants), the perceptive soul (animals), and the rational/linguistic soul (humans). Each form accomplishes a kind of union with its environment: the nutritive soul incorporates the matter of food through digestion; the perceptive soul takes in the sensitive form of things without the matter; and the rational soul takes in the intelligible form. In both perception and cognition there is a joining of the sense and the mind with the thing sensed and thought: each case is a *single* actualization of the joint potentialities of a sense to perceive a thing, of a thing to be perceived, of a mind to think a thing, and of a thing to be thought. See *De Anima* 425b27–29, 426a16–18, 429a13–17, 429b3–431a1, and 431b16–18.

106. Even Searle's focus on intentionality and the human brain retains an internalist assumption of intelligence that is held distinct from ecological factors in the lived world. See Shaun Gallagher, "Social Cognition, the Chinese Room, and the Robot Replies," in *Knowing Without Thinking: Mind, Action, Cognition, and the Phenomenon of the Background*, ed. Zdravko Radman (New York: Palgrave Macmillan, 2012), 83–97. Searle's important notion of a tacit background that animates semantic meaning is also construed in mentalistic, representational terms. See in the same volume, Daniel D. Hutto, "Exposing the Background: Deep and Local," 37–56.

107. For a stimulating overview of evolution and its philosophical ramifications, see Dennett, *Darwin's Dangerous Idea*, hereafter *DDI*.

108. Part of this section is drawn from my "From Animal to Dasein: Heidegger and Evolutionary Biology," in *Heidegger on Science*, ed. Trish Glazebrook (New York: SUNY Press, 2012), 93–111.

109. For the coalescence of nature and culture, nature and nurture, see Gabriel Alejandro Torres Colón and Charles A. Hobbs, "The Intertwining of Culture and Nature," *Journal of the History of Ideas* 76, no. 1 (January 2015): 139–62.

110. See Maarten Boudry and Massimo Pigliucci, "The Mismeasure of Machine: Synthetic Biology and the Trouble with Engineering Metaphors," *Studies in History and Philosophy of Biological and Biomedical Sciences* 44 (2013): 660–68. See also John

Dupré, *Processes of Life: Essays in the Philosophy of Biology* (Oxford: Oxford University Press, 2012).

111. Richard Gregory calls this "kinetic intelligence." See *Mind in Science: A History of Explanations in Psychology and Physics* (Cambridge: Cambridge University Press, 1981). See also Marc D. Hauser, *Wild Minds* (New York: Henry Holt and Co., 2000). Hauser sees animal intelligence as a set of mental "tools" or various capacities for solving environmental problems that may be basic across species, as in capacities for recognizing objects, counting, and navigating.

112. *DDI*, chap. 8.

113. See Stuart Kauffman, *The Origins of Order: Self-Organizations and Selections in Evolution* (New York: Oxford University Press, 1993).

114. See Richard Dawkins, *The Selfish Gene*, second edition (Oxford: Oxford University Press, 1989), and E. O. Wilson, *Sociobiology: The New Synthesis* (Cambridge, MA: Harvard University Press, 1975).

115. See Larry Arnhart's discussion in *Darwinian Natural Right: The Biological Ethics of Human Nature* (Albany, NY: SUNY Press, 1998), 36ff, and Dennett's discussion of the "Baldwin effect," in which the exploratory behavior of the phenotype creates fitness characteristics that are then favorable for selection, in *DDI*, 77ff. See as well J. Scott Turner, *The Extended Organism* (Cambridge, MA: Harvard University Press, 2000); also Alvaro Moreno and Matteo Mossio, *Biological Autonomy: A Philosophical and Theoretical Inquiry* (Dordrecht: Springer, 2015).

116. For a defense of "organismic" fitness over "trait" fitness, see Charles H. Pence and Grant Ramsey, "Is Organismic Fitness at the Basis of Evolutionary Theory?" *Philosophy of Science* 82, no. 5 (December 2015): 1081–91.

117. It should be noted that an Aristotelian sense of teleology is still relevant in modern biology. See James G. Lennox, "Teleology," in *Keywords in Evolutionary Biology*, eds. Evelyn Fox Keller and Elizabeth A. Lloyd (Cambridge, MA: Harvard University Press, 1992), 324–33.

118. Richard Dawkins concedes that there seem to be purposes in living behavior, but this is an objective error due to our constrained sense of time. Natural life in itself is a product of blind physical forces. See *The Blind Watchmaker* (New York: Norton, 1996).

119. *DDI*, 39, 56, 66.

120. Ibid., 144, 368.

121. Ibid., 80–83.

122. Ibid., 50ff.

123. Ibid., 143, 342ff, 362ff. Dennett seems to grant that a scientific tracking of memes and their "descent" is unlikely owing to the complexity and fluidity of culture, but he attributes this to *epistemological* limits rather than to any inadequacy in the evolutionary algorithm as such (356).

124. For an attempt at a sociobiological reduction of culture, see E. O. Wilson, *Consilience: The Unity of Knowledge* (New York: Random House, 1999). For critiques of such approaches see Philip Kitcher, *Vaulting Ambition* (Cambridge, MA: MIT Press, 1985), and Stephen Jay Gould, "Sociobiology and the Theory of Natural Selection," in *Sociobiology: Beyond Nature/Nurture?* Eds. G. W. Barlow and J. Silverberg (Boulder, CO: Westview Press, 1980), 257–69.

125. On these points, see H. Allen Orr, "Dennett's Strange Idea," *Boston Review* 21, no. 3 (1996): 28–32.

126. *DDI*, 470.

127. Ibid., 471, 491.

128. See Jean Aitchison, *The Seeds of Speech: Language Origin and Evolution* (Cambridge: Cambridge University Press, 2000), 21, 177.

129. For an overview of different theories on the evolution of language, see Tao Gong et al., "Evolutionary Linguistics: Theory of Language in an Interdisciplinary Space," *Language Sciences* 41 (January 2014): 243–53.

130. See Aitchison, *The Seeds of Speech*, 96–97.

131. See Peter F. MacNeilage, *The Origin of Speech* (Oxford: Oxford University Press, 2008).

132. Much of what follows is drawn from the work of Michael Tomasello: *The Cultural Origins of Human Cognition*, *Origins of Human Communication* (Cambridge, MA: MIT Press, 2008), and *A Natural History of Human Thinking* (Cambridge, MA: Harvard University Press, 2014).

133. For an account of how mirror neurons may be implicated in the evolution of language, see Michael A. Arbib, *How the Brain Got Language: The Mirror Systems Hypothesis* (Oxford: Oxford University Press, 2013).

134. Most of the research in this regard (including the work of Tomasello) deploys notions of mind reading and intentional agency to describe an infant's social sense, which I take to be an expositional distortion of the underlying (and ecstatic) intimation of a social-world.

135. Primate hunting practices seem more competitive than collaborative and less prone to sharing food after a hunt.

136. See Corbalis, *The Recursive Mind*, chap. 4.

137. See Thomas Nagel, *Mind and Cosmos: Why the Materialist and Neo-Darwinian Conception of Nature Is Almost Certainly False* (Oxford: Oxford University Press, 2012), 28.

Chapter Four

Language and Truth

1. PRESENTATIONAL TRUTH

A philosophical treatment of the lived world and language calls for an account of how the question of truth can be treated in a phenomenological analysis. If we confine the discussion of truth to matters of language, the ecstatic immersion that is characteristic of communicative speech practices allows the notion of *presentational* truth, as distinguished from representational models (for instance, the "correspondence" of propositions and states of affairs, which follows from presuming the subject-object binary). Presentational truth need not be restricted to linguistic matters. It can also be surmised in more experiential conditions of direct disclosive effects in intimation, know-how, and immersed engagement, which presuppose grasping the meaning of a situation and its components. Yet as was argued in chapter 3, even such nonarticulated bearings are constituted by background effects of language, and the articulation of meaning and sense is a natural possibility in these factical circumstances.

Presentational truth can be applied to a host of appropriately disclosed conditions that are not experienced as a bridging of discrete spheres and that do not or need not involve procedures of justification. Nevertheless, such a discussion will have to show what "appropriate disclosure" means because truth is conceptually juxtaposed against "untruth" (error or deception) in any human culture and from the start of any person's development as a language speaker. Presentational truth can be understood from a number of angles. Consider my furniture-restoring example, in which what is said is immediately presumed as duly disclosive (absent some contravention) without justification. Much of ordinary utterance and conversation is presumed to be disclosive in a similar way. Only a hyper-skepticism would toy with a standard that required justification for any and all utterances before genuine truth conditions could be satisfied. Such a standard is not only impractical but unrealistic in a substantive sense when considering how language functions in everyday life.

Presentational truth involves the default assumption of disclosiveness that marks much of human discourse in the manner of tacit *trust*. Indeed, the word *truth* is etymologically connected with trust by way of the word *troth*, pertaining to faith in a pledge, as in betrothal.[1] Trust by definition is not a matter of certainty or justification but rather a kind of faith, as in trust that someone will be "true" to their word, but it is not blind faith because degrees of trust-*worthiness* must be in the mix, at least implicitly. Outside of philosophical analysis, the default trust in truth is not usually a conscious or deliberate comportment; we simply are normally predisposed to take speech as sincere and disclosive. In fact, a specific awareness or articulation of trust usually unfolds only when the possibility of violating trust is intimated. The stronger the trust, the less it is voiced or put in view. The deep background of trust in truth is a matter of tacit immersion, not theoretical exposition or inferential application of beliefs. Yet trust should not be taken as simply an attitude devoid of rationality. Aligning trust with presentational truth speaks to the myriad ways in which reasoning relies on a tacit background of trust.[2] It is hard to imagine human life functioning well without such an implicit predisposition of trust in presentational truth. Of course, deception is a common phenomenon in human communication, but it is driven by contextual and specific motivational conditions—and it relies on normal veridical trust for its prospects of success. Truth is the default expectation in human speech.[3] Veridical trust is also implicated in the extensive role that testimony plays in knowledge, in which deference to disciplinary findings, expertise, and presumed authority compensates for the absence or impossibility of firsthand engagement.[4] The trust in testimony shows the interpersonal, even intergenerational structure of a good deal of knowledge; it also implies a fideistic disposition, which belies a monological epistemology and a baseline notion of rational autonomy, self-sufficiency, or self-constitution.

Contraventions can disturb trust and open up the problem of truth and untruth, as well as space for representational conceptions of truth—in which presentational immediacy is exposited as a partition of the language-world correlation into distinct spheres of propositions and states of affairs. Recalling the concept of differential fitness, it is the fitness of language that bestows presentational truth and the differential element allows for the possibility of untruth, a disjunction between what is said and what is the case (whether it be error, distortion, or deception), especially concerning the diachronic distance of past and future conditions, which may not bear the same degree of trust as present-situated speech.[5] In any case, a default presentational trust in truth would seem to be a necessary condition for the normal course of life. Except in extreme circumstances, skepticism could not serve well as a first-order disposition.

Presentational truth does not rule out or replace representational truth, but names a more original dimension that can cover more ground and dissolve some of the puzzles attached to representational formats. The correspondence theory, for example, defines truth as the matching of a statement with a state of affairs, so that "the cat is on the mat" is true if in fact there is a cat on the mat and false if not. Yet in the background of this example there are a host of meanings and conceptions that are tacitly involved and already understood: what "cat" and "mat" mean, taking something *as* a cat or a mat, what "on" means, the context of relations into which cat and mat fit, what "statement" means, the relatedness of statements and states of affairs, and more generally the ecstatic openness to a meaningful world—which is to say that prior to any particular disclosive event, we are predisposed to find things meaningful and understandable.[6]

Presentational truth can address the complex tacit background of a correspondence relation, and the ecstatic character of presentational immersion can sidestep puzzles pertaining to how something like a linguistic proposition can "match" something like an actual cat on a mat or how a mental state can "represent" an external state of affairs. Because such binaries arise as an exposition out of an original condition of ecological dwelling, the puzzle is such only if we take representational relations as the exclusive model for thinking about truth.[7] In most direct experiences and everyday speech practices, the theoretical problem of correspondence does not arise; language can be immediately disclosive. Think of me looking for my cat and someone in another room says, "Hey, your cat is on the mat." This is a directly disclosive utterance and its reception is saturated with caring about my (not the) cat. The ecological character of dwelling shows that *before* language and world are divided by exposition they already coalesce in ecstatic speech practices, where they do not need to be bridged.

The matter of untruth most clearly prompts the distinction between statements and states of affairs due to a "misfit" of what is said and what is the case. Yet such differentiation can still be seen to emerge out of a prior field of linguistic immersion, and real-life matters of untruth arise from contraventions (doubt, for instance) that prompt expositional attention to the possible divergence of what is said from what is the case. Expositional differentiation is derived from, and does not override, the undifferentiated field of ecstatic immersion. The mistake is taking expositional contexts, in which something like representation can make sense, as the grounding model for linguistic activity—thus presuming that language as such must be based on representational relations.

The differential character of language and temporal distance can bring about contexts in which the issue of the proper disclosive function of language can arise ("I saw your cat earlier this morning"), thus opening the issue of a statement fitting or not fitting a now absent direct experience. The correspondence theory has some bearing here, but in its own discursive context it deals abstractly with statements yanked out of actual settings, now simply taken as examples in the reflective question of how statements can be true or false.[8] The *theoretical* deployment of formal constructions such as beliefs and propositions in relation to things and events stems from and reinforces an abstract model of mental subjects in relation to external objects, which then conjures up the problem of how, or even if, these two spheres can be joined. Yet such a theory misses or distorts much of the way in which language functions in ordinary life. In my cat example, theoretical questions of correspondence would not arise, or if something comparable did arise ("Are you sure it was my cat?"), it would not be framed in terms of mental representations linked up with external objects but simply the matter of fitting or unfitting disclosure in a lived world of concerns. Even everyday expositions concerning the relationship between what is said and what is the case do not readily fit the technical contours of a "representational" relation and its bridging structure. A number of nontechnical meanings of the word *true* show some relevance here: a steady and faithful reliance (being true to someone), what properly belongs to something (a true friend), to fit properly, loyalty, a mutual pledge.[9] Accordingly, there are ways to talk about truth as *fitting discourse* without assuming a binary representational division between subjects and objects. Outside of philosophical theories of truth—which bank on and abstract from the ordinary expositional distinction between what is said and what is the case—in the normal course of things the very *issue* of truth and untruth does not arise until contraventions disturb the tacit trust in presentational truth.[10]

2. PHENOMENOLOGY AND TRUTH

A phenomenological approach to truth would begin with how truth functions in the lived world and its existential conditions. First of all, truth must exhibit some sense of authority in its differentiation from untruth and its allowance of judgment—to provide a robust response to radical versions of skepticism, subjectivism, relativism, conventionalism, or constructivism. Yet second, truth cannot be a purely objective matter because truth must first *matter*, we must care about it, and truth serves the meanings and interests that mark factical life. Third, the finite character of the lived world and the vicissitudes of natural language call for an orientation toward truth that permits its authoritative sense without a requirement of indefeasibility or strict certainty. The default character of veridical trust does not normally presume incorrigibility but something closer to plausibility and probability. Fourth, truth should not be taken as uniform because it can function in different ways and in different interpretive *settings*—in science, history, ethics, politics, religion, technology, art, and so on. A setting for truth is a hermeneutical perspective that "sets up" a manner of inquiry or engagement—like a scene setting in the theater—and that sets out the as-indicators marking the modes of enactive interpretation.[11] Different settings stem from different contexts of meaning—causal explanation, understanding the past, evaluative concerns, instrumental tasks, social roles, practical engagements, artistic endeavors—which issue truth conditions and norms that can disclose the world in ways appropriate to the specific setting (more on this shortly). Given the ecological character of the lived world, different perspectives on the world can track different ways in which an *environment* is opened up, which is therefore not a reduction to human constructs but a responsiveness to the environment at hand. Perspectival responsiveness is different from radical relativism (in which all perspectives have equal authority) and it can even allow a kind of realism that is different from strict objectivism.[12]

2.1. Objectivity and Realism

Truth would have to satisfy *some* sense of objectivity to warrant its authority. We can notice several meanings of the word *objective*, not all of which have to do with the strictest sense of objective truth operating in some epistemological theories. I suggest that the most basic meaning of being objective is being *responsive*, in the sense that one is responding *to* something in the world on its terms rather than merely subjective terms (whether it is personal subjectivity or the cognitive faculties of a rational subject). Being objective can also mean *unbiased*, an open-minded disposition that does not presume the validity of a certain viewpoint, or *impartial*, in which one's interests are not assumed to be decisive. Objectivity can also refer to something *observable* in the world rather than simply imagined, *public* in the sense of something shareable, or *real* in the manner of common sense realism, in which something is extant in the surrounding world and not reducible to our thoughts and desires. There are stronger senses of objectivity, such as being *value-free*, in which no values or interests obtain, or *really-real* in the manner of metaphysical realism, in which the world is the way it is *independent* of human thought, awareness, or response. In the proto-phenomenological approach I am taking, only the value-free and the really-real would be put in question. All the other meanings can be seen to fit the lived world and various forms of disclosure. Such meanings involve seemingly ineliminable conditions of human discourse and normal existence, which thus allows for a modest and expanded notion of objectivity and truth. The proviso is that there can be different perspectives on truth depending on the context of discovery, the kind of phenomenon involved, and the kind of question posed (What is the history of love? What is the physiology of love? What is the meaning of love? Do you love me?). Each area can have a different rendering of sense in a specific domain.

One way to open up a looser sense of objectivity is to consider the history of the words *subject* and *object*, which originally denoted the reverse of what these words have come to mean since the modern period (as noted in chapter 2). The current prevailing notion of objectivity in philosophy is itself a historically emergent rendition of truth. Following the ascent of scientific methodologies and schematics, the notion of truth has commonly been restricted to "objective" empirical or conceptual standards, to verifiable facts or a priori structures of thought.[13] Yet a pluralistic conception of truth can follow from the precedence of natural language and the different ways in which the world is engaged. As indicated with the example of a tree in chapter 2, a phenomenon can be responsively engaged from many perspectives and the notion of a single standard language governing all other modes of expression is unnecessary and unworkable. Here I might borrow from Nietzsche and suggest an aggregate sense of "objectivity" that takes in as many different perspectives that can be brought to bear on a given phenomenon.[14]

The expanded sense of objectivity suggested here, along with the presumption of immanence at the heart of proto-phenomenology, allows for a modest realism that can speak to classic philosophical problems.[15] First, we have already seen how radical skepticism can be intercepted by a factical perspective on engaged immersion, which also challenges the primacy of the subject-object distinction that guides most treatments of realism and anti-realism. Second, the phenomenon of contravention—resistance, disturbance, obstacles, surprises, and so on—shows the way in which the world has its own course, which can override any human standpoint. Such override seems more consistent with a realist than an anti-realist posture. Third, with a common sense ontology that deems ordinary things in the lived world to be fully real, a derivative reality can be assigned to exposited and reflective occasions that unfold out of factical immersion. Accordingly, there can be phenomenological support for the "reality" of values, properties, propositions, the future, and other notions that have been troublesome in philosophy because they do not satisfy prevailing standards of objective being and reification: How can values be real without empirical status or consensus? How can properties be real apart from substances? How can future states be real if they are not currently in being? If, as I have argued, valuation and temporality are intrinsic to factical life, and if properties are expositionally emergent out of engaged immersion, such notions can be deemed either intrinsically or derivatively real. Standard philosophical conceptions of objective being are themselves derivative as a refined process of exposition out of the lived world, and so they should not stand as exclusive measures for what counts as real. With a factical anchor, even things like propositions and numbers can be called derivatively real when they are understood in terms of emergent technologies of writing and graphics. In any case, the modest realism advanced here is a factical alternative to metaphysical realism, if the latter assumes a strong sense of mind independence that exceeds the bounds of phenomenology. The brute existence of a tree is not mind-dependent, but the very idea of mind-independence is mind-dependent as a hermeneutical orientation geared toward thinking about the world in a philosophical manner.

Phenomenological realism is not based on various models that treat mind independence or dependence by way of direct or indirect relations between perceptions or representations and the outside world. Generally, such projects aim to show how (or whether) perceptual, propositional, or intentional states can be coordinated with the world and distinguished from errors or illusions by way of satisfaction conditions. But in factical terms, say I am working with someone to position, measure, and hang a painting on a wall. In the *immersed practice*, the question of whether the scene is as it appears or is mind-independent would not arise (unless I am working with a manic metaphysician, which would not be wise). Even from an expositional standpoint, it would not make sense to wonder if the wall, for example, might really be different from what *dealing with it* presupposes. The same incongruence would pertain to a number of philosophical questions regarding the scene that might be posed to us as *participants* in something being *done*: Is the wall real? Are walls and paintings less real than natural things? Does your partner have a mind? Can you really know what she was thinking when she gave you a measurement? Are numbers real? Is that painting on the wall something dependent on or independent of your perception and belief?

The modest and pluralized approach to objectivity and reality suggested here is an alternative to binary models that mandate exclusive conceptions of what satisfies truth conditions. The debates between realist and anti-realist postures in various philosophical domains are generally predicated on unilateral or reductionist standards for what counts as real and unreal, as when common sense realism deems scientific constructs to be fictions and scientific realism deems ordinary beliefs to be imprecise errors.[16] A contextual approach to expositional derivation need not get trapped in questions of whether common sense and science are more or less "real" (even though common sense retains a certain phenomenological priority).

2.2. Truth Conditions

How can a pluralistic conception of truth allow for a sense of warrant? As long as we assume a contextual focus that appropriately gathers different discourses, we can rest with an orchestration of such interpretive contexts without the need for reducing different kinds of disclosure to one form, as in the case of scientism, in which only scientific descriptions are said to provide decisive truth. Contextualism reiterates the interrogative and phenomenological pluralism discussed in chapter 3. Whatever the context, what would the conditions be for truthful discourse? I offer the following *inhabitive* truth conditions, namely measures that shore up different ways of dwelling in the world: 1) *Responsive fit*. In line with the fitness-character of language, truth is fitting for phenomena, in that what we say is responsive to what is going on and where the world (in its full phenomenological sense) is responsive to what we say.[17] Such co-responding suggests something like the correspondence theory but without its theoretical baggage or a restriction to certain kinds of claims (factual description or object designation). Responsive fit simply calls for being "true" to phenomena by attending carefully and thoroughly to matters at hand and avoiding omissions, distortions, or confusion with other kinds of phenomena. Responsiveness also implies a disposition of openness *to* phenomena, of *letting* things show themselves and being wary of prejudgment. 2) *Reliability*. Truth has a continuity that is not utterly unstable, instantaneous, or unrepeatable; we can go on with it. This is not to be confused with eternal truth or absolute certainty. 3) *Workability*. Truth is effective, it renders us fit to engage and navigate the world successfully. The pragmatic theory of truth applies here, but we would not want to say that truth is only a matter of practical utility or problem solving. 4) *Agreement*. Truth is shareable and communicable rather than mere subjective opinion. This is not to say that agreement is sufficient for truth (fitness and workability show that truth cannot be merely conventional) or that seamless unanimity could or should be the aim of thought. 5) *Consociation*. Given the importance of upbringing, inheritance, trust, and corroboration, truth is a cooperative, socially structured endeavor rather than a monological construction. 6) *Sense*. Truth gathers experience into a shape that allows understanding, orientation, and familiarity, in which things make sense. This has nothing to do with a rigid, systematic structure or a single governing order.

Overall, inhabitive truth conditions indicate responsiveness to the world rather than mere belief. They also overlap and can reinforce each other in combination. Judgments following these truth conditions will generally stem, either explicitly or implicitly, from attention to a claim's temporal scope in terms of the figure-eight structure of past, present, and future, of how well antecedent and consequent elements have been taken into account. In any case, inhabitive truth allows for warrant without having to presume the modern division between a reflective subject and a freestanding object. Although it seems right to call hallucination a "subjective" occasion, for some experience to first *count* as a hallucination it amounts to a misfit with reliability, workability, and agreement. Historically, of course, certain novel claims or proposals have been *deemed* illusory or deranged, but in time such estimations fade and give way if the innovation comes to register as reliable, workable, and agreeable.[18]

In line with this analysis, "untruth" would involve failures or diminishments of inhabitive truth conditions. Suppositions of truth can generate or encounter contraventions, and that is when critique is possible, both synchronically and diachronically—the latter meaning that over time something taken as true might no longer exhibit fitness, reliability, or workability owing to changing conditions or new findings. Such contravening circumstances can bring about innovation or even revolution in everything from social movements to science. It is important to note that uniformity and systematic order are challenged not only by a plurality of settings, but also by diachronic and synchronic tensions between settings of truth. Hume was right to stress the logical "break" between facts and values, between an "is" and an "ought." Any orchestration of divergent settings need not involve a global measure but rather a contextual dwelling with such divergence, marked by appropriate shifts from one setting to another (which I have named enactive interpretation). There are also critical tensions *within* settings, which account for hermeneutical disagreements and challenges regarding disciplinary assumptions or analyses. Accordingly, the history of settings (in everything from ethics to science) shows that truth is not something absolute, rigid, or indefeasible, but rather a coalescing *achievement*, the contingent *enactment* of inhabitive truth by the settled determinations of discursive communities, enactments that are and always have been subject to revision.

A phenomenology of truth need not be restricted to sophisticated models of rational adjudication because it can include more original capacities of natural language. The priority of language over rationality in this regard can be located in the history of the Greek word *logos*. With Plato and Aristotle, *logos* generally came to mean a rational account, explaining or justifying a belief with an inferential chain that could survive scrutiny. But the more original meaning of *logos* had to do simply with speech and conversation, derived from the verb *legein*, to say, speak, gather, and show. *Logos* could also mean narrative, notice, measure, and proportion. Even though philosophers focused on rational accounts, which were formalized in Aristotle's "logic," a speaker of Greek could intimate the wide range of meanings in the use of *logos*.[19] Accordingly, discourse outside of philosophical logic would not be irrational or disoriented because the common overarching meaning of *logos* was "speech that makes sense to an audience."[20] Because we have defined language as *communicative* speech practices, *logos*— as a *gathering of sense*—would be intrinsic to language. Thus "nonsense" is understood against the backdrop of expecting sense. Yet nonsensical uses can play a formative role in differentiating sense, especially in early language acquisition. From childhood on, language is a communicative field, the default impetus of which is to share meaning (even if one expresses disagreement, there is a shared sense of what that means), to come together on usage in repeatable ways, with connotations that broaden comprehension beyond immediate events. Natural language therefore in its very constitution exceeds individual speakers and brute experiences in order to gather sense. So-called rational thinking is simply an extension and refinement of the communicative sense of natural language—an extension that can go astray if it forgets its native base.

2.3. Rationality

As in the discussion of objectivity, it is possible to lay out a range of meanings for rationality, which need not be restricted to traditional epistemological standards. What is meant by being "rational"? The following examples of what I call *existential* rationality can be seen to function in the usual course of life. To be rational in this sense is to be *explicative*, as in ordinary reason giving and the capacity to articulate reasons for acting; *dialogical*, in which one's reasons can make sense to other people and one is willing to engage objections; *realistic*, in which one is responsive and attentive to how things manifest themselves; *discerning*, in which one can make appropriate practical judgments; *well-disposed*, in which one is interested in truth, open-minded, curious, fair, and heedful; *consistent*, in which one follows through on the implications of professed beliefs; and *organized*, in which one's thinking is not sporadic or chaotic. From these meanings can be distinguished a *regimented* rationality advanced in many philosophical systems (especially in the modern period), which push existential rationality in the direction of foundationalist guarantees. Regimented rationality is *disengaged*, in terms of cognition fashioned apart from interests, desires, customs, and traditions; *apodictic*, as measured by universality and necessity, by way of principles or findings that no rational person could dispute; and *demonstrative*, in guaranteeing conclusions solely by the logical force of a reasoning process. My contention is that existential rationality has central importance in factical life and that regimented rationality, apart from certain appropriate contexts, does not always serve philosophy well.[21]

Regimented rationality is an understandable but questionable consequence of the philosophical impulse to find truth and defend it against objections. The possibilities of success in this endeavor have naturally prompted a vision of ideal success marked by strict certainty. A standard of indefeasible truth has operated in direct and indirect ways in philosophical pursuits, especially in epistemology. Radical skepticism, for example, has banked on indefeasibility by demonstrating failures to meet that standard. And philosophical adjudication often involves purported defeat of a position by citing counter-examples, from empirical exceptions all the way to logically possible cases in possible worlds. In the face of such tests, advancing a philosophical position often aims to satisfy indefeasibility with constructions such as "if and only if . . ." and "in any possible world . . ." In factical life, contraventions stimulate analysis, interrogation, and criticism. Philosophy goes further in anticipating and even looking for contraventions, not only actual contraventions but possible ones, even logically possible contraventions. I am not saying that such rigor is useless. It can bear fruit, but suspicion is called for if the prime concern is indefeasibility. Philosophical discipline should pay heed to contraventions and disagreements in real life before it considers virtual possibilities. When imaginative scenarios are advanced, they should retain proximity and applicability to the actual world. Thought experiments have an important place in philosophy, but sometimes they amount to an extravagant conceit driven by uncritical preoccupation with a given theory or set of assumptions.[22]

Short of indefeasibility, there can be degrees of truth across different disciplines that need not measure up to perfection, as will be argued shortly. There is exactitude in mathematics, but the philosophy of mathematics is a different story. When it comes to factical life, at least, philosophy could follow what I call an *adequation theory*, in the sense that sometimes we can rest with an adequate degree of truth and probability, which is "true enough" despite exceptions that are not fatal to the notion at hand (as in "smoking causes cancer") and despite fantastical but logically possible exceptions (zombie smokers).[23] Exceptions need not invalidate or challenge the aptness of a concept or truth claim. What should be challenged is the aptness of a standard with zero tolerance for exceptions. Outside of mathematical exactitude and logical necessity, truth in various settings can function in a scalar fashion. The advantage of adequation is its undogmatic openness to contingency and revisability.

2.4. Ethics and Truth

Inhabitive conditions can admit the possibility of truth in settings outside of science that are no less evident in their ecological domains, an important example being ethics.[24] We can find a way around familiar critiques of moral claims, for instance that they cannot satisfy correspondence with empirical facts or the necessity of conceptual principles. A moral setting can exhibit inhabitive truth, which helps overcome theories that presume to ground ethics in "subjective preferences" because we locate ethics in its environing-world. Are objections to torture simply a matter of personal preference? If the objections are shared, is the agreement here simply a matter of collusion or a collection of preferences? Are objections to fraud in scientific research simply a function of interior estimations superimposed upon value-free practices?

Disagreement and lack of settlement shown in moral matters have often been cited as a reason for turning to inner attitudes: If one and the same act can be considered moral by one person and immoral by another, how can the moral "property" inhere in the act or in the world? It must then stem from a subjective state. The assumption here, however, is that limits and disagreements are a decisive threat to truth, which would follow only from traditional standards of strict objectivity and regimented rationality. Such an assumption, though, is out of line with the actual course and practice of human thinking anyway, in any form.

Scientific inquiry, both diachronically and synchronically, is marked by limits, disagreement, controversies, and unsettlement at certain levels. We could distinguish between science and ethics in terms of the *degree* of agreement and uncertainty, but one need not divorce truth from ethics simply because of disagreement and uncertainty.

I have maintained that strict objective conditions do not have priority over existential meaning. Prior to "knowing," we are *moved* by interest, involvement, and mattering, which are not strictly "cognitive" dispositions. A focus on ethical disposition can be related to noncognitivist ethical theories, which take moral life to stem more from feeling and emotion than from rational constructions or inferences. One advantage of considering affect in ethics is that it speaks well to questions of moral constitution and motivation. For example, if I witness the wanton beating of a child, I take this *as* an ethical situation not by way of some classification technique but through affective reactions of revulsion and compassion, which also motivate me to condemn the act and to do something about it. In other words, we can take certain emotions as modes of disclosive "moral perception" that first give access to the ethical sphere and to a kind of mattering that prompts involvement and commitment. We have located elements of interest, disposition, and mood in all areas of thought, science included. Ethical and cognitive domains can be bridged not simply by valorizing ethical interests and dispositions, but also by attending to moods like wonder, curiosity, and excitement in science. If one resists calling curiosity in science a "mere feeling," one might be able to do the same with ethical dispositions. Other bridging effects can be shown by considering normative elements in science, such as truthfulness, and certain virtues that mark critical thinking, such as open-mindedness, courage, and responsiveness.

The ecstatic character of disclosure advanced in this investigation brings some relief from the subject-object binary that prompts an account of affects as merely subjective phenomena. Certain moods involve being captivated by something in the world and not simply an inner state; so advancing the role of emotion in ethics need not face the problem of subjectivism that has haunted noncognitivist ethical theories. It is possible to address philosophical questions of moral constitution and motivation without being pressed into a subjective or internal sphere distinct from some world-disclosive sphere. Recalling the many senses of objectivity discussed in this chapter, we can suggest an objective character in certain affective responses, in that they can be called appropriate disclosures of some ethical import in the world and not simply an interior mental state. Regarding the example above, it is possible to talk of appropriate revulsion at the beating of an innocent child. We might even say that someone who takes an indifferent or detached stance toward such an act is not responding appropriately, is not being morally objective in a way.

Ethical comprehension can be construed as a form of interpretation, in the manner of certain background intimations that elicit as-indications. With the example of child beating, the pre-reflective intimation of human vulnerability constitutes taking this situation *as* an ethical one, as a situation prompting a response to the ethical bearing of the act or agent, unlike other human endeavors such as technical skill or cognitive investigation. The understanding of human finitude is implicated in the ethical disclosure of various modes of care and neglect, help and harm, *as* matters that are appropriately scalable as better and worse performances in the context of existential weal and woe. The ethical sphere, then, is hermeneutically distinct from other spheres of life. And then within the ethical sphere itself there is the hermeneutical element that issues interpretive variations and disagreements as to what counts as better or worse performances and to what degree. For instance, the scenario above might be different if it involved a parent spanking a disobedient child.

With questions of child neglect, which often prompt drastic interventions into families and the abrogation of parental rights, we can recognize inhabitive truth conditions that show such judgments and responses to be anything but arbitrary: judgments about the immorality of child abuse are appropriately *responsive*, given the suffering involved and what is known about a child's developmental needs. There is also widespread *agreement* about such judgments; the ethical norms involved are certainly *reliable* and *workable* with respect to child-rearing practices in general terms.

It is important to spotlight inhabitive modes of ethical truth to avoid overestimating the contingency of ethical assessment. We should not overstate the degree of disagreement in ethics, despite the obvious range of variations and disputes in moral matters. From a pedagogical standpoint, although ethical controversies are an excellent setting for cultivating critical thinking skills, and even though there is much controversy in ethical concerns, students are misled when we concentrate primarily on dilemmas and disputes in moral considerations or on the shortcomings of moral paradigms. We should at least start with areas of agreement (all students believe that they should be graded fairly) before we take up controversies to block the impression (very common among students) that moral values are completely undecidable. Stressing "lifeboat" scenarios, for example, is like beginning physics instruction with the uncertainty principle or the wave-particle paradox. Moral disagreements often turn on the extent of a norm (Is it always right to tell the truth?) rather than its status *as* a norm.[25] Ironically, it may be the standard of indefeasibility that creates an overly distorted picture of conflict in ethics, in that we are prompted to consider any imaginable objection in order to shore up the validity of a proposed norm. We might do better to begin with our actual proclivities and wait for sincere, forthright disputes. For instance, let us wait for actual radical egoists to advance (and live by) their positions, and let us gauge ethical prospects here by way of actual dealings with such persons. Many moral cases do not arouse interrogation because they do not contravene established and projected ethical bearings. There is little controversy in cases of indiscriminate or wanton killing, for instance. We might be interested in questions concerning why someone goes on a killing spree for thrills, yet who would question the wrongness of such an action? Of course, one might pose such a question as a theoretical exercise, and someone who commits such an action might sincerely claim to be in the right. Yet if someone actually were to defend killing for thrills, there is little that philosophical debate could contribute. Such a person, I would think, is not really interested in ethics as a question (and is probably a sociopath).

The lived world is always already saturated with values and norms. We dwell ethically as a matter of course. Everyday social interactions, habits, competencies, and expectations enact a host of evaluations, ranging from common courtesy to basic social customs and ethical routines. Say I walk into a shop, exchange greetings with the clerk, carefully browse the merchandise, choose an item, take my place in line to purchase it, move aside as someone needs to get by, stumble on something and fall, injuring myself. People immediately come to my aid, and someone says, "I'm a doctor, let me help," and I let her come to my aid. This episode is filled with spontaneous performances of social values and norms—concerning manners, decorum, respect for property, fairness, unobtrusiveness, heedfulness, beneficence, truthfulness, and trust. Such routines play out without reflection or some theoretical application of rules to cases. And the aptness of the behaviors can well illustrate inhabitive signs of truth, namely responsive fit, workability, reliability, and sense. Such unreflective ethical capacities can trace back to child-rearing and educational training in that how we are raised enculturates and incorporates values and norms into a habitual competence. We can recognize different levels of ethical competence, ranging from somewhat automatic customs to a kind of proficient facility in responding to moral situations without much reflective effort.[26]

Because moral philosophy pursues interrogation and justification programs that depend on contravention and disagreement to shape their procedures, it is easy to miss the positive aspect of ethical behaviors that are simply given or expected. Teaching ethics to undergraduates might benefit from acknowledging and articulating normal ethical competency and also admirable ethical actions—which can show something important to students, namely that not everything in ethics need be subject to examination. Of course, there is much in ethical life that bears interrogation and critical analysis. This happens when normative dwelling and immersion are interrupted by contravening circumstances or events. We confront novel situations that do not fit expected patterns: for example, the prospect of gay marriage or animal rights. We might come across disparate patterns, as in the case of different customs from other cultures. We can experience the unexpected contravention of a pattern: questions do not arise about being thanked for a gift but about not being thanked. We confront situations marked by a conflict of norms: if a friend asks me about something that will hurt him, here loyalty, honesty, and beneficence collide. In times of historical crisis, new patterns emerge as a critical force when old ways are no longer experienced as fitting or workable, as in the feminist movement, and familiar conceptions can reveal their ambiguity and contestability, as in the Vietnam era, when the meaning of "patriotism" was claimed by both hawks and doves. This is where moral philosophy is important in trying to think through such scenarios. But ethical dwelling must also be kept in mind in order to situate ethics in a background environment that does not require justification or critical review.

3. PHILOSOPHY AND REASON

In the light of existential rationality and philosophy's assignment to the lived world, including its own factical background discussed in chapter 2, I will highlight what I think is common to any form of philosophy. I am comfortable calling this a commitment to human reason, yet in a modest sense that need not be confined to standard rational principles and procedures, which have tended toward a regimented rationality that supposedly governs thinking in advance and supervises other modes of thought. The modest sense of reason I have in mind can be gleaned by considering how philosophy emerged and took shape in ancient Greece.

We have noted the pre-logical senses of *logos*, which could function apart from philosophical expectations. We can recognize forms of "reasoning" in nonphilosophical domains in the Greek world: What does the king (or god) want? What does his command mean? What will follow from obeying or not obeying? In Greek philosophical reasoning, *logos* did take on specific differences that have marked it ever since, but that need not be restricted to logical formats or rational principles. How so? Early Greek culture was informed by religion and myth, which exhibited two prominent features: 1) The gods were extra-natural entities in the sense of being concealed from normal awareness and everyday phenomena and of being the controlling forces behind natural life; 2) Because of this extra-natural concealment, access to divine dimensions was a matter of extraordinary insight granted to special individuals such as kings, seers, oracles, and poets.[27] In this pre-philosophical world, knowledge of the deepest and most important domains was inaccessible to most people, who therefore were in a position of dependency on both the gods and their select conduits.

With Thales, purported to be the first philosopher, the contours of philosophical reason can be shown in his supposed first principle—Everything comes from water—and how it departs from the earlier mythical world. Aside from the innovation of a unified account of things, there is a turn to natural, commonly accessible experience. The reference to water is different from sacred sources, and the claim that water is a grounding source can be discerned as a process of thinking drawn from available evidence: The crucial importance of water for life and the larger extent of water compared to land—which are readily grasped by anyone—could support the proposal of water's primacy.[28] The key feature here is not the truth or falsity of Thales's claim, but the way in which one might come to believe it on the basis of one's own experience and its possible implications. One could reject the claim or even point to another element as a better candidate (perhaps air). In any case, the path of thinking does not involve hidden mysteries or passive reliance on privileged mentalities or authorities, but rather self-directed inferences stemming from the common ground of available experience.

Even though we can surmise these aspects of early philosophical thinking, the sources we have do not offer much specific attention to methodological questions. Indeed, the texts are often more declarative than inquisitive, at times even oracular in tone. Perhaps this is why such thinkers are called Presocratics because Socrates clinched the full spirit of philosophy with his interrogative and dialogical posture (as depicted in Plato's writings). With Socrates, questioning goes all the way down; anything of importance deserves critical examination. The prosecution of Socrates is at least understandable in light of his counter-traditional provocations. No belief could be taken for granted or protected from criticism. Such radical interrogation was joined with the counter-secretive path of starting with accessible common ground, which allows self-directed discovery and which was intrinsic to Socrates's dialogical method. He would not begin with a proposed theory but with a question posed to an interlocutor, whose own answer would be the focus of examination—so that the course of discussion would never exceed self-professed beliefs and experiences. Wherever the discussion went, it would proceed according to stipulations evident to the conversation partners. The dialogical method also followed the erstwhile notion of *logos*—speech that makes sense to an audience—in assuming that one's beliefs and actions could not assume a solipsistic posture. This is one reason why Socrates refused the offer of escape from prison in the *Crito* because he would be sending the signal that anyone could renounce the law if they saw fit. Assuming that one is not the only person in the world, or the only person who counts in the world, one's beliefs and actions are an offering for public consideration as a possible way of being for others as well.

What is emphasized here is distinct from any metaphysical or epistemological commitments that might be operating in Plato's dialogues, likewise any successful or unsuccessful arguments that might be identified. I am highlighting constituent features of a modest sense of reason that is intrinsic to the inception of philosophy, concerning how it gets off the ground in the first place as a living phenomenon. These features can be gathered as an *interrogative dialogical immanence*: Philosophical reason puts anything in question (even itself); interrogation elicits a shared, interactive exploration of possible answers; dialogue must at least start out from evident common ground, which sets up the possibility of persuasion and agreement. As in the case of Socrates, radical interrogation is much more than a disciplinary obligation or procedure; it can be a genuine disturbance of established cultural norms and beliefs. In this way, philosophy embodies the tension between individuation and socialization, divergence and coherence, as discussed in chapter 1. Philosophy is not sheer individuation because it presumes an audience of interlocutors in mutual pursuit of truth and persuasion (whether it is face-to-face conversation or an exchange between writers and readers). Persuasive truth differs from obedient compliance in being mutual self-discovery that stems from already apparent beliefs and evidence. This baseline conception of reason shows how philosophy exhibits its own personal-social-world. It also makes possible subsequent developments of epistemological methods, rational principles, and logical structures. Yet this erstwhile sense of reason is more factical than technical in nature, and the possibility of persuasion on the basis of accessible common ground shows that philosophy should not drift too far from the lived world, which is the original and immanent common terrain.

A relevant example in this regard is the familiar juxtaposition of reason and rhetoric. Plato is well-known for identifying the problem of rhetoric and its supposed threat to truth, especially in the political sphere. Since then we are inclined to say that reason pertains to the logical force of an argument, while rhetoric pertains to the psychological force of an argument with an appeal to emotions, desires, and interests that might override truth. Although this distinction can have much relevance, a more complex phenomenology of language and disclosure speaks against a binary division of reason and rhetoric. We have seen that affect is not always out of place in cognition, and the range of existential factors in factical life shows that meaning, value, and purpose cannot be sectioned off apart from so-called objective truth. Argumentation need not always be divorced from felt concerns.[29] This is not to invite irrationality but simply to complicate the reach of, or what is meant by, reason and logic.[30] We have indicated how embodiment is central to cognition and language, especially in the degree to which tangible metaphors inform all ranges of thinking. This is why the traditional preserve of reason apart from corporeal forces is suspect.

The contextual pluralism of language usage opens the door for a less regimented and more flexible approach to rational persuasion. Oratorical gifts in politics can certainly be problematic, but the setting of politics makes such gifts far from merely ornamental. The stirring of an audience may be the lifeblood of politics, without which motivation might be lost. Narrative features of language can also be crucial in legal proceedings. The facts of the case, even if stipulated, can emit different stories that carry different meanings, each being admissible to conceptions of justice.[31] Effective storytelling can therefore be decisive in legal and political arguments.[32] In general terms, different dialogical settings carry different purposes, expectations, and appropriate measures, which cannot be governed by a single or purified rubric of logic. Within domains of persuasion, inquiry, negotiation, deliberation, or eristic debate, for instance, different appeals, styles, and evidentiary forces apply.[33] Developments in natural language semantics, pragmatics, and dynamics have shown the limitations in traditional models of reason and have suggested modified formats of structure, procedure, and agency that can take into account variable practices, actors, processes, and competency levels, particularly when "knowledge" is redescribed as a matter of coming-to-know in conjunction with learning.[34] Plato's dialogues—which offer the first full-blooded display of philosophical thinking—themselves exhibit rhetorical, situational, narrative, existential, even mythical and poetic elements that cannot be separated from the distinctly rational character of these seminal texts.[35]

4. PLURALISM

The set of truth conditions sketched earlier shows in a rough sense how truth can be both one and many. The unity of truth here is certainly not the kind sought in traditional concepts of one kind of truth or a single universal standard. The set of conditions simply shows a range of features or functions that any claim to truth would satisfy. But the range is such that it could fit different ways of engaging the world, in science, ethics, art, and other settings.[36] The word *truth*, then, can cut across different settings as a focal term with an indicative function rather than a single standard with a regulating function. The indicative meaning of truth would simply point to different modes of *appropriate disclosure*.

Inhabitive truth conditions open up the validity of pluralism when a certain setting or context can lose its manner of inhabitive truth if subjected to undue assessment from another setting or context—which would go against the interrogative and phenomenological diversity outlined in chapter 2. For instance, if the interrogative context is causal explanation in the sphere of physical entities, natural science is appropriate; all six truth conditions can be met and spiritual or mentalistic notions would be out of place. But if such a setting is presumed to be universally applicable, what can follow is a physicalistic explanation for anything that pertains to mental life. Then we run into truth-conditional failure in a shifting context—neurological descriptions of my brain states at the time of composing this sentence would not be able to convey its meaning (thus violating responsive fitness and workability). Not every engagement with the world is a matter of physical causation. Say that I have a brain tumor and my surgeon is showing me its location on an MRI. "There it is," he says, "and we will be able to remove it safely. Don't worry." I say, "OK, but I am still really afraid for some reason." He points to another location on the MRI and says, "Here's why you're afraid; that's where fear is produced." This would be a startling response (violating fitness and sense) and I am quite sure that it would not arise in a situation like this. We continually orchestrate and navigate different phenomenological contexts (in enactive interpretation) and there are times when certain philosophical notions make for "false moves" in factical situations. Accordingly, untruth can be shown both within settings and between settings when there is an undue incursion from one setting to another (such as "creation science," in which the intimation of something supernatural violates all the conditions of truth in natural science).[37]

With respect to an account of phenomena, we can ask about its truth in terms of the following questions: Is it fitting, reliable, and workable? Is there agreement and sense? Is it contextually appropriate? Then various answers regarding truth and untruth can be worked out. Moreover, truth will often be a complex matter because the six conditions are inter-relatable and many areas of thought involve a combination or orchestration of different settings and contexts. Think of a murder trial, for instance, with an array of empirical, conceptual, normative, scientific, psychological, and historical factors that can be brought to bear. The different settings involved overlap in being gathered by the meaning and purpose of a trial. And the shifts of enactive interpretation (for instance between normative, empirical, and psychological settings) are typically automatic, without a need for explanation or transitional steps. In any case, being "true" to phenomena will often require polyvocal complexity, which can be suppressed by a preference for univocal or unmitigated accounts. A true history of the Civil War, for example, calls for a wide range of perspectives. Indeed, the truth of something like war requires a factical depth that perhaps only literature or poetry can provide.

Given the complexity of truth, we might notice the inadequacy of overly simple or one-dimensional models of truth. Consider the "deflationary" theory, wherein "P is true" is eliminable in an explanation of P; it is simply an ornament on "P." The theory likely stems from frustration following problems attached to other models of truth, which can be jettisoned by calling off the search for something substantive called "truth." There is nonetheless evasion shown in the word *simply*, because how P *is* P (and thus true) can involve a complex amalgamation of factors. Any "explanation" will imply its own tacit conditions of disclosure that run far and wide within thinking. Truth need not be a redundancy but rather indicative attention to a deep background behind and within propositions. Moreover, the *question* of truth—in real life—unfolds out of expositional contraventions of a prior trust in presentational truth, a process that is more complex than simply the confines of a proposition.

Nevertheless, there is saliency in a deflationary focus when considering some baseline elements of complex philosophical topics. Familiar self-reference problems arise when governing principles are interrogated reflexively. Is the correspondence theory itself true? To what does it correspond? Can the standard of empirical verification be verified empirically? How can any principle of justification itself be justified? The traditional response to this problem mandated the underivability of first principles in the manner of being "self-evident," which meant immediately certain and beyond question. Such reliance on self-evidence is suspect today in part because historically it was often traced to a divine mind or intuition. The notion of presentational truth, however, can apply to the reflexive problem of governing principles in the following way. Such principles are established *starting points* for thinking that are taken as *given*.[38] Yet taking them as given is not arbitrary because 1) a certain interrogative or phenomenological context can grant saliency (such as scientific confirmation in matters of causal explanation), 2) the establishment of starting points is not out of the blue because it stems from a host of background determinations, and 3) inhibitive truth conditions can flesh out the cogency of first principles. Presentational "self-evidence" does not entail unquestionability or indefeasibility; it simply designates a starting point that shapes inquiry without itself being interrogated—*any longer*. The deepest levels of philosophical debate do often involve questioning such starting points, but it is no wonder that few if any such debates get resolved, precisely because the pathway to starting points is not a matter of demonstrative certainty.

And even with agreement over starting points, contextual pluralism argues against their universal or uniform applicability. So there are a number of ways in which human discourse can issue truth, but not on the basis of some indubitable or absolute foundation.

As an example, consider the presumption of immanence at the heart of this investigation. It is a precondition for much of my analysis, and it has some muscle in being based on our normal access to the world without any initial importation outside of lived experience. Yet in putting off transcendent realities and scientistic reductionism, how can it be said that this presumption is rationally compelling? I am sure that not everyone will be sold. What can be offered at that baseline level of inquiry? If someone aimed for a religious foundation in divine creation or thought that scientific explanation is the decisive criterion for all questions, I might still try to persuade, but at some point the issue is no longer a matter of rational argument but disposition in the manner of affective attunement. The lived world, especially its temporal structure and limit conditions, is disruptive of common human preferences for order, stability, and secured foundations. In the end, people simply differ in dispositional bearings toward these conditions—which is where the personal-world figures in intellectual life. Some people are more comfortable with plurality, contingency, and openness; others more inclined toward unity, necessity, and closure.[39] Such dispositions are existential orientations that are not usually susceptible to debate or persuasion.

I doubt that coming to be a pluralist is simply a matter of following an argument or drawing inferences, although some manner of persuasion is surely involved (otherwise why write this book?). In keeping with the lived elements of disclosiveness sketched in chapter 2, coming to a philosophical position is a complex result of personal, historical, social, practical, affective, cognitive, and intimated factors. The same holds for established orientations and convictions in various disciplines, which are not absolute and fixed given the rarity of unanimity and the pliancy exhibited in the (ongoing) history of disciplines.[40] Whatever truth there may be in a discipline is, in accordance with inhabitive conditions, an achieved consensus that *settles* in a community of inquirers and holds on by force of that settlement. Such *enacted* knowledge is not mere social constructivism because the settings of truth will not countenance sheer conventionalism. If such a picture of truth and knowledge is resisted because it cannot satisfy a more secured condition of warrant, it can only be said that actual occasions of knowledge in human history have always played out in the enactive sense here described, even when inquirers may have thought they had an absolute or securely grounded warrant.

An enacted sense of knowledge and truth, along with its factical environment and contingencies, is a reiteration of the central position given to interpretation in proto-phenomenology, especially with respect to perspectival and enactive interpretation. Accordingly, baseline disputes are a matter of hermeneutics. Yet even with interpretation going all the way down, the truth conditions suggested in this chapter are meant to intercept a relativistic interpretation of interpretation, in which any and all positions are self-warranted and beyond critique. Absolutism and relativism differ only in the extent of uncontestability: in the former, only one position is uncontestable; in the latter, all positions are uncontestable. This is why interpretive pluralism is different from relativism because it affords contextual measures and perspectival constraints.

5. THE MIND-BODY QUESTION AND LINGUISTIC PLURALISM

I conclude this chapter with a pluralistic analysis of the mind-body question because it touches on many fundamental issues that proto-phenomenology aims to address. The two prominent metaphysical positions in the mind-body question are dualism, which argues that mental and physical properties are a function of two separate substances, and physicalism, which holds that only material entities are real. Physicalism is the dominant theory in contemporary philosophy, and two versions stand out: the identity theory, which maintains that whatever is meant by a mental state, it is numerically identical to a brain state, and eliminativism, which argues that any talk of mental states should be rejected in favor of neurophysiological descriptions.

I have already broached an alternative phenomenological approach to this question, which here will be developed further. Given the phenomenological priority of language and the cogency of veridical pluralism, different and incommensurable linguistic meanings can suffice to stand against reductive incursions that disallow, replace, or take over other established modes of expression. It must be kept in mind that the starting point for this venture of contextual pluralism is natural language and its disclosive power in factical speech. A phenomenology of mental and physical language has no metaphysical pretensions, it simply tracks the patterns of enactive interpretation, which shifts to different meanings in different contexts without any suppositions about the existence of the mind as some kind of immaterial entity or even about the body in purely physical terms divorced from the existential significance of lived embodiment. The words *mind* and *body* can function as nonreified indicative concepts that simply point to the ways in which mental and physical dimensions of normal life are understood and interpreted—along with their immersed, ecological, and temporal elements that exceed any expositional/reified focus on a mind or a body. In addition, with language understood in the manner of ecological dwelling, the probative approach to linguistic usage in this discussion is not advancing linguistic idealism, nor is it simply about the semantic meaning of words, because it has to do with ways of being in the world and inhabitive truth disclosed in language.

Natural language usage shows different interpretive spheres that have their own integrity, which should not be colonized by other hermeneutical perspectives. With respect to the mind-body question, mental and physical indications amount to a linguistic, rather than metaphysical, dichotomy.[41] There may be a certain weight given to "physical" descriptions, not in terms of advanced scientific accounts but simply because so many mental terms are metaphorically drawn from concrete sensory meanings, especially with respect to vision: seeing the point, an unclear idea, and so on. Yet such metaphors involve an interpretive shift from physical-sensory occasions (one does not clarify an idea with a cleaning cloth). In any case, a linguistic dichotomy can be shown by noting nonsensical transfers between forms of speech with comparable grammatical structures but incommensurable meanings. If I say, "I am heavier than last year," someone might reply, "You don't look heavier. Are you sure? Have you checked recently?" If someone asks me how I am feeling, and I say, "I am a lot happier than last year," it would be odd to hear, "Are you sure? Have you checked?"[42] If I am thinking of a yardstick, someone would not ask how such a long thing can fit inside my head.[43] Grammatically speaking, nouns, adjectives, and verbs can apply respectively to both physical and mental *objects*, their *attributes*, and their *activities*—but not interchangeably. "A happy thought came to me" and "A red car approached me" have common grammatical structures, but with the former claim one would not ask, "From what direction, how fast?" Mixing and matching the different grammatical forms would result in nonsense: "A yellow hope hit my leg," "That pretentious rock is not very smart," or Chomsky's famous phrase, "colorless green ideas sleeping furiously." I should not be too dogmatic here. One can imagine poetical or satirical uses of such mismatches, and nonsensical uses can play a functional role in marking the boundaries of sense. And again, metaphorical combinations can make sense, as in a "pregnant pause," but not in a manner commensurable with actual pregnancy ("When is the pause due?"). The point is that linguistic pluralism and incommensurability can buttress objections to reductive physicalism. "Your hat is in your closet" makes sense while "Your fear is in your brain" would not. Such a linguistic divide can have legitimacy and salience in factual usage without countenancing metaphysical dualism.[44]

A dualist would take the linguistic divide as fitting an argument for an ontological divide between mental and physical substances. But this mirrors the error of physicalism in reifying on a different plane the grammar of mental descriptions. To say that my ideas are in my mind is at best a metaphor that should not tempt us to hypostasize ideas or minds into discrete realities apart from physical states. An identity theorist is right, in my view, to say that a linguistic divide is not equivalent to a metaphysical divide. But the different linguistic *meanings* cannot turn into an "identity" and established mental notions should not be deemed mere figures of speech. The problem with reductive physicalism can be gleaned from the different assessments of mental language in the identity theory and eliminativism. An identity theorist would likely acknowledge mental language yet maintain that any mental term is simply referring to, and identical with, a brain state. Eliminative physicalism takes a harder stance by not giving any status to mental language: If there are only brain states, we should reject mental language as having no significance and restrict an account of thoughts, desires, and so on to neurological descriptions.

It seems that eliminativism is the more consistent and honest version of reductive physicalism. Yet the sincere rejection of mental language only accentuates the shortcomings of physicalism in terms of what I call the *translation problem*. If an account of something is deemed mistaken, it would be reasonable to call for translating that account into the proper explanation, thereby discarding the former account. It was once believed that diseases are caused by spiritual beings such as demons. Attempts at healing would accordingly follow a spiritual script: praying, chanting, conjuring, or supplication. Since Hippocrates, spiritual causes have been challenged in favor of natural causes in the body or environment. Not only does this call for a therapeutic shift to physical treatments, it also mandates a wholesale translation of spiritual nomenclature into tangible natural descriptions. The viability of the translation turns on how we presumably lose nothing and gain much in the exchange of spiritual language for physio-somatic language.

It appears that eliminative physicalism sees the mind-body question in the same light, in which mental language is a historical superstition that should be exchanged for neuro-physiological accounts. Yet I do not think the two cases are comparable. I have no problem with the translation of disease references from spiritual to physical descriptions. It works well and we lose nothing in giving up something like demon language. But I do not see how we can give up mental language in favor of neurological descriptions without losing the existential meanings that animate normal life. As I have said before, translating the "ideas" in this sentence into the neurological states of my brain at the time of composition would be bereft of any communicative sense. And giving an anniversary card to my wife expressing my feelings for her by way of neurological data would be more than a translation problem.

I have argued for a distinction between causal explanation and phenomenological meaning. If the question concerns the natural "cause" of a feeling I have for my wife, I can side with physicalism on that score (so I am a causal physicalist).[45] But a reductive translation of "love" to such causal conditions in my brain is a pointless exercise that cannot be incorporated into natural life. Unlike the disease example, the exchange would not work in a pragmatic sense.[46] I have also argued for the phenomenological priority of language over an object-designation theory of language. Perhaps physicalism stems from a restriction to that theory, in which "love" fails to designate a discernible object and a neurological designation succeeds. But with proto-phenomenology, language is in the first place not a matter of object designation but the disclosure of factical *meanings*, which would evaporate if translated into object-language or physiological descriptions.[47]

Two prominent eliminativists, Paul and Patricia Churchland, have at least taken the translation problem to heart. Assuming that mental language is false in referring to nothing real, they see the need for exchanging that language for the only real domain of neuro-physiological facts.[48] This would apply not only to general terms stemming from folk psychology, such as beliefs, desires, intentions, and so on, but also to common descriptions of specific states of mind, as in "I am depressed,"

"I hate that movie," or "I am excited by your idea." The Churchlands call for, and foresee the possibility of, a translation of general and specific mental locutions into the scientific lexicon of neurological facts.[49] Consequently, "I am excited" would be replaced by . . . well, it is not entirely clear. Presumably it would be: "I am [insert the brain data causing the feeling]." But the "I" (as a traditional marker of a "self") might need translating too; perhaps: "There is [insert brain data] in my brain"—maybe not "my" brain but "the brain in this body." In fact, if *any* word in sentences like these can be associated at all with mental states, the translation would have to be exhaustive. I have argued that such an exchange would lose all factical sense. But even if we restricted the translation to discernible mental states like excitement, the exchange would still lose existential meaning.

Perhaps the eliminative project could compare with the disease example, in that we simply need to change all references and learn to live with them. The differential character of language would not rule this out. With semantic shift, we could simply gravitate toward using the new verbiage to replace the erroneous words we formally used. But if human communication is to be wholly transformed in this way, we would want to begin with children and train them to use neurological terms in place of the old-fashioned words that children learned in the past. Putting aside doubts about how or whether such translations could work in the practical-performative milieu of language acquisition (teaching these words to children could not be directly referencing neurological facts but ways of engaging the world), even if it were successful there would still arise *different contexts* in which a neurological term or phrase would be deployed, for instance the actual context of neurological research and findings as distinct from conversations about "how one is feeling" in everyday circumstances. Single words can have multiple meanings or count as homonyms, and the translation scheme could claim the virtue of having a single "true" denotation used in both settings.[50] But the meaning of those settings is so different that confusion could arise unless context could sort out the different meanings. But if proto-phenomenology allows for causal explanations in a distinct interrogative context, what is lost by retaining familiar mental words for the contexts that have spawned those words in the heretofore effective functioning of natural language? I cannot see why in child-rearing we need to (or can) replace "Did you enjoy the party, dear?" with "Was there [insert data] during the party, dear?" Because every word in the sentence has a neurological source, shouldn't we translate all the words into the new format? Are not "was there," "during," and "dear" slippery terms that need a more precise denotation? From a practical standpoint, this seems to be an enormous endeavor that taxes the imagination.[51] Even if it were possible to do this, if one grants the purported cogency of phenomenological pluralism, the only virtue of the translation would seem to be the satisfaction of a reductive fetish for the governance of thought by a uniform standard. It is hard to see how a factical utterance like "I love my wife" is infused with error because it is not couched in neurological terms and why it *needs* to undergo a neuro-translation at all (outside of a causal context) in order to purge the error and be in accord with a baseline truth.

As I have indicated, phenomenological pluralism is tracked contextually by interrogative pluralism in that the kind of question being posed can focus different ways of engaging the world. Yet one might ask about the context of a question like "What can everything be reduced to?" What kind of question is that? Is it a question that must be answered? Why is contextual pluralism unacceptable?[52] The same can be asked of dualistic tendencies that see the need for reifying mental phenomena. An alternative to both physicalism and dualism is the *indicative* function of words like mind, body, mental, physical, idea, and brain. Within such indications, further specified contexts can issue various modes of disclosure: causal explanations, empirical descriptions, practical tasks, normative concerns, affective attunement, and a wealth of nonreified engagements such as explaining, wondering, imagining, showing, loving, and so on.

The problem in the standard mind-body debate is that neither side would appear to be satisfied with indicative constraints and specifications. There seems to be a need for a stable ontology grounding mental and/or physical phenomena. That *need* can be isolated from the legitimate elements of mental and physical phenomena that each side has disclosed but that nevertheless may have triggered metaphysical overreach. It is no surprise that the tangibility of the body and the success of causal explanations have prompted physicalistic tendencies. Likewise, dualism can be prompted by the many facets of experience that seem so different from concrete physical states, especially in light of the linguistic divide treated above. On another level, perhaps the *sonic* element of speech—as distinct from a tangible body *seen* with the eyes—allows an intimation of something "invisible" compared to the body of a speaker, something dwelling "behind" the face, so to speak. I would add something that stems from the differential fitness of language.

With the separability of words from immediate engagement, a host of capacities can appear quite different from, and unconstrained by, concrete physical conditions: imagination, memory, and face-to-face conversations about past and future events. And the *fitness* character of such differential effects would give them a sense of being quite *real*.

While acknowledging these prompts, the metaphysical reach of physicalism and dualism can nevertheless be exchanged for a phenomenology of different interpretive contexts. In the bargain, indicative and contextual constraints free us from a number of problems that have accompanied both sides of the debate: How can a "mind" or "idea" interact with the "body" or "brain"? How can introspection be accessed by empirical science? Why does "love" seem so different from a brain state? How does the mind "supervene" upon, or emerge "out of," physical states? If the mental and physical terms involved here are revised as focal indications, their use simply points to disclosive effects *in context* without having to satisfy or comply with other contexts. Indeed, even the Cartesian "cogito" set apart from the body can bear some sense as indicative of the mathematical domain of physics detached from the ordinary experience of physical things. In any case, basic philosophical problems can be solved (or dissolved) by recasting them as linguistic shifts of interpretation. With the problem of interaction, for instance, substantive contraries—How can an unextended mind interact with an extended brain?—no longer apply. Instead we have the less puzzling question of how mental language interacts with physical language—less puzzling because a factual perspective shows the correlation achieved in natural orchestrations of enactive interpretation.

5.1. Selfhood

A comparable analysis can apply to the problem of the "self" and "identity" that continues to circulate in philosophy of mind. The word *self* can simply be indicative of the personal-world and all its various features without having to satisfy conditions of permanence, unity, and verification (at least not according to standard philosophical requirements) and without marking out a specific sphere of "consciousness." At the same time, a physicalist *dismissal* of consciousness is no less presumptuous than the notion that consciousness is a discrete "something" that can be ascertained apart from physical states. It is counterintuitive to be told that one's sense of being a conscious self is mistaken when *something* like self-awareness seems to be so obvious and evident. Even a "fictionalist" allowance of the conscious self, as something false but useful in explaining human behavior, falls short of what proto-phenomenology can offer.[53] The factical features of the personal-world provide a modest kind of truth with respect to selfhood, and the functions of first-person language in normal dealings seem to be ineliminable from a practical standpoint, in light of which a "useful fiction" would be a contradiction in terms.[54] It may be true that first-person language does not "designate" or "represent" a self, not because there is no self but because first-person language (and language generally) *first opens up* a sense of self in developmental terms (which will be argued in volume 2). Here I reiterate and paraphrase Helen Keller's remarkable claim that before she was able to learn language, she had no self-awareness, she lived in a no-world, she had no sense of action or desire or thinking; self-consciousness only first came to her when she learned the meaning of the words "I" and "me."

First-person language can suffice for selfhood in factical terms, and yet with limits that fall short of the supposed need for constancy and unity in theories of a *substantive* self, some permanent or unified self behind the flux of experience. The "linguistic person" cannot measure up to many conditions of selfhood proffered in metaphysical theories because it is caught up in the finitude of existence. Self-awareness ebbs and flows in the course of daily life (particularly in sleep), we talk of "not being ourselves" at times, and abnormal conditions can fracture and even rub out normal features of selfhood (as in multiple personality disorders, schizophrenia, or Alzheimer's disease). But within such limits, the capacity for, and effects of, first-person speech can do well enough to gather a workable sense of selfhood. And the temporal character of life (which is often posed as a problem for substantive conceptions of selfhood) can likewise be gathered as a kind of selfhood in *narrative* structures, in the stories and chronicles we tell about ourselves and our lives, which provide an adequate focus of a configured plot without having to exhibit metaphysically pure conditions of unity and constancy.[55] Here human "identity" is not a matter of *what* one is but *who* one is.[56]

Note that the formal background of narrative "unity" is the looping figure-eight structure of temporality, which provides a focal point to gather past, present, and future *together* in lived experience, especially because temporality here is not a matter of discrete "points" in time that seem to exclude each other. Such a narrative gathering remains a temporal phenomenon, which therefore does not satisfy substantive conceptions of permanence. Narrative unity need not mean that there is a *single* story that grounds all specific episodes. Rather, a life can involve many different narrative threads that are contextually distinct and even susceptible to being broken up or lost. Memory (following Locke) supplies enough coalescence for narrative identity, but memory is finite and far from perfect. Other persons can help in this regard, and indeed one's own story is intertwined with other stories in the social-world. Perhaps the only way to single out a human narrative and grasp it as a "whole" is to frame it between birth and death—a boundary marking an "outside" (before birth and after death) that fully outstrips the awareness of the main character, thus infusing the story with a radical finitude that is anything but substantive in a metaphysical sense.[57]

It should be added that the substantive sense of a subjective self and the reductive sense of the body as a physical object are not timeless concepts, but rather historical discoveries that are not evident in early Western languages, in the early experiences of a child, or in mature experiences of immersion. In all these cases, "selfhood" is dispersed and extended in an ecological field of multiple practices and the "body" is a lived phenomenon of meaning-laden engagements with the surrounding world.[58] Both physicalism and dualism therefore are selective theories that screen out other senses of experience and disclosure that have found a place in human language and that fit the phenomenology of the lived world.

By way of summation, "selfhood" is not a metaphysical entity but an indicative concept pointing to emergent meanings in factical life that would seem to be ineliminable. Indeed, exposition itself, *as* a phenomenon and *in* its articulation, opens space for a sense of selfhood that likely prompted dualistic ventures but that need not go that far. In an expositional circumstance, a *distinction* between myself and the world, between myself and my body, seems quite evident and articulable in first-person language, along with third-person descriptions of the world and my body: "My pen is out of ink"; "This pen is not comfortable in my hand." Other people would readily understand such talk but apply it to me in a second-person manner, as I would to them if they were to say such things. All of this amounts to an articulated personal-social-environing-world. As a refined form of exposition, scientific research is disclosive of the world in an acutely focused third-person manner. The problem with reductive physicalism is that it bypasses the first-person perspective that scientists themselves presumably must articulate in comprehending their own activity as working scientists, their own personal-science-world. With such a perspective, we have a mode of selfhood that is *true enough* (as adequation) to challenge reductive physicalism—not with a counter-reduction to a "mind" or a substantive "self," but simply with indicative attention to the lived world, which includes the very science-world that prompted the theory of physicalism in the first place.

This completes my account of truth from a phenomenological standpoint and how it applies to central philosophical questions. The next chapter offers a brief summary of the overall investigation thus far and a forecast of volume 2: *Language Acquisition, Orality, and Literacy*.

NOTES

1. See the *OED* under "truth" and "trust."
2. See Olli Lagerspetz, *Trust, Ethics, and Human Reason* (New York: Bloomsbury, 2015).
3. See Timothy R. Levine, "Truth-Default Theory: A Theory of Human Deception and Deception Detection," *Journal of Language and Social Psychology* 33, no. 4 (September 2014): 378–92.
4. See Paul Faulkner, *Knowledge in Trust* (Oxford: Oxford University Press, 2011), Benjamin McMyler, *Testimony, Trust, and Authority* (Oxford: Oxford University Press, 2011), and Thomas W. Simpson, "What Is Trust?" *Pacific Philosophical Quarterly* 93 (2012): 550–69.
5. Presentational truth and the differential potential for untruth together can account for two senses of "appearance," namely emergence (the actor appearing on stage) and semblance (he is only appearing to agree with you). Phenomenology, of course, is based on the first sense of appearance, but the second sense is an intrinsic possibility due to semiotic difference.
6. The network of implicit background comprehensions in presentational truth connects with the correlational scope of the lived world, which can compare with the coherence theory of truth, yet with an existential emphasis missing in that theory, which holds that the truth of a belief is grounded in its coherence with a range of other beliefs. Here the restriction to propositions does not measure up to the factical setting of presentational truth.
7. The distinction between a truth bearer (a proposition) and a truth maker (a fact) can be joined in presentational truth if making and bearing are taken in the *generative* sense of giving birth.
8. As an aside, I am willing to bet that "the cat is on the mat" has never actually been verified when used in epistemological discussions.
9. See the *OED* under "true" and "truth."
10. The immediacy of presentational truth fits the double-negative structure of disclosure mentioned in chapter 1, in which something simply comes to presence out of concealment. The word for truth in ancient Greek is *alētheia*, which indicates the double-negative sense of unhiddenness. Although *alētheia* was used by philosophers in ways familiar to modern usage, its earliest use included direct, sincere speech as op-

posed to deceptive speech that conceals truth. The strong association of *alētheia* with countering concealment is suggested by the fact that the word *pseudos* covered mistaken beliefs and lies with the same term. Especially in pre-literate Greek culture, a basic form of hiddenness or concealment was noted in the phenomenon of forgetting. A primary function of early poetry was the preservation of important things from passing into forgottenness, thus serving a kind of disclosive truth.

11. This is akin to what Ludwig Wittgenstein calls "stage setting" in *Philosophical Investigations,* trans. G. E. M. Anscombe (Oxford: Blackwell, 1953), section 257.

12. For an account of the perspectival character of science that shows how scientific thinking sets up its findings in a way that satisfies a kind of realism, see Ronald M. Giere, *Scientific Perspectivism* (Chicago: University of Chicago Press, 2006).

13. See Lorraine Daston and Peter Galison, *Objectivity* (New York: Zone Books, 2000).

14. See *On the Genealogy of Morality* III.12.

15. See Hubert Dreyfus and Charles Taylor, *Retrieving Realism* (Cambridge, MA: Harvard University Press, 2015), which emphasizes direct practices that are embodied and shared to counter "mediational" theories of cognition. See also Günther Figal, "Phenomenological Realism: Programmatic Considerations," *Meta,* Special Issue (2014): 15–20.

16. See Mario De Caro, "Realism, Common Sense, and Science," *The Monist* 98, no. 2 (April 2015): 197–214.

17. William James said that truth "fits" our dealings with the world: *Essays in Pragmatism* (New York: Free Press, 1970), 288.

18. Hallucinations and illusions are evident examples that likely figure in stressing the subject-object binary because it seems right to call them subjective misapprehensions of reality. Yet ecological factors should not be excluded in how such misapprehensions arise, and they can be corrected by truth conditions suggested here without committing to a primal subject-object model. In any case, hallucinations and illusions generally pertain to perception, and in this sphere it may be that representational theories apply (following the assumption that an illusion is best rendered as "X *appears* as Y *to* Z"). Yet given the wide range of possible misperceptions (from perspectival conditions to mistaken descriptions all the way to hallucinations) it is not clear that all forms of misperceptions are necessarily a function of representation. See Charles Travis, "The Silence of the Senses," *Mind* 113 (January 2004): 57–94, and Thomas Raleigh, "Phenomenology without Representation," *European Journal of Philosophy* 23, no. 4 (December 2015): 1209–37. For a direct realist/presentational account of perception that also challenges mind-dependency theories that bank on hallucinations and illusions, see Bill Brewer, *Perceptions and Its Objects* (Oxford: Oxford University Press, 2011). See also John Searle, *Seeing Things as They Are: A Theory of Perception* (Oxford: Oxford University Press, 2015).

19. See W. C. K. Guthrie, *A History of Greek Philosophy,* Vol. 1 (Cambridge: Cambridge University Press, 1979), 420–24.

20. See G. R. F. Ferrari, "Logos," in *Classical Papers* (Department of Classics, University of California at Berkeley, 1997). Even in Aristotle's work, *logos* is used in different senses, so that we get varying translations such as reason, argument, proposition, sentence, language, speech, and utterance. Sometimes the "rationality" of *logos* is different from modern expectations. See my "*Phainomenon* and *Logos* in Aristotle's Ethics," in *Phenomenology and Virtue Ethics,* eds. Kevin Hermberg and Paul Gyllenhammer (London: Bloomsbury, 2013), 9–28.

21. The work of Jürgen Habermas is an important contribution and a significant improvement over standard models of rationality. In place of monological, subject-based reason, Habermas works out the dialogical intersubjectivity of rational practices that permeate the life-world. Communicative action and discourse, the unforced search

for mutual understanding, consensus, and action-coordination goes all the way down in everyday life. Assumptions of objectivity, agent-responsibility, and validity claims are built into communicative practice. Philosophy can supposedly reconstruct this tacit rationality and draw from it implications of universal principles and norms. Everyday validity presupposes warrants that surpass individual cases, which together with the impulse toward mutual understanding implies, for Habermas, a direction toward universal agreement, in which all uncoerced discourse partners can come to a consensus. This does not presume what universal agreement entails from an a priori standpoint because it must be an achievement of actual conversants measured by standards of ideal speech conditions, conditions that are distortion-free, coercion-free, inclusive, without time constraints or a pressing need to make decisions. See *The Theory of Communicative Action*, 2 vols., trans. Thomas McCarthy (Cambridge, MA: MIT Press, 1984, 1987) and *Moral Consciousness and Communicative Action*, trans. Christian Lenhardt and Shierry Weber Nicholson (Cambridge, MA: MIT Press, 1990). Habermas presents a brilliant analysis of what I have termed existential rationality, which he then claims presupposes a graduation to elements of modernist rationality. This last step I take to be an unwarranted leap. And ideal speech conditions, even Habermas's dialogical version, can issue exclusionary effects by underwriting a charge of intransigence against one or more parties in a sustained disagreement that may simply be an intractable conflict that no amount of time or good will could resolve.

22. See James Chase and Jack Reynolds, *Analytic versus Continental: Arguments on the Methods and Value of Philosophy* (Montreal: McGill-Queen's University Press, 2010), chap. 8. Gettier cases have played a significant role in challenging the definition of knowledge as justified true belief by way of unusual scenarios that switch or secretly alter circumstances to show that one can have a justified true belief that is not in fact knowledge. That classic definition, which fits countless cases under normal circumstances, can be called into question here only if indefeasibility is the measure and only if one takes seriously implausible anomalies that seem pertinent only from a theoretical perspective. The point of such "armchair" constructions testing the definition of knowledge is quite different from actual cases in which beliefs are duly measured or called into question by standards of truth and justification. Even if a Gettier case actually transpired, one could simply marvel at a weird exception. See Avner Baz, *When Words Are Called For: A Defense of Ordinary Language Philosophy* (Cambridge, MA: Harvard University Press, 2012), chap. 3; also Yussif Yakubu, "Truth Analysis of the Gettier Argument," *Metaphilosophy* 47, no. 3 (July 2016): 459–66.

23. In medieval philosophy, the correspondence theory was rendered as *adequatio intellectus et rei*. The word *adequatio* did have a meaning of making equal, but also a looser meaning of adapting or adjusting. Aristotle distinguished "always" propositions and "for the most part" propositions, and the latter could still function in valid syllogisms, which would fit my sense of adequation. See *Physics* 198b35 and *Posterior Analytics* 87b20–25.

24. Parts of this section are drawn from my *Ethics and Finitude: Heideggerian Contributions to Moral Philosophy* (Lanham, MD: Rowman & Littlefield, 2000), chap. 3.

25. See Sisela Bok, "The Search for a Shared Ethics," *Common Knowledge* 1, no. 3 (Winter 1992): 12–25.

26. For an important essay on everyday ethical comportment, see Hubert L. Dreyfus and Stuart E. Dreyfus, "What Is Morality? A Phenomenological Account of the Development of Ethical Expertise," in *Universalism vs. Communitarianism*, ed. David Rasmussen (Cambridge, MA: MIT Press, 1990), 237–64. Here a nuanced articulation of skill acquisition is coordinated with the development of moral maturity. Deliberation and choice emerge out of a prior sphere of "spontaneous coping," and moral develop-

ment moves from more deliberate modes to more proficient modes of intuitive skill and to a mix of both modes in complex situations.

27. See my discussion in *Myth and Philosophy: A Contest of Truths* (Chicago, IL: Open Court, 1995), 56–62.

28. Something along these lines was suggested by Aristotle in *Metaphysics* 983b20ff.

29. See Douglas Walton, *The Place of Emotion in Argument* (University Park, PA: Penn State University Press, 1992).

30. See Calvin O. Schrag, *The Resources of Rationality: A Response to the Postmodern Challenge* (Bloomington, IN: Indiana University Press, 1992), especially chap. 5.

31. For example, a revenge killing in response to a heinous murder can receive a lesser charge or even acquittal out of mercy or sympathy.

32. Even the supposedly rarefied sphere of judicial review in the Supreme Court is not without its rhetorical strategies and machinations. See Bob Woodward, *The Brethren: Inside the Supreme Court* (New York: Simon and Schuster, 1979).

33. See Douglas Walton, *The New Dialectic: Conversational Contexts of Argument* (Toronto: University of Toronto Press, 1998).

34. See, for example, Johan Van Bentham, "Natural Language and Logic of Agency," *Journal of Logic, Language, and Information* 23, no. 3 (September 2014): 367–82.

35. See Drew A. Hyland, *Finitude and Transcendence in the Platonic Dialogues* (Albany, NY: SUNY Press, 1995).

36. For a recent attempt to sort out the unity and plurality of truth in functional terms, see Michael P. Lynch, *Truth as One and Many* (Oxford: Clarendon Press, 2009).

37. My analysis can admit the notion of truth in religion, but with phenomenological and pluralistic constraints. If religion is understood as a matter of factical life, as distinct from any metaphysical claims, then within religious communities inhabitive truth conditions can apply when various facets of the lived world and dwelling are the focus of attention, especially the deepest questions of meaning in a finite existence. Yet encroachment into other settings should be restricted, especially in the face of secularized developments since the modern period. A presumption of immanence can therefore grant respect to the phenomenology of religious *life* without countenancing full-blown atheism in the manner of a reductive dismissal of religion as a superstitious fiction that any rational person should reject.

38. The Greek word *archē* could refer to both a governing principle and a starting point.

39. Something like this is expressed in Isaiah Berlin's distinction between the Fox and the Hedgehog, between inclinations toward multiplicity and unity respectively. Nietzsche is unreserved in attributing a preference for unity to a psychological weakness in the face of finite natural life.

40. With respect to natural science, Thomas Kuhn issued a now classic conception of science as changeable in its orientation. "Normal" science is the familiar work of specific investigations grounded in certain paradigms setting the stage for that work. But science also exhibits historical contraventions, in which research runs into anomalies, followed by a shift to a new paradigm that can address these contraventions. Such is the "revolutionary" phase of science. How a new paradigm comes to be accepted and the old one replaced is not a matter of scientific inference because there is a certain "break" between paradigms. Here the sociology of science comes into view in terms of how individuals and groups react to the break in existential terms. Kuhn's major work is *The Structure of Scientific Revolutions*, fourth edition (Chicago: University of Chicago Press, 2012).

41. This gambit might be comparable to property dualism, but without any commitment to a substantial base of different properties.

42. This touches the difference between perception and introspection.

43. This touches the difference between abstract ideas and physical extension.

44. See Lynn Rudder Baker, *Naturalism and the First-Person Perspective* (Oxford: Oxford University Press, 2013), chap. 5.

45. Wittgenstein offers a comparable distinction between causal explanation and phenomenological description: "Now if it is not the causal connections which we are concerned with, then the activities of the mind lie open before us." This is from *The Blue and Brown Books*, trans. G. E. M. Anscombe (New York: Harper Torchbooks, 1965), 6. After this remark, Wittgenstein also spells out the difficulties of saying that thought takes place "in the mind."

46. The case of mental disorders such as depression shows the possibility of an orchestrated pluralism when it comes to therapy. A strictly physiological orientation would tend to see drug therapy as the proper targeting of the "cause" of depression. So-called talk therapy or cognitive therapy would engage first-person perspectives of experience and meaning. There is evidence that combining these therapies can produce more successful outcomes than either one alone. See Robert J. DeRubeis et al., "Cognitive Therapy versus Medication for Depression: Treatment Outcomes and Neural Mechanisms," *Nature Reviews Neuroscience* 9, no. 10 (October 2008): 788–96; and P. Crits-Christoph et al., "Combined Medication and Cognitive Therapy for Generalized Anxiety Disorder," *Journal of Anxiety Disorders* 25 (2011): 1087–94. Neurological states could apply to both therapies with respect to causal explanation, but talk therapy would require the shift of enactive interpretation away from the third-person standpoint in order to be effective.

47. So-called expansive materialism tries to avoid eliminativism and neurological reductions by seeing the brain as a complex production of rich psychological states (like affection), which would not be prone to the mereological fallacy. Yet this theory has been contrasted with "animalism" because the brain is distinguished from the rest of the organism, which supposedly cannot produce rich psychological states. The "thinking brain" is therefore different from the living organism. But expansive materialism in this way unwittingly reiterates something that actually began with Descartes, who rejected the Aristotelian notion of the soul—which was the seat of biological life functions, not simply thinking—by identifying the soul solely with the thinking mind and not the living body. (See Reply to Objections V.6, *The Philosophical Writings of Descartes*, Vol. 2, trans. John Cottingham, Robert Stoothoff, and Dugald Murdoch [Cambridge: Cambridge University Press, 1985], 246–47.) The body then has nothing to do with thinking and is now a purely physical mechanism. Ironically it was Descartes the dualist who set up a physicalistic framework for the body. Expansive materialism is not a mind-body dualism but a brain-organism dualism stemming from an exclusive focus on the brain and the separation of thinking from visceral processes of the living body, a separation that has been challenged by enactivism. See Eric T. Olson, *What Are We? A Study in Personal Ontology* (Oxford: Oxford University Press, 2007), and Carl Gillett, "Brains, Neurons, and Animalism: On the Implications of Thinking Brains," *Southern Journal of Philosophy* 52, no. S1 (September 2014): 41–52.

48. See Paul M. Churchland, *Matter and Consciousness*, third edition (Cambridge, MA: MIT Press, 2013), and Patricia S. Churchland, *Neurophilosophy: Toward a Unified Science of the Mind-Brain* (Cambridge, MA: Bradford Books, 1989). For a collection of debates concerning their work, see Robert McCauley, ed., *The Churchlands and Their Critics* (New York: Wiley-Blackwell, 1996).

49. The Churchlands are apparently experimenting with such a project in their interpersonal conversations.

50. I thank David Godden for this point.

51. For true accuracy, would the neural terminology have to denote the specific brain data of each speaker? If not, what would the more generalized description be? Would all the texts in human history have to be translated into the new format?

52. Wittgenstein again: "it has never been our job to reduce anything to anything, or to explain anything. Philosophy really *is* 'purely descriptive'" (*Blue and Brown Books*, 18).

53. See Daniel C. Dennett, *Consciousness Explained* (Boston, MA: Little, Brown and Co., 1991), especially chaps. 13–14.

54. For a critique of fictionalist accounts of common psychological concepts, see Daniel Hutto, "Fictionalism about Folk Psychology," *The Monist* 96, no. 4 (2013), 582–604. For a rich and detailed examination of human experience that revives common conceptions of human experience and challenges both dualism and reductive naturalism, see P. M. S. Hacker, *Human Nature: The Categorial Framework* (Oxford: Blackwell, 2007).

55. Daniel Dennett acknowledges narrative structure as providing a kind of selfhood, but he still dubs this a form of fiction. See "The Origin of Selves," *Cogito* 3 (1989): 163–73.

56. A classic source for the narrative character of selfhood is the work of Paul Ricoeur. See *Time and Narrative*, trans. Kathleen McLaughlin and David Pellauer (Chicago: University of Chicago Press, 1984, 1985, 1988) and *Oneself as Another*, trans. Kathleen Blamey (Chicago: University of Chicago Press, 1992). A good summary of narrative theories is David Lumsden, "Whole Life Narratives and the Self," *Philosophy, Psychiatry, and Psychology* 20, no. 1 (March 2013): 1–10.

57. This accords with Heidegger's concept of being-toward-death.

58. Ancient Greek language is the historical setting for the shift from a pre-theoretical sense of selfhood and physical life to familiar philosophical conceptions of mind and body. In Homer, words pertaining to selfhood or the mind did not exhibit modern criteria of unity, interiority, or autonomy. Mentality was expressed by different words carrying different functions: *psuchē* as life force, *thumos* as passion and emotion, *phrenēs* as heart, and *noos* as the receptacle of thoughts and images. These functions were simply portrayed in relevant contexts without being grounded in a unified "mind." The functions also reflected an embodied sense akin to physical organs, not in the modern objective sense but the "carnal" manifestations of certain mental states—for instance, "heart" as the site of both emotion and palpitation in the breast. If there is a sense of self in Homer, it is better rendered as a focal indication of various meanings, activities, and experiences that circulate in a person's life, which is embedded in social relations and worldly performance. In this way Homeric selfhood is an early manifestation of the pre-reflective personal-social-environing-world. The notion of a unified mind distinct from the body and the environing-world took shape in Plato's account of the *psuchē*, which was no longer simply life functions but a spiritual-intellectual entity marked by unity, interiority, and autonomy (*Republic* 443cff) and separated from the body after death. In Homer, *psuchē* was simply the living functions of the body; in fact, there was no unified concept of a body either, but rather various physical operations described contextually. The word *soma*, which later designated the "body," in Homer simply referred to a corpse. See my discussion of all this in *Myth and Philosophy*, 75–83, 210–16.

Chapter Five

Transition to Volume 2

Volume 1 of my investigation advances a proto-phenomenological analysis of the lived world, followed by its application to the question of language. Philosophy since the modern period has been based in the subject-object binary, largely in deference to scientific rationality, in which nature is construed in objective, material terms and stripped of human values, purposes, and meanings. Epistemological questions have been dominant and grounded in representational relations between the mind/brain and the external world. Cognition has been examined in monological terms as transactions between an individual mind and the world and between individual minds in communication formats.

A proto-phenomenological account of the lived world begins with the "first" world of normal everyday existence prior to reflective analysis and the subject-object division. This factical perspective displays a threefold personal-social-environing-world, which is meaning-laden rather than objectified, socially structured rather than individualized, and ecologically engaged rather than separated into internal and external spheres. Ecstatic immersion is more original than reflective disengagement, but contraventions call attention to exposited distinctions that allow space for subjective and objective angles that have spawned philosophical theories. The point is not that subjective, objective, and representational notions are false but that they are derived from an original field of ecstatic involvement that should be rendered in more immediate, presentational terms. Knowledge at this more original level is better understood as practical know-how and tacit intimation, as habitual conditions of second-nature aptitude. The first world of factical experience also shows itself as embodied, temporal, historically structured, and projected, the last term indicating circumstances and cultural domains that are not initially shaped by individual beliefs and intentions. The personal-world, however, allows for deviations from cultural assignments, which can generate revision, innovation, and historical change.

Disclosure of the world is not at first an objective description or a representational relation but a presentational field constituted by active engagement, affective attunement, and tacit intimation. Language is at the core of world-disclosure, but it too must be understood originally in ecstatic, embodied, and presentational terms. Yet the differential character of language allows for expositional articulation and a temporal, exponential expansion beyond immediate occasions of experience. Language, in sum, is the constitutive power that informs both factical world-disclosure and then, derivatively, the many refined expositions of disciplinary knowledge. Proto-phenomenology, however, calls for rational disciplines to not forget or conceal their factical base. Philosophy and science, for example, can each be understood as derived from, and animated by, factical energies in the lived world.

Such critical constraint placed upon philosophy and science can have persuasive force if one follows a phenomenological pathway, as I have done in studying Heidegger for almost fifty years. As stipulated early in this investigation, first-person attention to factical experience is the initial gateway to a proto-phenomenological account (which is not a matter of introspection but an opening to the personal-social-environing-*world*). I also indicated in chapter 4 how baseline philosophical orientations are not themselves inferential but existential bearings. That is why no baseline philosophical position, including mine, can ever be a slam dunk, can ever be established by demonstrative argument. Nevertheless, in the course of my career, I have come to embrace two avenues of analysis that can strengthen a proto-phenomenological account of language and that can supply a kind of tangible *evidence* backing the philosophical case at hand. Those avenues stem from research in 1) child development and language acquisition, and 2) the history of literacy and its alteration of oral language. The application of these research fields to the case I am making is the subject of volume 2: *Language Acquisition, Orality, and Literacy*. What follows is a brief preview. I will here forgo specific reference to research in these areas until the detailed discussions in volume 2.

1. LANGUAGE ACQUISITION AND CHILD DEVELOPMENT

Childhood and child-rearing have not been given sufficient consideration in philosophy, most likely because philosophy engages in complex conceptual reflections that are not evident in a child's experience and abilities, especially in pre-verbal stages. Childhood has been largely ignored, downplayed, or retrospectively described as a nascent prelude to, or deficiency of, mature rational competence. Even when child development is addressed positively in philosophical work, the framework of analysis is usually biased in favor of reflective processes that, I submit, are not exhibited in early experience and behavior—such as a child's "concept" of this or that or "theory" about this or that. The predominance of theoretical paradigms and expositional vocabulary has produced much distortion of a child's world and its relation to adult understanding.

I believe that proto-phenomenology is uniquely qualified to help make sense of a child's experience and development. Indicative concepts drawn from pre-reflective dwelling provide an orientation that can improve upon standard theories of child development that have overemphasized exclusive conditions or scientific suppositions: for instance, cognitive development (Piaget), psychosexual development and abnormal behavior (Freud), external conditioning (Skinner), and biogenetic forces (sociobiology). There are important advances in developmental psychology, however, that accord with a proto-phenomenological approach, that have called into question many standard assumptions in the field, which amount to uncritical imposition of adult perspectives and theoretical vocabulary drawn from the subject-object divide. What is especially helpful is a turn to so-called naturalistic studies of children in their actual environments and interactions with caregivers. Such a shift stems from a recognition that traditional research protocols and testing methods have controlled for and presumed theoretical criteria about cognition, behavior, and learning that screen out complex and variegated factical elements in a child's world. Such factical circumstances in natural settings, which have been recognized and thematized in the new research, match up well with proto-phenomenological findings: ecstatic dwelling, the personal-social-environing-world, the immersion-contravention-exposition dynamic, intimation, know-how, habit, second nature, projection, temporality, embodiment, and enactive interpretation. Yet even in this new research, there often persists an uncritical deployment of representational and epistemological assumptions that proto-phenomenology can well critique—to the betterment of the research, in my view.

The same kind of complementary relationship between proto-phenomenology and developmental psychology applies to research on language acquisition, in which indicative concepts can help focus, articulate, and revise research findings concerning how language emerges in a child's world and indeed prepares that emergence long before words are first spoken. Especially relevant here are the personal-social-environing-world, ecstatic immersion and imitation, joint attention, embodied practice, habituation, projection, temporality, and differential fitness. What follows are a few selected topics that illustrate the way in which proto-phenomenology contributes to understanding child development and language acquisition.

The important role of imitation in various linguistic, social, and behavioral circumstances in a child's life can be taken as a perfect illustration of ecstatic immersion. Mimetic behavior shows that what is "outside" in the child's environment precedes a fully formed self that is "inside," so to speak. Children may need to be shown what to imitate, but not how to imitate. An intrinsic mimetic capacity in children suggests that the direction toward self-formation is first cued by ecstatic absorption in environmental prompts. Evidence for the ecstatic nature of imitation can be found in the phenomenon of "invisible imitation," in which infants will operate imitatively with parts of the body such as the face that are not visible to the infant. Piaget maintained that such a capacity requires the development of a "body schema" around the age of eight to twelve months. But there is evidence of this mimetic capacity right after birth, for instance with tongue protrusion. This early capacity suggests an immediate outward immersion that need not require some inner formed sense directed outward.

What is particularly interesting in child development is the role of motor mimicry, which is essential to an extensive range of learning experiences. Motor mimicry is a kind of "empathic" embodiment in which, for example, we spontaneously wince at other people's pain, smile at their delight, recoil at their peril, ape their movements, and so forth. Such behavior has been generally perceived as a puzzle by psychologists. Why is it done, especially when we ourselves are not undergoing the movements? It seems, though, that the role of motor mimicry in early childhood provides answers, and ecstatic immersion greatly enhances an understanding of such behaviors. Mimetic response, especially in a child's early face-to-face engagements, would seem to be a fundamentally ecstatic phenomenon. In spontaneous mimicry, we can assume, as noted above, that the "outside" comes first and is productive of the child's "internal" states. Indeed, psychologists speculate that an infant comes to learn about the self primarily through the emotional responses to them by others, a process that can then be looped back to allow vicarious learning about the experiences of others around them.

With respect to language acquisition, it is no wonder that a child's first words are such a momentous event. Is this not the threshold of the child's emergence out of twilight, so to speak? When a child learns to talk, the world starts to open up, and the child begins to develop in ways that far exceed pre-linguistic conditions. It is interesting to note that the word *infant* comes from a Latin term meaning "incapable of speech." Such incapacity, of course, is not a sheer absence but an anticipation, and *naming* infancy as speech-less shows how central linguistic capacity is to human existence.

The setting of child-rearing shows that language should not be understood simply as the employment of words, but as a symbiotic development of the child's capacities for understanding and behavior in the midst of a prompting linguistic environment. It is clear that language is a multifaceted environmental influence on children from their first moments of life. If language were simply the speaking of words, all the verbal behaviors that we naturally engage in with infants before they learn to speak would seem to be a wasted activity. But research has shown that our instincts here are appropriate and crucial for the child's full development later on (even for brain development). This suggests that infants are exposed to a pre-verbal "rehearsal" of a complex linguistic environing-world from the very start: in terms of facial expressions, touch, physical interactions, gestures, sounds, rhythms, intonations, emotional cues, and a host of behavioral contexts. It should also be noted that a melodic, lilting, high-pitched pattern of speech directed toward infants (sometimes called "motherese") seems instinctive and universal across cultures, and that such tonal patterns seem to communicate basic meanings such as praise or danger, again found across cultures. It may be that the musicality of speech—which, of course, marks the common cultural forms of poetry and song—is not a mere ornament, but rather a function of a primal sensuous register of language beginning at the earliest periods of communication and expression.

In early stages of development, caregivers are in a sense interpreting the behavior of infants for them. In more advanced stages before the advent of speech, parents are constantly engaging the child's activities by way of the above complex together with now more focused and deliberate verbal associations, especially in terms of purposive behavior. Research in child psychology demonstrates that language acquisition, including pre-verbal rehearsals, is essentially an intersubjective process that precedes and makes possible later developments of focused individuation *out of* an original social nexus. In particular, the phenomenon of pointing, which is a precursor to language development, seems unique to humans and it exhibits a triangular structure because when infants point, they look back at adults to see if they notice it too (a ubiquitous feature of child behavior called "social referencing"). Such is the pre-lexical phenomenon of joint attention, which is the somatic precondition for language learning.

Even the emergence of self-consciousness can be shown to arise out of the social field of language practice. In developmental psychology, the notion of "inner speech" or "private speech"—meaning self-directed verbalization—accounts for how language is implicated in self-consciousness. Research shows that inner speech is the most important factor in the development of self-awareness, the capacity to become the object of one's own attention, one's own thoughts and behaviors. Such a process occurs originally in children but in adults as well. Fully immersed experience is not self-conscious. A kind of exposited "distance" between the observer and the observed is required for the self-awareness *of* observation. Inner speech provides this kind of distance. Such a development is derived from the original *social* milieu of language, and so self-awareness emerges from the *reproduction* of social mechanisms by way of self-directed language. The case of Helen Keller is again instructive because she claimed that consciousness first existed for her only after she gained access to language.

Private speech in young children (talking to oneself in task performance) has often been met with concern by parents, and Piaget had taken it to be a stage of ego-centrism. But L. S. Vygotsky initiated the dismissal of this scheme by arguing that private speech is essential for the cognitive and behavioral development of the child because here the child takes over the regulative role of the social world. Language begins as collaborative tasking and conversation; private speech is a redirection of this milieu toward independent functioning. Cognitive and behavioral capacities begin in a social-linguistic network and private speech begins a process that over time leads to the *internalization* of these capacities that now can operate "silently," as it were. In sum, mature development, individuation, and self-consciousness are the result of an internalization of the social-linguistic environment mediated by self-directed speech.

With respect to language acquisition, with the host of pre-verbal linguistic rehearsals in play right after birth and throughout early stages of development, an important insight emerges: What happens *before* a child learns to speak shows that language is a complex constellation of practices and is from the beginning an active, performative, affective, embodied, purposeful environing-world that first shapes a child's sense of things. The configurations of this engaged world are further articulated when the child learns to speak and develops linguistic competence in transactions with the social environment. This kind of linguistic saturation in a child's world from the start adds decisive weight to the phenomenological priority of language advanced in this investigation.

If proto-phenomenology is a fitting orientation for understanding child development and language acquisition, those developmental scenarios in return can provide substantive grounding for the validity of proto-phenomenology as a philosophical offering. We all begin our entry into the human world and culture in a thoroughly factical environment that exhibits all the indicative concepts at work in my analysis. Maturation surely expands horizons and develops powers and cognitive skills that traditional philosophy has emphasized and assumed to be the proper locus for understanding reality. Yet proto-phenomenology aims to situate these powers and skills in a more original environment, which attention to child development can secure as the generative origin of all human possibilities. Such an unfolding is not a periodic movement that strictly speaking leaves early stages behind. What has been called a "hybrid" or "nesting" effect shows that maturity builds *from within* its beginnings, which are *retained* in a kind of organic expansion and assimilation. The tacit background of immersed facticity—presumed in this investigation to be always already in play before reflection—is the persisting inheritance of having been born into the world, in every sense of the term, from biological birth to the unfolding of world-disclosive capacities.

2. ORAL AND WRITTEN LANGUAGE

There is another way to strengthen the findings of proto-phenomenology, by considering 1) the precedence of oral language as a lived world, 2) the derivative character of written language, and 3) the essential dependence of philosophy on the technology of writing and literate skills.

Proto-phenomenology investigates the lived world as the tacit background that standard philosophical theories have missed or distorted. The most important tacit element is language, understood as dwelling in speech. Volume 2 of this investigation in effect examines the background of this tacit background in terms of two developmental and historical factors. The first is language acquisition in childhood. That milieu exhibits all the phenomenological features of the lived world and language at their inception, a genetic account that clarifies and fortifies the phenomenological priority of dwelling. The second background factor is literacy. After children acquire speech, they learn to read and write—which, I hope to show, entails a momentous transformation of language and its relation to the world. Although child development has been taken up in some philosophical discussions, the difference between spoken and written language has rarely been given any attention. Yet I believe that the surest way to understand how philosophy has concealed the lived world is to recognize that philosophy is essentially a literate phenomenon, that it would not be possible in its fullest sense without writing, and that its typical assumptions, methods, and theoretical postulates are saturated with a literate inflection, an orientation toward the written word and its transformative effect on language. The general question occupying volume 2 concerns the relation between written and oral language, which helps focus the phenomenological interrogation of philosophy on behalf of a more original environment.

The acquisition of speech and literacy is the historical background for any individual who might come to philosophize. Moreover, the history of philosophy itself reaches back to ancient Greece, where there is a comparable scenario, because I want to argue that the advent of alphabetic writing in the Greek world was a necessary condition for the development of philosophy. Therefore an examination of literacy and orality, both historically and substantively, will give more depth to the questions animating this investigation. Here I will forecast some topics that will be treated in volume 2—in particular, how the history of literacy can provide instructive angles for rethinking philosophy in phenomenological terms.

Philosophy in Greece was born as a departure from traditional forms of understanding in myth and poetry. Although never completely breaking with tradition, philosophical modes of rationality began to contest the stories of gods and heroes that shaped the early Greek world. Myth and poetry, particularly the Homeric epics, expressed in both content and form elements of the lived world that have marked the present investigation—especially in being narratives of factical circumstances. Philosophers largely turned away from poetic narratives in favor of abstract concepts that would bring more order to thinking, especially in terms of unified principles. Mythical accounts of the gods were challenged in favor of more naturalized accounts of the world. Most importantly, divine mysteries gave way to unaided procedures of human thinking that could appeal to available experience and persuade through self-directed paths of understanding. Such developments have typically been described as a movement from the deficiencies of a primitive mentality to the truth-bearing character of rational thinking. Yet such a progressive model is suspect, in part because of the priority of lived experience assumed in proto-phenomenology. If early Greek culture was in fact more expressive of the lived world, the birth of traditional philosophical formulations should at least be open to interrogation if factical experience was unduly suppressed or marginalized.

The tension between myth and philosophy came to a head in the dialogues of Plato.[1] Plato's critique of traditional poetry was fundamental because it challenged both the material and formal elements at the heart of epic narratives and tragic drama. The material element can be summed up as the depiction of a tragic worldview, wherein mortals face inescapable limits in matters of knowledge, agency, and well-being. The formal element can be located in the psychological features of poetry's composition, performance, and reception—each of which involve forces that surpass conscious control and block critical reflection. For Plato, the formal and material constitution of traditional poetry represented a powerful cultural barrier that had to be overcome to clear the way for two new ideals: rational inquiry and an overarching justice governing the world and the soul.

The formal side of Plato's critique concerned the psychological structure of poetic production, performance, and reception. The traditional view was that poets were inspired receptacles for the sacred power of the Muses, a "revelation" more than a conscious construction.

This matter of absorption in a force beyond the conscious mind was implicated in Plato's objections to *mimēsis* in the *Republic*. In Greek, *mimēsis* referred not only to representational likeness, but also to psychological identification in poetic performance and audience reception, in which actors, reciters, and listeners were "taken over" by poetic imagery and its emotional power, which in my terms can be called a form of immersion. The central problem of mimetic immersion is that critical reflection is impeded by the captivating language of poetry. Philosophical thinking therefore runs counter to the force of poetic communication.

If we focus on the purported dangers of poetic language, it can be shown that Plato's posture was caught up in the larger story of momentous shifts in the Greek world stemming from the rise of literacy and its far-reaching effects in modifying the original and persisting oral character of Greek culture. Plato's critique of poetry suggests something essential for comprehending the development of philosophy in ancient Greece: that philosophical thinking, as we understand it, would not have been possible apart from the skills and mental transformations stemming from education in reading and writing and that primary features of oral language and practice were a significant barrier to the development of philosophical rationality (and also a worthy competitor for cultural status and authority). In this scenario, we are engaging the tensional relationship between an oral/mythical culture (which is embedded in the lived world) and a literate/rational culture (which developed thought patterns abstracted from the lived world). Such is the historical background that can help illuminate a proto-phenomenological analysis of language.

Before the emergence of writing, Greek culture was thoroughly oral, with spoken poetry being the primary vehicle for cultural transmission. Alphabetic script entered the Greek world most likely in the early part of the eighth century BC. It is important to note the difference between the alphabet and other forms of script. Unlike pictographic or hieroglyphic scripts, which involve symbolic or imagistic tokens of things in the world, the alphabet is a set of letters, the combinations of which are meant only to capture the *sounds* of speech, so that the written word will simply be a visual reproduction of a spoken word. And the actual lines of alphabetic letters are arbitrary in that they only indicate, and are learned as, elements of spoken sound—as opposed to representing some object of experience. So the written word t-r-e-e as such bears no relation to an actual tree or to the meaning of the word *tree* but only to the sound of the spoken word.

Writing is not simply the transfer of spoken words to graphic signs. If it were only that, we could not account for the far greater difficulty in learning to read and write compared to natural language acquisition. There are many ways to distinguish the nature and effects of writing from language confined to oral speech. Here I sketch ten distinctions between orality and literacy, with the latter marked against a strictly oral culture, the features of which can be gleaned from considering the pre-literate Greek world. But it must be said that it is impossible for us to directly access pure orality. The very idea of "studying" an oral culture is a function of literacy, and even a mere encounter with an oral culture could not help being influenced by literacy (if only by recognizing it *as* a nonliterate culture). The effects of reading and writing are so pervasive for us that it is hard to notice them or think outside them. But it is possible to intimate (indicatively) elements of orality through ethnographic research and by imagining what language would be like without texts, dictionaries, or grammatical constructs. In any case, intimations of orality will help put the effects of literacy in sharper relief. It should be kept in mind that the features of orality considered below do show their traces in oral elements of a literate culture (which elements apply well to the phenomenological notion of dwelling in speech).

2.1. Sound and Sight

Orality pertains to the sonic character of language in both speaking and hearing. Writing converts speech into a visual object inscribed on a perceptible medium. Yet orality is still very much a visual phenomenon because face-to-face speech engages a host of embodied factors, as we have seen.

2.2. Time and Space

Orality is exclusively temporal and a continual flow of appearing and disappearing. We can keep physical things from moving by holding or confining them, but linguistic sound cannot be stopped without losing it; absent the flow of words there would either be silence or continuous noise. Orality is therefore essentially a matter of becoming and not static being. The only way to preserve or "store" language in an oral culture is through memory. Many features of oral poetry involved mnemonic devices that would help prompt impact and recall: rhythmic and sonic patterns, epithets, formulaic settings, and so on. Yet memory is always subject to the limit of forgetfulness. Writing allows the spacialization of language, converting the flow of language into a stable visual object. Even though written language proceeds temporally when read, the words remain in their fixed location. Writing is a mode of storage that no longer relies on memory, thus providing a permanence that arrests the flow of speech and supercedes the possibility of forgetting. The transmission of tradition is no longer memorial but fixed by recorded documents.

2.3. Modification and Identity

With oral poetry, each performance would involve modifications of the narrative framework due to the contingencies of memory, variations in audience reaction, and different settings encountered by traveling bards. Writing allows an identical text to persist through time.

2.4. Embodiment and Disembodiment

Orality in its face-to-face character involves embodied speech and reception, given the communicative function of tone, rhythm, volume, emphasis, gesture, and facial expression. Literacy converts language into disembodied alphabetic lines that do not "speak" to the reader in a strict sense. The difference between a written text and live speech first opened space for a distinction that for us is taken for granted: that between a text per se and its meaning. Such a notion became evident in ancient Greek theater, with a written script meant to be performed by actors before an audience. The same script could issue different enactments and receptions owing to variations in live performance and audience interpretation. Subsequently, Greek thinkers began to conceive of language in a new way, in terms of the difference between what a text "says" and what it "means," between linguistic expression and interpretation, and therefore between "words" and their (now) "mental" significance—thus allowing for the representational theory of language, in which words are now "signs" for things or mental states.

2.5. Lived Context and Decontextualization

Orality is embedded not only in face-to-face speech, but also in multiple practical and situational settings. Writing permits a decontextualization that can open up abstract generalities that are not evident or functional in lived experience. That is why certain definitional or classification procedures are absent in oral cultures. Recall my tree example in the first chapter; in an oral culture, the "meaning" of a tree would be distributed (indicatively) throughout many different settings, each understood in context rather than by way of a universal definition covering all instances. A written text also opens up space for a disengaged "reader" and thus for an interiorized mentality and discrete sense of selfhood, unlike oral cultures in which a call for self-description would receive practical, performative, and situational scenarios in response.

2.6. Enchantment and Disengagement

In part because of the "memorable" requirement in orality, poetic performance conjured the power of ecstatic immersion and emotional absorption to capture an audience for full disclosive effect. This accounts for the "artistic" elements of enchanting imagery, elevated language, and musicality essential to oral delivery and reception. Indeed, Greek poetry in performance was *sung* and not separated from musical accompaniment. Poetic enchantment was precisely the force of mimetic immersion that Plato opposed on behalf of critical reflection *on* language, which is greatly enhanced by the disengaged consideration of a written text persisting right before one's eyes, thus diminishing the need for emotional attraction and creating space for detached analysis.

2.7. Performance and Reflection

The immediacy of an oral performance, its temporal expiration, and the limits of memory block a host of reflective skills made possible by the visible stability of a written work. One can move back and forth in a text and notice inconsistencies or deviations. One can notice patterns and relationships or disparities that could be reformed through organization. Here can emerge the sense of a "whole" text organized into parts. In fact, the very notion of a formal structure distinct from content can now be drawn out of language for the first time. Then a structural framework can be abstracted and identified as such, serving as a formalized requirement for future text writing, a regimen that characterized much of the Western tradition.

2.8. Narration and Abstraction

Orality is immersed in the lived world and poetic expression offers sensuous imagery and narrative depictions of action in life. So in Homer the gods are living, acting beings and the epics deal with ideals and purposes shown in the exploits of heroes. If a story concerns "justice," it is not in terms of an abstract principle but ways of being that are exemplified by a god or hero. The alphabetic lines of a written word as such present a nonsensuous, decontextualized object that is nothing like living speech or narrative situations. Oral poetry was a main source of education in ancient Greece. The narrative specificity of poetry meant that "learning" involved the "imitation" of role models depicted in stories. So learning about courage, for example, would not involve a definition but an exemplary maxim (Be like Achilles). Literate education involved learning letters, reading, writing, and grammar. Yet the two models of education could go together, as indeed they did in the Greek classical period. Young boys were taught to read primarily in order to recite poetic texts. In this way, familial, tribal, and civic values were still taught by way of oral transmission and emulation. Socrates challenged this kind of education by looking beyond familial tradition and exemplification to find the universal Form of, say, courage, which could not be satisfied by any particular instance. And literacy allowed for such a departure when no longer tied to recitation but pursuant of the abstract potential in language made possible by writing. I will argue that it is the visual graphics of writing that permits the new focus for philosophical thinking—an accessible *presence* for an abstraction stripped of factual specificity, which can then stand as a reference point for the revision of factual experience in the light of abstraction.

2.9. Tradition and Innovation

Even though repeat poetic performance in an oral culture would issue variations, the memorial requirement put a premium on staying within familiar narrative frameworks. This is why orality tends to be traditionalistic and inhospitable to significant deviation. Literacy opens the way for innovation in a number of ways. The portability of books allows for individual engagement with a text, as opposed to the social immersion of public performance. Even though a written text is more stable than an oral performance, portability separates a text from the "authorized" position of the speaker or writer, which opens space for extended variations of interpretation (given the differential character of language), especially across long stretches of time. Ironically, then, written texts both assure the maintenance of a tradition and allow for creative departures from "origins." And writing allows more extensive and individualized possibilities of composition.

2.10. Presentational and Representational Truth

Orality is immersed in what I have called presentational truth, especially in face-to-face disclosure, action-saturated speech, and poetic performance. The Greek word for truth, *alētheia*, had a connotation of unconcealment (disclosure), which fits the oral requirement of preservation from the oblivion of forgetting, as well as the direct, unmediated element of revelation from "inspired" speech (as in oracles and poetry granted by the Muses). The freestanding character of written letters permits the notion that "words" are "labels" for things or thoughts, which is not possible in primary orality. What follows is the model of language as signification and truth as a representational relation between propositions and states of affairs. The first formal account of such notions is Aristotle's *On Interpretation* 1–5, in which he distinguishes between written and spoken "signs" of "mental states," which are "representations" of things in the world. The chain of signification is as follows: things are represented in mental states, which are then represented by spoken words, which are then represented by written words. But the very notion of "representation," it seems, would not be possible apart from the *perceived* difference of written words marked off against the lived world of orality. Aristotle goes on to talk of linguistic "propositions" as bearers of truth about the world. So when we talk of mental "representations" and "propositional attitudes," we have inherited the literate transformation of language from ecstatic speech in lived experience to self-referential linguistic entities.

Volume 2 will draw on this historical background to examine how philosophical thinking altered factical language by way of literate skills and how learning to read and write is the precondition for such alteration. Yet the derivative character of written language keeps in play a relation to oral language and points to what is covered up when the derived power is presumed to be sufficient access to the nature of language. The critical stance assumed by proto-phenomenology in the second volume, however, faces a significant difficulty. The effects of literacy are so pervasive and transformative that a direct critique is impossible. My investigation is a literate endeavor. The notion of "orality" is a literate creation, as is any "study" of orality. The initial problem cited at the start of volume 1, of how reflection can address pre-reflective experience, is magnified even further with respect to a literate investigation of oral language. Nevertheless, proto-phenomenological discipline and attention to relevant research can at least provide an indicative lens for engaging this vexing but illuminating problem.

Such a conundrum and its possible resolution imply something noteworthy. Orality is part of a proto-phenomenological project. But a purely oral world would allow none of the expositional articulation and reflection made possible by literacy. If the philosophical pathway of phenomenology succeeds to any significant degree, the result could be an account of language inhabiting the best of both worlds: 1) a sensitivity to the factical base of dwelling in oral speech, which a hyper-literate framework would miss or suppress, and 2) a comprehensive picture of language that includes and requires literate exposition, which would remain concealed in a purely oral domain. Literate philosophical analysis can both attend indicatively to dwelling in speech and open up a reflective dwelling *on* language in a rich and thoroughgoing manner, which is illuminating and fulfilling in its own right if philosophy is one's calling.

NOTE

1. Some of what follows can be found in my "Orality, Literacy, and Plato's Critique of Poetry," *Epochē* 11, no. 2 (Spring 2007): 319–32.

Bibliography

Aitchison, Jean. *The Seeds of Speech: Language Origin and Evolution.* Cambridge: Cambridge University Press, 2000.

———. *Words in Mind: An Introduction to the Mental Lexicon.* Malden, MA: Wiley-Blackwell, 2012.

Arbib, Michael A. *How the Brain Got Language: The Mirror Systems Hypothesis.* Oxford: Oxford University Press, 2013.

Arnhart, Larry. *Darwinian Natural Right: The Biological Ethics of Human Nature.* Albany, NY: SUNY Press, 1998.

Austin, J. L. *Philosophical Papers.* Oxford: Clarendon Press, 1961.

Baddeley, Alan. "Working Memory and Language: An Overview." *Journal of Communication Disorders* 36 (2003): 189–208.

Bar, Moshe. "The Proactive Brain: Memory for Predictions." *Philosophical Transactions: Biological Sciences* 364, no. 1521 (May 2009): 1235–43.

Bargh, John A. "Bypassing the Will: Toward Demystifying the Role of Nonconscious Control of Social Behavior." In *The New Unconscious,* edited by Ran R. Hassin, James S. Uleman, and John A. Bargh, chap. 2. Oxford: Oxford University Press, 2005.

Bargh, John A., and Erin L. Williams. "The Automaticity of Social Life." *Current Directions in Psychological Science* 15, no. 1 (February 2006): 1–4.

Bashour, Bana, and Hans D. Muller, eds. *Contemporary Philosophical Naturalism and Its Implications.* New York: Routledge, 2014.

Baslow, Morris H. "The Language of Neurons: An Analysis of Coding Mechanisms by Which Neurons Communicate, Learn and Store Information." *Entropy* 11, no. 4 (December 2009): 782–97.

Bates, Elizabeth et al. "Innateness and Emergentism." In *A Companion to Cognitive Science,* edited by William Bechtel and George Graham, 590–601. Oxford: Blackwell, 1998.

Baz, Avner. *When Words Are Called For: A Defense of Ordinary Language Philosophy.* Cambridge, MA: Harvard University Press, 2012.

Bengson, John, and Marc A. Moffet, eds. *Knowing How: Essays on Knowledge, Mind and Action.* Oxford: Oxford University Press, 2011.

Bennett, M. R., and P. M. S. Hacker. *Philosophical Foundations of Neuroscience.* Oxford: Blackwell, 2003.
Benson, Janette B., and Marshall H. Haith, eds. *Language, Memory, and Cognition in Infancy and Early Childhood.* New York: Academic Press, 2009.
Benzaquén, Adrianna S. *Encounters with Wild Children: Temptation and Disappointment in the Study of Human Nature.* Montreal: McGill-Queen's University Press, 2006.
Bergen, Benjamin K. *Louder Than Words: The New Science of How the Mind Makes Meaning.* New York: Basic Books, 2012.
Bok, Sisela. "The Search for a Shared Ethics." *Common Knowledge* 1, no. 3 (Winter 1992): 12–25.
Bonnvillian, John D. et al. "Observations on the Use of Manual Signs and Gestures in the Communicative Interactions between Native Americans and Spanish Explorers of North America." *Sign Language Studies* 9, no. 2 (Winter 2009): 132–65.
Boronat, Consuelo B. et al. "Distinction between Manipulation and Function Knowledge of Objects." *Cognitive Brain Research* 23 (2005): 361–73.
Bouchard, Denis. *The Nature and Origin of Language.* Oxford: Oxford University Press, 2014.
Boudry, Maarten, and Massimo Pigliucci. "The Mismeasure of Machine: Synthetic Biology and the Trouble with Engineering Metaphors." *Studies in History and Philosophy of Biological and Biomedical Sciences* 44 (2013): 660–68.
Bourdieu, Pierre. *Language and Symbolic Power.* Translated by Gino Raymond. Cambridge, MA: Harvard University Press, 1999.
Brewer, Bill. *Perceptions and Its Objects.* Oxford: Oxford University Press, 2011.
Brown, Jessica A. "Knowing How: Linguistics and Cognitive Science." *Analysis* 73, no. 2 (April 2013): 220–27.
Bruya, Brian, ed. *Effortless Attention: A New Perspective in the Cognitive Science of Attention and Action.* Cambridge, MA: MIT Press, 2010.
Cain, Mark. *Fodor: Language, Mind, and Philosophy.* New York: Polity, 2002.
Carel, Havi, and Darian Meacham, eds. *Phenomenology and Naturalism: Examining the Relationship Between Human Experience and Nature.* Cambridge: Cambridge University Press, 2013.
Carijó, Filipe Herkenhoff et al. "On Haptic and Motor Incorporation of Tools and Other Objects." *Phenomenology and the Cognitive Sciences* 12, no. 4 (December 2013): 685–701.
Carpenter, Melinda et al. "Social Cognition, Joint Attention, and Communicative Competence from 9 to 15 Months of Age." *Monographs of the Society for Research in Child Development* 255 (1998): 1–74.
Carr, David. *Experience and History: Phenomenological Perspectives on the Historical World.* Oxford: Oxford University Press, 2014.
———. *Phenomenology and the Problem of History.* Evanston, IL: Northwestern University Press, 1974.
Carruthers, Peter. "The Cognitive Function of Language." *Behavioral and Brain Sciences* 26, no. 6 (December 2002): 657–726.
———. *Language, Thought, and Consciousness: An Essay in Philosophical Psychology.* Cambridge: Cambridge University Press, 1996.
Carruthers, Peter, and Jill Boucher, eds. *Language and Thought.* Cambridge: Cambridge University Press, 1998.
Casey, Edward. *The Fate of Place: A Philosophical History.* Berkeley: University of California Press, 1998.
Cavell, Stanley. *In Quest of the Ordinary: Lines of Skepticism and Romanticism.* Chicago: University of Chicago Press, 1988.
Charlton, William. *Metaphysics and Grammar.* New York: Bloomsbury, 2014.

Chartrand, Tanya L. et al. "Beyond the Perception-Behavior Link: The Ubiquitous Utility and Motivational Moderators of Nonconscious Mimicry." In *The New Unconscious*, edited by Ran R. Hassin, James S. Uleman, and John A. Bargh, chap. 13. Oxford: Oxford University Press, 2005.

Chase, James, and Jack Reynolds. *Analytic versus Continental: Arguments on the Methods and Value of Philosophy.* Montreal: McGill-Queen's University Press, 2010.

Chernis, Anthony. *Radical Embodied Cognitive Science.* Cambridge, MA: MIT Press, 2009.

Christensen, Wayne et al. "Cognition in Skilled Action: Meshed Control and the Varieties of Skill Experience." *Mind and Language* 31, no. 1 (February 2016): 37–66.

Chun, Marvin M. et al. "A Taxonomy of External and Internal Attention." *Annual Review of Psychology* 62 (2011): 73–101.

Churchland, Paul M. *Matter and Consciousness*, third edition. Cambridge, MA: MIT Press, 2013.

Churchland, Patricia S. *Neurophilosophy: Toward a Unified Science of the Mind-Brain.* Cambridge, MA: Bradford Books, 1989.

Clark, Andy. *Supersizing the Mind: Embodiment, Action, and Cognitive Extension.* Oxford: Oxford University Press, 2011.

———. "Extended Cognition and Epistemology." *Philosophical Explorations* 15, no. 2 (June 2012): 87–90.

Clark, Herbert H. *Using Language.* Cambridge: Cambridge University Press, 1996.

Clarke, Randolph. "Skilled Activity and the Causal Theory of Action." *Philosophy and Phenomenological Research* 80, no. 3 (May 2010): 523–50.

Coates, Paul, and Sam Coleman, eds. *Phenomenal Qualities: Sense, Perception, and Consciousness.* Oxford: Oxford University Press, 2015.

Cole, Jonathan. "The Origin of Consciousness: The Background of the Debate." *Pragmatics and Cognition* 18, no. 3 (2010): 481–95.

Collins, Harry. *Tacit and Explicit Knowledge.* Chicago: University of Chicago Press, 2010.

———. "Three Dimensions of Expertise." *Phenomenology and the Cognitive Sciences* 12, no. 2 (June 2013): 253–73.

Colombetti, Giovanna. "Enactive Affectivity, Extended." *Topoi* (2015): DOI:10.1007/s11245-015-9335-2.

———. *The Feeling Body: Science Meets the Enactive Mind.* Cambridge, MA: MIT Press, 2014.

Colón, Gabriel Alejandro Torres, and Charles A. Hobbs. "The Intertwining of Culture and Nature." *Journal of the History of Ideas* 76, no. 1 (January 2015): 139–62.

Consentino, Erica. "Self in Time and Language." *Consciousness and Cognition* 20, no. 3 (2011): 777–83.

Coplan, Amy, and Peter Goldie. *Empathy: Philosophical and Psychological Perspectives.* Cambridge: Cambridge University Press, 2011.

Corbalis, Michael C. *The Recursive Mind: The Origins of Human Language, Thought, and Civilization.* Princeton, NJ: Princeton University Press, 2011.

Crease, Robert P. *The Play of Nature: Experimentation as Performance.* Bloomington, IN: Indiana University Press, 1993.

Crick, Francis. *Astonishing Hypothesis: The Scientific Search for the Soul.* New York: Scribner's, 1995.

Cristensen, Carelton B. "Meaning Things and Meaning Others." *Philosophy and Phenomenological Research* 57, no. 3 (September 1997): 495–522.

Crits-Christoph, P. et al. "Combined Medication and Cognitive Therapy for Generalized Anxiety Disorder." *Journal of Anxiety Disorders* 25 (2011): 1087–94.

Csikszentmihalyi, Mihalyi. *Flow: The Psychology of Optimal Experience.* New York: Harper Perennial, 1991.

Cuccio, Valentina, and Marco Carapezza. "Is Displacement Possible Without Language?" *Philosophical Psychology* 28, no. 3 (April 2015): 369–86.
Cuffari, Elena Clare et al. "From Participatory Sense-Making to Language: There and Back Again." *Phenomenology and the Cognitive Sciences* 14, no. 4 (December 2015): 1089–125.
Curtis, Susan. *Genie: A Psycholinguistic Study of a Modern-Day "Wild Child."* New York: Academic Press, 1977.
D'Oro, Guiseppina, and Constantine Sandis, eds. *Reasons and Causes.* New York: Palgrave Macmillan, 2013.
Damasio, Antonio. *Descartes' Error: Emotion, Reason, and the Human Brain.* New York: Penguin Books, 2005.
Daprate, Elena, and Angela Sirigu. "How We Interact with Objects: Learning from Brain Lesions." *Trends in Cognitive Sciences* 10, no. 6 (June 2006): 265–70.
Daston, Lorraine, and Peter Galison. *Objectivity.* New York: Zone Books, 2000.
Davidson, Donald. *Inquiries into Truth and Interpretation.* Oxford: Clarendon Press, 1984.
Davis, Mark H. *Empathy: A Social Psychological Approach.* Boulder, CO: Westview, 1996.
Dawkins, Richard. *The Blind Watchmaker.* New York: Norton, 1996.
———. *The Selfish Gene*, second edition. Oxford: Oxford University Press, 1989.
De Caro, Mario. "Realism, Common Sense, and Science." *The Monist* 98, no. 2 (April 2015): 197–214.
De Sousa, Ronald. *The Rationality of Emotion.* Cambridge, MA: MIT Press, 1987.
de Vignemont, Frederique, and Tania Singer. "The Empathic Brain: How, When, and Why?" *Trends in Cognitive Sciences* 10, no. 10 (2006): 435–41.
Dennett, Daniel C. *Consciousness Explained.* Boston, MA: Little, Brown and Co., 1991.
———. *Darwin's Dangerous Idea: Evolution and the Meanings of Life.* New York: Penguin Books, 1995.
———. "The Origin of Selves." *Cogito* 3 (1989): 163–73.
Derrida, Jacques. *Of Grammatology.* Translated by Gayatri Chakravorty Spivak. Baltimore, MD: Johns Hopkins University Press, 1998.
DeRubeis, Robert J. et al. "Cognitive Therapy versus Medication for Depression: Treatment Outcomes and Neural Mechanisms." *Nature Reviews Neuroscience* 9, no. 10 (October 2008): 788–96.
Descartes, René. *Meditations on First Philosophy.* In *The Philosophical Writings of Descartes*, Vol. 2, translated by John Cottingham, Robert Stoothoff, and Dugald Murdoch. Cambridge: Cambridge University Press, 1985.
Dewey, John. "Does Reality Possess Practical Character?" In *Middle Works, 1899–1924*, Vol. 5, edited by Jo Ann Boydston, 125–42. Carbondale, IL: Southern Illinois University Press, 1997.
———. *Human Nature and Conduct: An Introduction to Social Psychology.* Amherst, NY: Prometheus Books, 2002.
———. "Propositions, Warranted Assertibility, and Truth." In *Later Works, 1925–1953*, Vol. 14, edited by Jo Ann Boydston, 168–88. Carbondale, IL: Southern Illinois University Press, 1997.
Dezechache, Guillaume et al. "An Evolutionary Approach to Emotional Communication." *Journal of Pragmatics* 59 (2013): 221–33.
Dijksterhuis, Ap et al. "The Power of the Subliminal: On Subliminal Persuasion and Other Potential Applications." In *The New Unconscious*, edited by Ran R. Hassin, James S. Uleman, and John A. Bargh, chap. 4. Oxford: Oxford University Press, 2005.
Dreyfus, Hubert L. "Overcoming the Myth of the Mental." *Proceedings and Addresses of the American Philosophical Association* 79, no. 2 (November 2005): 47–65.

———. *Skillful Coping: Essays on the Phenomenology of Everyday Perception and Action*. Edited by Mark A. Wrathall. Oxford: Oxford University Press, 2014.
———. *What Computers Can't Do: A Critique of Artificial Reason*. New York: Harper and Row, 1972.
———. *What Computers Still Can't Do*. Cambridge, MA: MIT Press, 1992.
———. "Why Heideggerian AI Failed and How Fixing It Would Require Making It More Heideggerian." *Philosophical Psychology* 20 (2007): 247–68.
Dreyfus, Hubert L., and Stuart E. Dreyfus. "From Socrates to Expert Systems: The Limits of Calculative Rationality." *Technology in Society* 6, no. 3 (1984): 217–33.
———. "What Is Morality? A Phenomenological Account of the Development of Ethical Expertise." In *Universalism Vs. Communitarianism*, edited by David Rasmussen, 237–64. Cambridge, MA: MIT Press, 1990.
Dreyfus, Hubert, and Charles Taylor. *Retrieving Realism*. Cambridge, MA: Harvard University Press, 2015.
Dummett, Michael. "A Nice Derangement of Epitaphs: Comments on Davidson and Hacking." In *Truth and Interpretation: Perspectives on the Philosophy of Donald Davidson*, edited by Ernest LePore, 450–76. Oxford: Blackwell, 1989.
———. *Frege's Philosophy of Language*. London: Duckworth, 1973.
Dupré, John. *Processes of Life: Essays in the Philosophy of Biology*. Oxford: Oxford University Press, 2012.
Eisenberg, Nancy, and Janet Strayer, eds. *Empathy and Its Development*. Cambridge: Cambridge University Press, 1987.
English, Andres R. *Discontinuity in Learning: Dewey, Herbart, and Education as Transformation*. Cambridge: Cambridge University Press, 2013.
Estany, Anna, and Segio Martinez. "Scaffolding and Affordance as Integrative Concepts in the Cognitive Sciences." *Philosophical Psychology* 27, no. 1 (February 2014): 98–111.
Evans, Dylan. *Emotion: The Science of Sentiment*. Oxford: Oxford University Press, 2001.
Evans, Vyvyan. *The Language Myth: Why Language Is Not an Instinct*. Cambridge: Cambridge University Press, 2014.
Fauconnier, Gilles, and Mark Turner. *The Way We Think: Conceptual Blending and the Mind's Hidden Complexities*. New York: Basic Books, 2002.
Faulkner, Paul. *Knowledge in Trust*. Oxford: Oxford University Press, 2011.
Faye, Jan. *The Nature of Scientific Thinking: On Interpretation, Explanation, and Understanding*. New York: Palgrave, 2014.
Feest, Uljana. "Phenomenal Experiences, First-Person Methods, and the Artificiality of Experimental Data." *Philosophy of Science* 81 (December 2014): 927–39.
Ferrari, G. R. F. "Logos." In *Classical Papers*. Department of Classics, University of California at Berkeley, 1997.
Ferretti, Francesco, and Erica Cosentino. "Time, Language, and Flexibility in the Mind: The Role of Mental Time Travel in Linguistic Comprehension and Production." *Philosophical Psychology* 26, no. 1 (February 2013): 24–46.
Figal, Günther. "Phenomenological Realism: Programmatic Considerations." *Meta*, Special Issue (2014): 15–20.
Fodor, Jerry. *The Language of Thought*. Cambridge, MA: Harvard University Press, 1980.
———. *The Language of Thought Revisited*. Oxford: Oxford University Press, 2008.
Foucault, Michel. *Discipline and Punish*. Translated by Alan Sheridan. New York: Vintage Books, 1995.
Freeman, Lauren. "Toward a Phenomenology of Mood." *Southern Journal of Philosophy* 52, no. 4 (December 2014): 445–76.

Fridland, Ellen. "Knowing-How: Problems and Considerations." *European Journal of Philosophy* 23, no. 3 (September 2015): 703–24.

———. "They've Lost Control: Reflections on Skill." *Synthese* 191, no. 12 (August 2014): 2729–50.

Friedman, Michael. *Kant's Construction of Nature: A Reading of the Metaphysical Foundations of Natural Science*. Cambridge: Cambridge University Press, 2013.

Fuchsman, Ken. "Empathy and Humanity." *Journal of Psychohistory* 42, no. 3 (Winter 2015): 176–86.

Fulkerson, Matthew. *The First Sense: A Philosophical Study of Human Touch*. Cambridge, MA: MIT Press, 2014.

Gadamer, Hans Georg. *Dialogue and Dialectic: Eight Hermeneutical Studies on Plato*. Translated by P. Christopher Smith. New Haven, CT: Yale University Press, 1980.

———. *Plato's Dialectical Ethics*. Translated by Robert M. Wallace. New Haven, CT: Yale University Press, 1991.

———. *Truth and Method*. Translated by Joel Weinsheimer and Donald G. Marshall. London: Continuum, 2004.

Gallagher, Shaun. "Defining Consciousness: The Importance of Non-Reflective Self-Awareness." *Pragmatics and Cognition* 18, no. 3 (2010): 561–69.

———. "Inference or Interaction: Social Cognition Without Precursors." *Philosophical Explorations* 11, no. 3 (2008): 163–74.

———. *How the Body Shapes the Mind*. Oxford: Oxford University Press, 2005.

———. "Pragmatic Interventions into Enactive and Extended Conceptions of Cognition." *Philosophical Issues* 24, no. 1 (2014): 110–26.

———. "Social Cognition, the Chinese Room, and the Robot Replies." In *Knowing Without Thinking: Mind, Action, Cognition, and the Phenomenon of the Background*, edited by Zdravko Radman, 83–97. New York: Palgrave Macmillan, 2012.

Gallagher, Shaun, and Daniel Schmicking, eds. *Handbook of Phenomenology and Cognitive Science*. New York: Springer, 2010.

Gallagher, Shaun, and Dan Zahavi. *The Phenomenological Mind*. New York: Routledge, 2008.

Gallagher, Timothy J. "A Mead-Chomsky Comparison Reveals a Set of Key Questions on the Nature of Language and Mind." *Journal for the Theory of Social Behavior* 44, no. 2 (June 2014): 148–67.

Gallese, Vittorio. "Mirror Neurons and the Social Nature of Language." *Social Neuroscience* 8 (2008): 317–33.

Gallese, Vittorio, and George Lakoff. "The Role of the Sensorimotor System in Conceptual Knowledge." *Cognitive Neuropsychology* 21 (2005): 455–79.

Gerrans, Philip, and David Sander. "Feeling the Future: Prospects for a Theory of Implicit Prospection." *Biology and Philosophy* 29, no. 5 (September 2014): 699–710.

Gibbs, Raymond W. "A Dynamical Self-Organized View of the Context for Linguistic Performance." *International Review of Pragmatics* 5 (2013): 70–86.

Gibson, James J. "The Theory of Affordances." In *Perceiving, Acting, and Knowing: Toward an Ecological Psychology*, edited by Robert Shaw and John Bransford, 67–82. Hillsdale, NJ: Erlbaum, 1977.

Giere, Ronald M. *Scientific Perspectivism*. Chicago: University of Chicago Press, 2006.

Gill, Jerry H. "Language as Gesture: Merleau-Ponty and American Sign Language." *International Philosophical Quarterly* 50, no. 1 (March 2010): 25–37.

Gillett, Carl. "Brains, Neurons, and Animalism: On the Implications of Thinking Brains." *Southern Journal of Philosophy* 52, no. S1 (September 2014): 41–52.

Ginev, Dimitri. "Perspectives on the Hermeneutic Philosophy of Science." *Hermeneia* 12 (2012): 107–25.

———. "Two Accounts of the Hermeneutic Fore-Structure of Scientific Research." *International Studies in the Philosophy of Science* 26, no. 4 (December 2012): 423–45.

Glock, Hans Johann. "Philosophy, Thought, and Language." *Royal Institute of Philosophy Supplement* 42 (March 1997): 151–69.

Goldberg, Sanford C. *Relying on Others: An Essay in Epistemology.* Oxford: Oxford University Press, 2010.

Goldin-Meadow, Susan, and Dedre Gentner, eds. *Language in Mind.* Cambridge, MA: MIT Press, 2003.

Goldman, Alvin I. *Joint Ventures: Mindreading, Mirroring, and Embodied Cognition.* Oxford: Oxford University Press, 2013.

Goleman, Daniel. *Emotional Intelligence: Why It Can Matter More than IQ.* New York: Bantam Books, 2006.

Gong, Tao et al. "Evolutionary Linguistics: Theory of Language in an Interdisciplinary Space." *Language Sciences* 41 (January 2014): 243–53.

Gorden, Susan, ed. *Neurophenomenology and Its Applications to Psychology.* New York: Springer, 2013.

Gould, Stephen Jay. "Sociobiology and the Theory of Natural Selection." In *Sociobiology: Beyond Nature/Nurture?* Edited by G. W. Barlow and J. Silverberg, 257–69. Boulder, CO: Westview Press, 1980.

Greco, John. "Common Sense in Thomas Reid." *Canadian Journal of Philosophy* 41, no. S1 (2014): 142–55.

Gregory, Richard. *Mind in Science: A History of Explanations in Psychology and Physics.* Cambridge: Cambridge University Press, 1981.

Grethlein, Jonas. *The Greeks and Their Past: Poetry, Oratory, and History in the Fifth Century BCE.* Cambridge: Cambridge University Press, 2010.

Grice, Paul. *Studies in the Way of Words.* Cambridge, MA: Harvard University Press, 1991.

Guthrie, W. C. K. *A History of Greek Philosophy*, Vol. 1. Cambridge: Cambridge University Press, 1979.

Habermas, Jürgen. *Moral Consciousness and Communicative Action.* Translated by Christian Lenhardt and Shierry Weber Nicholson. Cambridge, MA: MIT Press, 1990.

———. *The Theory of Communicative Action.* 2 vols. Translated by Thomas McCarthy. Cambridge, MA: MIT Press, 1984, 1987.

Hacker, P. M. S. *Human Nature: The Categorial Framework.* Oxford: Blackwell, 2007.

Hackett, Edward J. et al. *The Handbook of Science and Technology Studies.* Cambridge, MA: MIT Press, 2007.

Hamilton, William, ed. *The Works of Thomas Reid*, Vol. 2. New York: Elibron Classics, 2005.

Hassin, Ran R., James S. Uleman, and John A. Bargh, eds. *The New Unconscious.* Oxford: Oxford University Press, 2005.

Hatab, Lawrence J. "Can We Drop the Subject? Heidegger, Selfhood, and the History of a Modern Word." In *Phenomenology, Existentialism, and Moral Psychology*, edited by Hans Pedersen and Megan Altman, 13–30. New York: Springer, 2015.

———. *Ethics and Finitude: Heideggerian Contributions to Moral Philosophy.* Lanham, MD: Rowman & Littlefield, 2000.

———. "From Animal to Dasein: Heidegger and Evolutionary Biology." In *Heidegger on Science*, edited by Trish Glazebrook, 93–111. New York: SUNY Press, 2012.

———. *Myth and Philosophy: A Contest of Truths.* Chicago, IL: Open Court, 1995.

———. "Orality, Literacy, and Plato's Critique of Poetry." *Epochē* 11, no. 2 (Spring 2007): 319–32.

———. "*Phainomenon* and *Logos* in Aristotle's Ethics." In *Phenomenology and Virtue Ethics*, edited by Kevin Hermberg and Paul Gyllenhammer, 9–28. London: Bloomsbury, 2013.

———. "The Point of Language in Heidegger's Thinking: A Call for the Revival of Formal Indication." *Gatherings: The Heidegger Circle Annual* 6 (2016): 1–22.

Haugeland, John. *Artificial Intelligence: The Very Idea.* Cambridge, MA: MIT Press, 1989.

Hauser, Marc D. *Wild Minds.* New York: Henry Holt and Co., 2000.

Hodges, John R., Josef Spatt, and Karalyn Patterson. "'What' and 'How': Evidence for the Dissociation of Object Knowledge and Mechanical Problem-Solving Skills in the Human Brain." *Proceedings of the National Academy of Sciences* 96 (August 1999): 9444–48.

Honneth, Axel. *The Struggle for Recognition: The Moral Grammar of Social Conflicts.* Translated by Joel Anderson. Cambridge, MA: MIT Press, 1996.

Hookway, Christopher. "Affective States and Epistemic Immediacy." *Metaphilosophy* 34, no. 1–2 (January 2003): 78–96.

Hume, David. *An Enquiry Concerning Human Understanding.* Edited by Thomas L. Beauchamp. Oxford: Oxford University Press, 1999.

———. *A Treatise of Human Nature.* Edited by David Fate Norton and Mary J. Norton. Oxford: Oxford University Press, 2000.

Husserl, Edmund. *The Crisis of European Sciences and Transcendental Phenomenology.* Translated by David Carr. Evanston, IL: Northwestern University Press, 1970.

Hutto, Daniel. "Fictionalism about Folk Psychology." *The Monist* 96, no. 4 (2013): 582–604.

Hutto, Daniel, and Erik Myin. "Neural Representations Not Needed: No More Pleas, Please." *Phenomenology and the Cognitive Sciences* 13, no. 2 (June 2014): 241–56.

———. *Radicalizing Enactivism: Basic Minds without Content.* Cambridge, MA: MIT Press, 2013.

Hyland, Drew A. *Finitude and Transcendence in the Platonic Dialogues.* Albany, NY: SUNY Press, 1995.

Inkpin, Andrew. *Disclosing the World: On the Phenomenology of Language.* Cambridge, MA: MIT Press, 2016.

James, William. *Essays in Pragmatism.* New York: Free Press, 1970.

Jennings, Carolyn Dicey. "Consciousness Without Attention." *Journal of the American Philosophical Association* 12 (July 2015): 276–95.

Johnson, Mark. "Experiencing Language: What's Missing in Linguistic Pragmatism." *European Journal of Pragmatism and American Philosophy* 6, no. 2 (2014): 14–27.

Kagan, Jerome, and Sharon Lamb, eds. *The Emergence of Morality in Young Children.* Chicago: University of Chicago Press, 1987.

Kahneman, Daniel. *Thinking Fast and Slow.* New York: Farrar, Straus and Giroux, 2011.

Kant, Immanuel. *The Critique of Pure Reason.* Translated by Werner S. Pluhar. Indianapolis, IN: Hackett, 1996.

Kauffman, Stuart. *The Origins of Order: Self-Organizations and Selections in Evolution.* Oxford: Oxford University Press, 1993.

Kekes, John. *The Nature of Philosophical Problems: Their Causes and Implications.* Oxford: Oxford University Press, 2014.

Keller, Helen. *The Story of My Life.* New York: Bantam, 1990.

———. *The World I Live In.* New York: NYRB Classics, 2004.

Kim, Jaegwon. *Philosophy of Mind*, third edition. Boulder, CO: Westview Press, 2010.

Kitcher, Philip. *Preludes to Pragmatism: Toward a Reconstruction of Philosophy.* Oxford: Oxford University Press, 2012.

———. *Science in a Democratic Society.* New York: Prometheus Books, 2011.

———. *Vaulting Ambition.* Cambridge, MA: MIT Press, 1985.
Kiverstein, Julian, and Michael Wheeler. *Heidegger and Cognitive Science.* New York: Palgrave Macmillan, 2012.
Klein, Stanley B. "The Self and Its Brain." *Social Cognition* 30, no. 4 (2012): 474–518.
Kögler, Hans Herbert, and Karsten R. Steuber, eds. *Empathy and Agency: The Problem of Understanding in the Human Sciences.* Boulder, CO: Westview, 2000.
Kuhn, Thomas. *The Structure of Scientific Revolutions*, fourth edition. Chicago: University of Chicago Press, 2012.
Küpers, Wendelin M. "Embodied Pheno-Pragma-Practice-Phenomenological and Pragmatic Perspectives on Creative 'Inter-Practice' in Organizations between Habits and Improvisation." *Phenomenology and Practice* 5, no. 1 (2011): 100–139.
La Rock, Eric. "Aristotle and Agent-Directed Neuroplasticity." *International Philosophical Quarterly* 53, no. 4 (December 2013): 385–408.
Lagerspetz, Olli. *Trust, Ethics, and Human Reason.* New York: Bloomsbury, 2015.
Lakoff, George, and Mark Johnson. *Metaphors We Live By.* Chicago: University of Chicago Press, 1980.
———. *Philosophy in the Flesh.* New York: Basic Books, 1999.
Lalumera, Elisabetta. "Whorfian Effects in Color Perception: Deep or Shallow?" *The Baltic International Yearbook of Cognition, Logic, and Communication* 9 (December 2014): 1–13.
Larkin, Michael et al. "Interpretive Phenomenological Analysis and Embodied, Active, Situated Cognition." *Theory and Psychology* 21, no. 3 (2011): 318–37.
Laugier, Sandra. *Why We Need Ordinary Language Philosophy.* Translated by Daniela Ginsburg. Chicago: University of Chicago Press, 2013.
Laure-Ryan, Marie. *Narrative as Virtual Reality: Immersion and Interactivity in Literature and Electronic Media.* Baltimore, MD: Johns Hopkins University Press, 2003.
Lavelle, Jane Suilin. "Theory-Theory and the Direct Perception of Mental States." *Review of Philosophy and Psychology* 3, no. 2 (2012): 213–30.
Leder, Drew. *The Absent Body.* Chicago: University of Chicago Press, 1990.
Lennenberg, Eric H. *Biological Foundations of Language.* New York: Wiley, 1967.
Lennox, James G. "Teleology." In *Keywords in Evolutionary Biology*, edited by Evelyn Fox Keller and Elizabeth A. Lloyd, 324–33. Cambridge, MA: Harvard University Press, 1992.
Levine, Timothy R. "Truth-Default Theory: A Theory of Human Deception and Deception Detection." *Journal of Language and Social Psychology* 33, no. 4 (September 2014): 378–92.
Levinson, Stephen C. *Presumptive Meanings: The Theory of Generalized Conversational Implicature.* Cambridge, MA: MIT Press, 2000.
Locke, John. *An Essay in Human Understanding.* Edited by Peter Nidditch. Oxford: Oxford University Press, 1975.
Low, Douglas. "Merleau-Ponty on Causality." *Human Studies* 38, no. 3 (September 2015): 349–67.
Lum, Jarrad A. G. et al. "Procedural and Declarative Memory in Children with and without Specific Language Impairment." *International Journal of Language and Communication Disorders* 45, no. 1 (2010): 96–107.
Lumsden, David. "Whole Life Narratives and the Self." *Philosophy, Psychiatry, and Psychology* 20, no. 1 (March 2013): 1–10.
Luna, Laureano. "Indefinite Extensibility in Natural Language." *The Monist* 96, no. 2 (2013): 295–308.
Lynch, Michael P. *Truth as One and Many.* Oxford: Clarendon Press, 2009.
MacNeilage, Peter F. *The Origin of Speech.* Oxford: Oxford University Press, 2008.
Malafouris, Lambros. *How Things Shape the Mind: A Theory of Material Engagement.* Cambridge, MA: MIT Press, 2013.

Malt, Barbara C., and Phillip Wolff, eds. *Words and Mind: How Words Capture Human Experience*. Oxford: Oxford University Press, 2010.

Maoz, Uri et al. "On Reporting the Onset of the Intention to Move." In *Surrounding Free Will: Philosophy, Psychology, Neuroscience*, edited by Alfred R. Mele, chap. 10. Oxford: Oxford University Press, 2015.

McCauley, Robert, ed. *The Churchlands and Their Critics*. New York: Wiley-Blackwell, 1996.

McCrone, John. *The Myth of Irrationality: The Science of Mind from Plato to Star Trek*. New York: Carroll and Graf, 1994.

McDermott, J. J., ed. *The Philosophy of John Dewey*. Chicago: University of Chicago Press, 1981.

McDowell, John. *Mind and World*. Cambridge, MA: Harvard University Press, 1994.

McGuirk, James. "Phenomenological Considerations of Habit: Reason, Knowing, and Self-Presence in Habitual Action." *Phenomenology and Mind* 6 (2014): 112–21.

McLaughlin, Brian P., and Jonathan Cohen, eds. *Contemporary Debates in Philosophy of Mind*. Malden, MA: Blackwell, 2007.

McMyler, Benjamin. *Testimony, Trust, and Authority*. Oxford: Oxford University Press, 2011.

McNeill, David. *Gesture and Thought*. Chicago: University of Chicago Press, 2005.

McNeill, William E. S. "On Seeing That Someone Is Angry." *European Journal of Philosophy* 20, no. 4 (2012): 575–97.

Mead, George Herbert. "A Behaviorist Account of the Significant Symbol." *Journal of Philosophy* 19 (1922): 157–63.

Medina, José. *Language: Key Concepts in Philosophy*. New York: Continuum, 2005.

———. "On Being 'Other-Minded': Wittgenstein, Davidson, and Logical Aliens." *International Philosophical Quarterly* 43, no. 4 (2003): 463–75.

Meltzoff, Andrew, and Rebecca Williamson. "Imitation: Social, Cognitive, and Theoretical Perspectives." In *Oxford Handbook of Developmental Psychology*, Vol. 1, edited by P. R. Zelazo, 651–82. Oxford: Oxford University Press, 2013.

Merleau-Ponty, Maurice. *Consciousness and the Acquisition of Language*. Translated by Hugh J. Silverman. Evanston, IL: Northwestern University Press, 1973.

———. *Phenomenology of Perception*. Translated by Colin Smith. Atlantic Highlands, NJ: Humanities Press, 1962.

———. *The Primacy of Perception*. Edited by James Edie. Evanston, IL: Northwestern University Press, 1964.

———. *The Visible and the Invisible*. Translated by Alphonso Lingus. Evanston, IL: Northwestern University Press, 1968.

Mervis, Carolyn B., and Angela M. Becerra. "Language and Communicative Development in Williams Syndrome." *Mental Retardation and Development Disabilities Research Review* 13 (2007): 3–15.

Miller, John William. *The Midworld of Symbols and Functioning Objects*. New York: W. W. Norton, 1982.

Moreno, Alvaro, and Matteo Mossio. *Biological Autonomy: A Philosophical and Theoretical Inquiry*. Dordrecht: Springer, 2015.

Mueller, Erik T. *Commonsense Reasoning*. San Francisco, CA: Morgan Kaufmann Publishing, 2006.

Nagel, Thomas. *Mind and Cosmos: Why the Materialist and Neo-Darwinian Conception of Nature Is Almost Certainly False*. Oxford: Oxford University Press, 2012.

Natsoulas, Thomas. *Consciousness and Perceptual Experience: An Ecological and Phenomenological Approach*. Cambridge: Cambridge University Press, 2013.

Neal, David T., Wendy Wood, and Jeffrey M. Quinn. "Habits—A Repeat Performance." *Current Directions in Psychological Science* 15, no. 4 (August 2006): 198–202.

Nelson, Katherine. *Young Minds in Social Worlds: Experience, Meaning, and Memory.* Cambridge, MA: Harvard University Press, 2007.

Newell, Ben R., and David R. Shanks. "Unconscious Influences in Decision Making: A Critical Review." *Behavioral and Brain Sciences* 37 (2014): 1–61.

Niemeier, Susanne, and René Driven. *Evidence for Linguistic Relativism.* Amsterdam: John Benjamins Co., 2000.

Noë, Alva. *Action in Perception.* Cambridge, MA: MIT Press, 2004.

Nussbaum, Martha. *Upheavals of Thought: The Intelligence of Emotions.* Cambridge: Cambridge University Press, 2001.

O'Canaill, Donnchadh. "The Space of Motivations." *International Journal of Philosophical Studies* 22, no. 3 (2014): 440–55.

Okrent, Mark. *Heidegger's Pragmatism: Understanding, Being, and the Critique of Metaphysics.* Ithaca, NY: Cornell University Press, 1988.

Olson, Eric T. *What Are We? A Study in Personal Ontology.* Oxford: Oxford University Press, 2007.

Orr, H. Allen. "Dennett's Strange Idea." *Boston Review* 21, no. 3 (1996): 28–32.

Ott, Walter. "Phenomenal Intentionality and the Problem of Representation." *Journal of the American Philosophical Association* 2, no. 1 (March 2016): 131–45.

Papineau, David. "In the Zone." *Royal Institute of Philosophy Supplement* 73 (October 2013): 175–96.

Pence, Charles H., and Grant Ramsey. "Is Organismic Fitness at the Basis of Evolutionary Theory?" *Philosophy of Science* 82, no. 5 (December 2015): 1081–91.

Polanyi, Michael. *The Tacit Dimension.* London: Routledge and Kegan Paul, 1966.

Preston, John, and Mark Bishop, eds. *Views into the Chinese Room: New Essays on Searle and Artificial Intelligence.* Oxford: Oxford University Press, 2002.

Price, Huw. *Expressivism, Pragmatism, and Representationalism.* Cambridge: Cambridge University Press, 2013.

Radman, Zdravko, ed. *The Hand: An Organ of the Mind, What the Manual Tells the Mental.* Cambridge, MA: MIT Press, 2013.

Raleigh, Thomas. "Phenomenology without Representation." *European Journal of Philosophy* 23, no. 4 (December 2015): 1209–37.

Ramsey, William M. *Representation Reconsidered.* Cambridge: Cambridge University Press, 2007.

Repetto, Claudia et al., "The Link between Action and Language: Recent Findings and Future Perspectives." *Biolinguistics* 6, no. 3–4 (2012): 462–74.

Ricoeur, Paul. *Memory, History, and Forgetting.* Translated by Kathleen Blamey and David Pellauer. Chicago: University of Chicago Press, 2004.

———. *Oneself as Another.* Translated by Kathleen Blamey. Chicago: University of Chicago Press, 1992.

———. *Time and Narrative.* 3 vols. Translated by Kathleen Blamey and David Pellauer. Chicago: University of Chicago Press, 1984, 1985, 1988.

Rigoni, Davide, and Marcel Brass. "From Intentions to Neurons: Social and Neural Consequences of Disbelieving in Free Will." *Topoi* 33, no. 1 (April 2014): 5–12.

Rizzolatti, Giacomo, and Laila Craighero. "The Mirror-Neuron System." *Annual Review of Neuroscience* 27 (2004): 168–92.

Rizzolatti, Giacomo, and Corrado Sinigaglia. *Mirrors in the Brain: How Our Minds Share Actions and Emotions.* Oxford: Oxford University Press, 2006.

Robinson, John M., ed. *The Philosophical Works of Francis Bacon.* Translated by Robert L. Ellis and James Spedding. London: Routledge, 1905.

Roochnik, David. *Retrieving Aristotle in an Age of Crisis.* Albany, NY: SUNY Press, 2013.

Rorty, Richard M., ed. *The Linguistic Turn: Essays in Philosophical Methodology.* Chicago: University of Chicago Press, 1992.

Rosenberg, Alexander. "Disenchanted Naturalism." In *Contemporary Philosophical Naturalism and Its Implications*, edited by Bana Bashour and Hans D. Muller, chap. 19. New York: Routledge, 2014.

Rotchie, Jack. *Understanding Naturalism*. Durham, England: Acumen, 2009.

Rouse, Joseph. *Articulating the World: Conceptual Understanding and the Scientific Image*. Chicago: University of Chicago Press, 2015.

———. *Engaging Science: How to Understand Its Practices Philosophically*. Ithaca, NY: Cornell University Press, 1996.

Rowlands, Mark. *The New Science of the Mind: From Extended Mind to Embodied Phenomenology*. Cambridge, MA: MIT Press, 2010.

Roy, Jean-Michael. "Anti-Cartesianism and Anti-Brentanism: The Problem of Anti-Representationalist Intentionalism." *Southern Journal of Philosophy* 53, Spindel Supplement (2015): 90–125.

Rudder Baker, Lynn. *Naturalism and the First-Person Perspective*. Oxford: Oxford University Press, 2013.

Rutter, Michael. *Genes and Behavior: Nature-Nurture Interplay Explained*. Malden, MA: Blackwell, 2006.

Ryle, Gilbert. *The Concept of Mind*. Introduction by Daniel C. Dennett. Chicago: University of Chicago Press, 2000.

Sacks, Harvey. *Lectures on Conversation*. Oxford: Blackwell, 1992.

Sacks, Oliver. *Seeing Voices: A Journey into the World of the Deaf*. Berkeley: University of California Press, 1989.

Sandel, Adam Adatto. *The Place of Prejudice: A Case for Reasoning within the World*. Cambridge, MA: Harvard University Press, 2014.

Satel, Sally, and Scott Lilienfield. *Brainwashed: The Seductive Appeal of Mindless Neuroscience*. New York: Basic Books, 2013.

Sauer, Hanno. "Educated Intuitions: Automaticity and Rationality in Moral Judgement." *Philosophical Explorations* 15, no. 3 (September 2012): 255–75.

Schatzki, Theodore. "Temporality and the Causal Approach to Human Activity." In *Heidegger and Cognitive Science*, edited by Julian Kiverstein and Michael Wheeler, 343–64. New York: Palgrave Macmillan, 2012.

Schrag, Calvin O. *The Resources of Rationality: A Response to the Postmodern Challenge*. Bloomington, IN: Indiana University Press, 1992.

Searle, John. *The Construction of Social Reality*. New York: Free Press, 1997.

———. *Intentionality*. Cambridge: Cambridge University Press, 1983.

———. *Seeing Things as They Are: A Theory of Perception*. Oxford: Oxford University Press, 2015.

Seemann, Axel, ed. *Joint Attention: New Developments in Psychology, Philosophy of Mind, and Social Neuroscience*. Cambridge, MA: MIT Press, 2011.

Sellars, Wilfrid. *The Space of Reasons*. Cambridge, MA: Harvard University Press, 2007.

Semin, Gün R., and Eliot R. Smith. "Socially Situated Cognition in Perspective." *Social Cognition* 31, no. 2 (2013): 125–46.

Shear, Joseph K., ed. *Mind, Reason, and Being-in-the-World: The McDowell-Dreyfus Debate*. New York: Routledge, 2013.

Sheets-Johnstone, Maxine. "Embodiment on Trial: A Phenomenological Investigation." *Continental Philosophy Review* 48, no. 1 (March 2015): 23–39.

———. "From Movement to Dance." *Phenomenology and the Cognitive Sciences* 11, no. 1 (March 2012): 39–57.

Simpson, Thomas W. "What Is Trust?" *Pacific Philosophical Quarterly* 93 (2012): 550–69.

Slote, Michael. *From Enlightenment to Receptivity: Rethinking Our Values*. Oxford: Oxford University Press, 2013.

Sokolov, Alexander N. *Inner Speech and Thought.* Translated by George T. Onischenko. New York: Plenum, 1972.
Sorrell, Kory. "Our Better Angels: Empathy, Sympathetic Reason, and Pragmatic Moral Progress." *The Pluralist* 9, no. 1 (Spring 2014): 66–86.
Sparrow, Tom, and Adam Hutchinson. *A History of Habit: From Aristotle to Bourdieu.* Lanham, MD: Lexington Books, 2014.
Sprevak, Mark. "Fictionalism about Neural Representations." *The Monist* 96, no. 4 (2013): 539–60.
Stanley, Jason. *Know How.* Oxford: Oxford University Press, 2011.
Stanley, Jason, and John M. Krakhauer. "Motor Skill Depends on Knowledge of Facts." *Frontiers in Human Neuroscience* 7 (August 2013): 1–11.
Steiner, Pierre. "The Bounds of Representation: A Non-Representationalist Use of the Resources of the Model of Extended Cognition." *Pragmatics and Cognition* 18, no. 2 (2010): 235–72.
Stern, Daniel N. *The First Relationship: Infant and Mother.* Cambridge, MA: Harvard University Press, 2004.
Stevenson, Leslie. "Who's Afraid of Determinism?" *Philosophy* 89, no. 3 (July 2014): 431–50.
Tabery, James. *Beyond Versus: The Struggle to Understand the Interaction of Nature and Nurture.* Cambridge, MA: MIT Press, 2014.
Talero, Maria. "Merleau-Ponty and the Bodily Subject of Learning." *International Philosophical Quarterly* 46, no. 2 (June 2006): 191–203.
Tallis, Raymond. *Aping Mankind: Neuromania, Darwinitis and the Misrepresentation of Humanity.* Durham, England: Acumen, 2011.
Taylor, Charles. *The Language Animal: The Full Shape of the Human Linguistic Capacity.* Cambridge, MA: Belknap Press of Harvard University Press, 2016.
———. *Philosophical Arguments.* Cambridge, MA: Harvard University Press, 1995.
———. *Sources of the Self: The Making of Modern Identity.* Cambridge, MA: Harvard University Press, 1989.
Thagard, Paul. "The Passionate Scientist: Emotion in Scientific Cognition." In *The Cognitive Basis of Science*, edited by Paul Carruthers, et al., 235–50. Cambridge: Cambridge University Press, 2002.
Tomasello, Michael. *A Natural History of Human Thinking.* Cambridge, MA: Harvard University Press, 2014.
———. *The Cultural Origins of Human Cognition.* Cambridge, MA: Harvard University Press, 2000.
———. *Origins of Human Communication.* Cambridge, MA: MIT Press, 2008.
Travis, Charles. "The Silence of the Senses." *Mind* 113 (January 2004): 57–94.
Turner, J. Scott. *The Extended Organism.* Cambridge, MA: Harvard University Press, 2000.
Uher, Jana. "What Is Behavior? And When Is Language Behavior?" *Journal for the Theory of Social Behavior* (February 2016): DOI:10.1111/jtsb.12104.
Van Bentham, Johan. "Natural Language and Logic of Agency." *Journal of Logic, Language, and Information* 23, no. 3 (September 2014): 367–82.
van der Zande, Patrick et al. "Hearing Words Helps Seeing Words: A Cross-Modal Word Repetition Effect." *Speech Communication* 59 (2014): 31–43.
Varela, Francisco. "Neuro-Phenomenology: A Methodological Remedy for the Hard Problem." *Journal of Consciousness Studies* 3, no. 4 (1996): 330–49.
Varela, Francisco et al. *The Embodied Mind: Cognitive Science and Human Experience.* Cambridge, MA: MIT Press, 1991.
Vygotsky, Lev. *Thought and Language.* Translated by Alex Kozulin. Cambridge, MA: MIT Press, 1986.

Wagner, Petra et al. "Gesture, Brain, and Language." *Brain and Language* 101 (2007): 181–84.
Wallis, Charles. "Consciousness, Context, and Know-How." *Synthese* 160 (January 2008): 123–53.
Walton, Douglas. *The New Dialectic: Conversational Contexts of Argument.* Toronto: University of Toronto Press, 1998.
———. *The Place of Emotion in Argument.* University Park, PA: Penn State University Press, 1992.
Weinberg, Steven. *The First Three Minutes: A Modern View of the Origin of the Universe.* New York: Basic Books, 1993.
Wheeler, Michael. "Cognition in Context: Phenomenology, Situated Robots, and the Frame Problem." *International Journal of Philosophical Studies* 16, no. 3 (2008): 323–49.
Wiggins, David. "Practical Knowledge: Knowing How To and Knowing That." *Mind* 121 (January 2012): 97–130.
Willems, Roel M., and Peter Hagoort. "Neural Evidence for the Interplay Between Language, Gesture, and Action: A Review." *Brain and Language* 101 (2007): 278–89.
Wilson, E. O. *Consilience: The Unity of Knowledge.* New York: Random House, 1999.
———. *Sociobiology: The New Synthesis.* Cambridge, MA: Harvard University Press, 1975.
Wilson, Margaret. "The Case for Sensorimotor Coding in Working Memory." *Psychonomic Bulletin and Review* 9 (2001): 49–57.
Windsor, Jennifer et al. "Language Acquisition with Limited Input: Romanian Institution and Foster Care." *Journal of Speech, Language, and Hearing Research* 50, no. 5 (October 2007): 1365–86.
Wittgenstein, Ludwig. *The Blue and Brown Books.* Translated by G. E. M. Anscombe. New York: Harper Torchbooks, 1965.
———. *Philosophical Investigations.* Translated by G. E. M. Anscombe. Oxford: Blackwell, 1953.
Woodward, Bob. *The Brethren: Inside the Supreme Court.* New York: Simon and Schuster, 1979.
Wrathall, Mark, and Jeff Malpas, eds. *Heidegger, Coping, and Cognitive Science.* Cambridge, MA: MIT Press, 2000.
Yakubu, Yussif. "Truth Analysis of the Gettier Argument." *Metaphilosophy* 47, no. 3 (July 2016): 459–66.
Yousef, Nancy. "Savage or Solitary: The Wild Child and Rousseau's Man of Nature." *Journal of the History of Ideas* 62, no. 2 (April 2001): 245–63.
Zahavi, Dan. "Empathy and Direct Social Perception: A Phenomenological Proposal." *Review of Philosophy and Psychology* 2, no. 3 (2011): 541–58.
———. *Husserl's Phenomenology.* Stanford, CA: Stanford University Press, 2003.
———. *Self and Other: Exploring Subjectivity, Empathy, and Shame.* Oxford: Oxford University Press, 2014.
———. "Subjectivity and the First-Person Perspective." *Southern Journal of Philosophy* 45, Spindel Supplement (2007): 66–84.
Zahidi, Karim. "Non-Representationalist Cognitive Science and Realism." *Phenomenology and the Cognitive Sciences* 13, no. 3 (September 2014): 461–75.

Index

affect (feeling, emotion mood), 73–75
affordance, 23, 53, 65n10
Aitchison, Jean, 175n34, 180n128, 181n130
alētheia, 216n10
alphabet, 232–233
American Sign Language, 133–134
animals, 148–149, 155, 162–163, 166–168
appearance, 216n5
Arbib, Michael A., 181n133
archē, 219n38
Aristotle, 17n7–17n8, 68n51, 99, 100, 103, 165, 174n22, 176n49, 177n70, 179n105, 217n20, 218n23, 219n28
Arnhart, Larry, 180n115
artificial intelligence, 98–102; and language, 159–161; vs. natural intelligence, 102
atomism, 82
Austin, J. L., 144, 146, 177n62
authenticity, 51
automaticity, 37, 39–40

Bacon, Francis, 13
Badderly, Alan, 174n19
Baker, Lynn Rudder, 65n8, 220n44
Bar, Moshe, 70n86

Bargh, John A., 68n44
Baslow, Morris H., 112n39
Baz, Avner, 176n57, 218n22
being, 27, 53, 70n83
Benzaquén, Adriana S., 178n97
Bergen, Benjamin K., 112n47
Berlin, Isaiah, 219n39
binary thinking, 106–107
bi-directionality of immersion and exposition, 30, 33, 121
bio-intelligence, 99, 100, 161
biology, 99, 102, 162–164, 166–168
Bok, Sisela, 218n25
Bouchard, Denis, 175n40
Bourdieu, Pierre, 175n47
brain in a vat, 65n6, 112n44
Brewer, Bill, 217n18
Brown, Jessica A., 68n40

Cain, Mark, 177n69
capaciousness, 24, 36, 149
Carr, David, 71n91, 111n32
Carruthers, Peter, 177n74–177n75, 179n102
Casey, Edward, 71n98
causal explanation, 84; limits of, 87–88; vs. phenomenological description, 84–87, 91–92, 210

Cavell, Stanley, 144, 176n56
Charleton, William, 173n17
Chernis, Anthony, 112n40
child development, 6–7, 46, 225–229; and language acquisition, 226–229
Chinese room thought experiment, 159; and proto-phenomenology, 160–161
Chomsky, Noam, 176n52
Churchland, Patricia, 210–211, 220n48–220n49
Churchland, Paul, 210–211, 220n48–220n49
circumspection, 24
Clark, Andy, 67n33, 174n18, 174n27, 175n32
Clark, Herbert H., 173n11, 174n25
Clarke, Randolph, 110n18
cognitive science, 90–98; 4E model, 112n40; and embodied cognition, 96–98; and enactivism, 95–96
Cole, Jonathan, 66n27
Collins, Harry, 66n20, 68n53
Colombetti, Giovanna, 112n43, 113n57
common sense, 9, 101–102
concepts, 15, 97; abstract vs. factical, 63–64; proto-, 15
consciousness, 31–32, 213–214
Consentino, Erica, 174n20
contextualism, 80–81, 191, 203–204
contravention, 25–26, 27–28; and philosophy, 106–107
Corbalis, Michael C., 175n45, 181n136
correlational scope, 77
Crease, Robert P., 110n13
creativity, 60–61
Crick, Francis, 110n16
Cristensen, Carelton B., 173n9
Csikzentmihalyi, Mihalyi, 65n14
culture: exceeding nature, 166–168; and nature, 141–143, 162–168
Curtis, Susan, 179n98

Damasio, Antonio, 109n5
Darwin, Charles, 162
Davidson, Donald, 83, 176n53, 177n68

Davis, Mark H., 70n70–70n71
Dawkins, Richard, 165, 180n114, 180n118
De Caro, Mario, 217n16
De Sousa, Ronald, 109n7
Dennett, Daniel, 102, 114n69, 162, 163, 165, 166, 179n107, 180n115, 180n119–180n123, 180n126–180n127, 221n53, 221n55
depression, 220n46
Derrida, Jacques, 175n38
Descartes, René, 11–12, 20–21, 31, 99, 220n47; and modern science, 11–12
design, 102
determinism, 88–89
Dewey, John, 33, 66n15, 66n18
differential fitness, 136–141, 169–170; and cognitive functions, 137–139
disclosure, 3, 73, 216n10; and language, 126–127
Dreyfus, Hubert L., 36, 65n14, 66n21, 67n37, 113n64, 113n67, 156–157, 217n15, 218n26
dualism, 207–213
Dummett, Michael, 110n15, 173n16
Dupré, John, 2n14 3n110
dwelling, 2–3, 14, 22, 163; field-character of, 2, 34, 44; in speech, 5, 121–122, 148; and meaning, 42–43

ecological structure, 23–24, 65n10, 100–101, 131–132
ecstatic experience, 19, 44–45, 97; and empathy, 48–49; and touch, 62
embodied jointure, 160–161
embodiment, 61–62; and cognition, 96–98; and ecstatic immersion, 97; and language, 125, 132–135, 160–161, 234; metaphors from, 96
empathy, 47–49, 93, 94; and ethics, 49; and immersion, 48–49
empiricism, 18n16
environing-world, 23–44; and meaning, 42–43
English, Andrea R., 66n17

essentialism and anti-essentialism, 140–141
ethics, 195–199; as interpretation, 197; and interrogation, 199; and truth, 197–199
Evans, Dylan, 109n6
Evans, Vyvyan, 178n84
evolution, 102, 162–172; and language, 168–172
expansive materialism, 220n47
exposition, 24–29; degrees of, 27; everyday, 28–29; of language, 130–131; scientific, 28–29; scope and importance of, 78–79. *See also* bi-directionality
extended cognition, 35
externalism-internalism debate, 32

fact-value distinction, 42, 69n59, 172
factical life, 8, 92
Faulkner, Paul, 216n4
Faye, Jan, 69n57
Feest, Uljana, 113n59
feral children, 157–158
Ferrari, G. R. F., 217n20
fiction, 139
Figal, Günther, 217n15
finitude, 25, 43, 53, 61–62
first-person standpoint, 14, 23, 46–47, 65n8, 84, 98, 214; bypassed in research, 74, 97–98
Fodor, Jerry, 148, 177n67
Foucault, Michel, 71n92
freedom, 88–90, 107; contextual and situated, 89–90
Freeman, Lauren, 109n2
Frege, Gottlob, 173n16, 177n66
Freud, Sigmund, 225
Fridland, Ellen, 68n41, 69n55
Freedman, Michael, 17n11
Fuchsman, Ken, 70n74
Fulkerson, Matthew, 71n96
functionalism, 113n65

Gadamer, Hans Georg, 71n94, 109n11, 114n76, 175n46
Gallagher, Shaun, 65n8, 66n24, 111n26, 111n30, 112n36, 112n40, 112n43, 179n106
Gallagher, Timothy J., 176n52
Gallese, Vittorio, 173n14
Gentner, Dedre, 175n43
gesture, 132–134; and the evolution of language, 171
Gettier cases, 218n22
Gibbs Jr., Raymond W., 176n61
Gibson, James J., 65n10
Giere, Ronald M., 217n12
Gill, Jerry H., 175n31
Gillett, Carl, 220n47
Ginev, Dimitri, 69n57, 110n13
Glock, Hans Johann, 177n63
Godden, David, 220n50
Goldberg, Sanford C., 69n63
Goldin-Meadow, Susan, 174n30
Goldman, Alvin I., 111n35
Goleman, Daniel, 109n4
Gómez, Juan-Carlos, 178n93
Gordon, Peter, 177n80
Gould, Stephen Jay, 180n124
grammar, 173n17
Greco, John, 17n12
Gregory, Richard, 180n111
Grethlein, Jonas, 71n93
Grice, Paul, 173n8
Guthrie, W. C. K., 217n19

Habermas, Jürgen, 217n21
habit, 30–31, 39–40
Hacker, P. M. S., 221n54
hallucination, 217n18
Haugeland, John, 113n64
Hauser, Marc D., 180n111
Hegel, G. W. F., 46, 106
Heidegger, Martin, xi–xiii, 170
history, 58–59, 60–61; and language, 129; and philosophy, 104–106
Honneth, Axel, 69n67
Hookway, Christopher, 109n7

Hume, David, 21, 35
Husserl, Edmund, 4, 90–91, 92, 111n32, 177n66
Hutto, Daniel, 112n40–112n41, 179n106, 221n54
Hyland, Drew A., 219n35

imitation, 38, 97, 226–227; and motor mimicry, 226–227
immanence: circularity of, 9, 80, 121; presumption of, 9–11, 105–106, 206
immersion, 19, 24–27, 29–31, 33–34, 168; and conscious direction, 40–41; degrees of, 27; and reflection, 29–30, 78–79; and social relations, 44–46, 94; when problematic, 78–79, 107. *See also* bi-directionality
improvisation, 59–60
indicative concepts, 14–17, 79, 94
individualism, 44–46
individuation, 46; and socialization, 50–51, 126
Inkpin, Andrew, 17n4
intellectualism and anti-intellectualism debate, 36–38
interpretation, 79–83, 102–103, 109n12, 167, 197, 207; enactive, 82–83, 90, 101–102, 131–132, 192; not theoretical, 83; and pluralism, 80–82; settings for, 187
intimation, 75–78; and as-indicators, 76–77; and correlational scope, 77; and knowledge by acquaintance, 77
introspection, 46–47, 124
intonation, 134–135

James, William, 217n17
Jennings, Carolyn Dicey, 66n25
Johnson, Mark, 112n45, 176n61
joint attention, 45–46, 125, 155

Kahneman, Daniel, 68n46
Kant, Immanuel, 13, 17n11, 31, 89, 106, 146

Kaufman, Stuart, 180n113
Kekes, John, 114n81
Keller, Helen, 119, 151, 177n78
Kemmerer, David, 178n92
Kierkegaard, Søren, 89
Kim, Jaegwon, 67n28
Kitcher, Philip, 65n12, 69n60, 180n124
Klein, Stanley B., 111n31
know-how, 24, 36–38; and propositional knowledge, 36–38
knowledge/cognition: acquaintance, 77; and affect, 74–75; Greek words for, 37; and language, 137–139; monological, 44; and rhetoric, 202–203; social, 44
Kuhn, Thomas, 219n40
Küpers, Wendelin, 71n94

Lagerspetz, Olli, 216n2
Lakoff, George, 112n45, 113n51
Lalumera, Elisabetta, 178n84
language: acquisition, 226–229; and animals, 169–171; and artificial intelligence, 159–161; and biology, 154; and child development, 148–150, 154–155, 227–229; as communication, 117–118, 123–124; communicative theory of, 118, 147, 173n6; constitutive vs. nativist theories, 147, 152–157; and core knowledge, 154–155; deprivation, 157–158; as dialogical address, 123, 126, 128; as differential fitness, 136–141, 169–170; as disclosive field, 126–127; and dwelling, 117, 121–122, 130–131, 142–143, 147–148; and embodiment, 132–135; as environing-world, 119–120, 227–229; and evolution, 168–172; and experience, 119–120; extensibility, 136, 160, 169; factical, 117–118; and gesture, 132–134, 171; and history, 129, 140; and joint attention, 155, 170–171; and lexical-factical distinction, 127, 150–151,

152; and lived world, 148, 161; material character, 122; meaning-laden, 122; and memory, 128; natural, 117, 141; and nesting effect, 156, 229; as personal-social-environing-world, 122–126, 135; phenomenological priority of, 118–120, 148–151; and presentation, 118; and psychological thinking, 147–151; recessed effects of, 149–151, 153; and relativism, 146; and self-consciousness, 228–229; and sound, 134–135; and temporality, 127–129, 140, 169, 233–234; and thought, 146–158; and tradition, 140; traditional approach to, 1–3
language of thought theory, 148

La Rock, Eric, 110n21

Laugier, Sandra, 176n57
Laura-Ryan, Marie, 64n2
Lavelle, Jane Suilin, 112n36
Leder, Drew, 71n95, 177n73
Lennenberg, Eric H., 178n96
Lennox, James G., 180n117
Levine, Timothy R., 216n3
Levinson, Stephen C., 173n8, 174n18, 178n86, 178n88
linguistic idealism, 119–120, 143, 148
linguistic relativism, 152–153
linguistic turn, 119, 172n2
literacy, 7, 230–231, 232–238
lived world, 2, 4–5, 8–11, 103; priority of, 12–14, 92
Locke, John, 31, 215
logos, 193, 200, 201, 217n20
love, 86
Low, Douglas, 111n26
Luna, Laureano, 179n104
Lynch, Michael P., 219n36

Malafouris, Lambros, 67n34
Marx, Karl, 106

MacNeilage, Peter F., 181n131
McCrone, John, 178n97
McDowell, John, 66n19, 66n21, 85, 110n19, 156–157
McGuirk, James, 68n52
McMtler, Benjamin, 216n4
McNeill, David, 174n26–174n28
MacNeill, William E. S., 112n36
Mead, George Herbert, 65n11
meaning/meaningfulness, 3, 23, 42–43, 85; and finitude, 25–26, 43; and immersion, 42–43, 77–78; and language, 119–120, 122, 130–132, 161; of life, 43
mechanistic thinking, 82
Medina, José, 173n10, 176n53, 176n58
memes, 165–166
memory, 55, 128, 215
Merleau-Ponty, Maurice, 36, 61, 68n51, 70n88, 71n97, 112n42, 173n4, 174n24, 175n35
middle voice, 53, 90
Miller, John William, 69n56, 173n3
mind-body question, 207–213; and the translation problem, 209–212
mind-reading theories, 47, 93–94, 124
mirror neurons, 92–94, 125–126
Mueller, Erik T., 114n68
Myin, Erik, 112n40–112n41
myth, 18n15, 200, 231–232

Nagel, Thomas, 181n137
naturalism, 8, 83; existential, 10, 86–87; reductive, 83–89, 110n16, 172
nature: and convention, 141–142; and culture, 141–143, 162–168; and disenchantment, 165; as environing-world, 43; and invariance, 141–142; in modern science, 13, 28; and nurture, 142
Nelson, Katherine, 174n20
Nietzsche, Friedrich, 106, 189
Noë, Alva, 113n48
nominalism, 18n18

Nussbaum, Martha, 109n3

objectivity, 12, 28–29, 188–189
O'Canaill, Donnchadh, 110n17
Okrent, Mark, 65n12
Olson, Eric T., 220n47
orality, 7; and literacy, 230–238; and narration, 236; and presentational truth, 237; and tradition, 236–237
ordinary language philosophy, 144–146
organism, 163–164
Orr, H. Allen, 180n125
Ott, Walter, 66n16

Papineau, David, 68n42
personal-world, 22–23, 52, 86; and philosophy, 104
persons vs. things, 49–50, 70n77, 100
phenomenology, 4; in analytic philosophy, 26, 69n68; vs. causal explanation, 84–87; and cognitive science, 90–98; and truth, 187–193
philosopher's fallacy, 33
philosophy, 102–109; analytic, 106; beginnings in ancient Greece, 200–203, 230–232; and the circularity of immanence, 9; and contravention, 106–107; and dialogue, 104; as engaged openness, 103; and existential background, 103–104, 108; and history, 104–106; as interrogative mood, 104; importance of, 107–109; and literacy, 230–232; modern, 11–12; and pre-philosophical experience, 7–8, 108; professional, 114n81; and reason, 199–203; and traditional critique of the lived world, 11–12; teaching, 114n74; texts, 114n79
phonology, 135
physicalism, 83, 85–86, 204; vs. dualism, 207–213
Piaget, Jean, 225
Plato, 11, 104, 106, 177n71, 202, 231–232

pluralism, 80–82, 189, 203–207; and the mind-body question, 207–213
poetry, 231–232
Polanyi, Michael, 39
pragmatics, 145–146
pragmatism, 65n12
presentation, 3; vs. representation, 33–35
Price, Huw, 176n60
projection, 51–53; active and passive, 52; and selfhood, 52–53
proposition, 129–131
propositional attitude, 129
proto-phenomenology, xii, 4, 8–11, 26–27, 64, 79, 85; and artificial intelligence, 98–102; and child development, 225–229; comprehensiveness of, 41–42; and evolution, 162–164; and language acquisition, 226–229; as naturalism, 8–10; and neuroscience, 84–87, 95; of science, 41–42; summary of, 223–224
pseudos, 216n10
psychologism, 148

Raleigh, Thomas, 217n18
Ramsey, William M., 112n38
realism, 189–190; and anti-realism, 190
reason/rationality, 30, 183–194; existential vs. regimented, 193–195; in philosophy, 199–203; and rhetoric, 202–203
reasons and causes, 84–85
recursion, 138
reductionism, 81–82, 163–164, 165, 212
reflection, 103; and pre-reflective experience, 14–17, 38, 79, 108
Reid, Thomas, 17n12
reification, 26–27
religion, 17n10, 219n37
representation, 2–4, 32–35, 94–95, 98, 129–132, 137, 190; coloring research, 151, 152, 155–156;

factionalist account of, 112n38; vs. presentation, 33–35, 130
rhetoric, 202–203
Ribeiro, Rodrigo, 66n20
Ricoeur, Paul, 174n21, 221n56
Roochnik, David, 17n7
Rosenberg, Alexander, 110n16
Rotchie, Jack, 110n16
Rouse, Joseph, 110n13, 110n19, 111n23, 178n95
Rousseau, Jean-Jacques, 46
Rowlands, Mark, 67n33
Roy, Jean-Michael, 113n60
Ryle, Gilbert, 36

Sacks, Harvey, 173n7
Sacks, Oliver, 175n31
Sandel, Adam Adatto, 109n11
Sartre, Jean-Paul, 89
Sauer, Hanno, 66n21
scaffolding, 53
Schatzki, Theodore, 70n88
Schrag, Calvin O., 219n30
science, 28–29, 81, 196; as a lived world, 41–42; modern, 11–12, 13
science and technology studies, 42
Searle, John, 67n31, 70n81, 145, 159–161, 177n68, 179n106, 217n18
second nature, 30–31, 142
selfhood, 22, 213–215; and exposition, 215; in Homer, 221n58; and identity through time, 54; as indicative concept, 215–216; and language, 151, 228–229; non-substantive, 214–216; and personal-world, 214; and projection, 52–53; and recognition, 46; social, 44–47; and temporality, 214–215
selfish gene, 163–164
Sapir-Whorf hypothesis, 152–153
Sellars, Wilfrid, 85, 110n19
semantic shift, 137–138
Sheets-Johnstone, Maxine, 69n65, 113n61
Simpson, Thomas W., 216n4

skepticism, 20–21, 64n3; and language, 124
Skinner, B. F., 225
Slobin, Daniel I., 174n18, 178n83
Slote, Michael, 70n76
social-world, 44–47, 86, 93–94; and immersion, 44–46, 97; and individuation, 45–47, 50–51, 140
Socrates, 18n18, 37, 68n45, 106, 201
Sokolov, Alexander N., 177n76
Sorrell, Kory, 70n75
space and place, 62–63
speech-act theory, 145
Spelke, Elizabeth S., 178n90
Spinoza, Benedict, 69n59
Sprevak, Mark, 112n38
Stanley, Jason, 67n38–67n39
Steiner, Pierre, 67n34
Stern, Daniel N., 176n51
Stevenson, Leslie, 111n28
subject-object distinction, 2, 11–12, 26, 35, 42, 44, 89, 94, 97, 105, 108, 188–189, 196–197
subjectivism, 42, 196
Supreme Court, 219n32

Tabery, James, 176n50
tacit knowledge, 39–40; and explicit knowledge, 40
Talero, Maria, 68n51
Tallis, Raymond, 111n24
Taylor, Charles, 17n4, 18n15, 34, 217n15
temporality, 53–58, 103, 104; and the derivation of objective time, 56–58; and freedom, 55–56; figure-eight structure of, 54–55, 58, 87, 128; and language, 127–129; and memory, 55; and now-time, 54, 57–58; and priority of the future, 54–55
Thagard, Paul, 109n8
Thales, 200
third-person standpoint, 23, 47, 85, 98
Tomasello, Michael, 69n63, 173n13, 178n91, 181n132

touch, 62
Travis, Charles, 217n18
trust, 184–185
truth: as adequation, 195; coherence theory of, 216n6; conditions of, 191–192, 204; and context, 203–204, 211–213; and correspondence, 186, 191; deflationary theory of, 205; and differential fitness, 185–187; enacted, 206–207; and enactive interpretation, 192; and ethics, 195–199; and first principles, 205–206; as fitting discourse, 187; and hallucination, 192; and indefeasibility, 194–195; inhabitive, 191; and lived world, 187; and natural language, 193; and objectivity, 188–189; pluralistic, 189; presentational, 183–187; and realism, 189–190; representational, 183, 185–187; settings for, 187; and temporality, 192; and trust, 184–185; and untruth, 183–185, 186–187
Turing test, 159
Turner, J. Scott, 180n115

Uher, Jana, 175n39

values, 42–43; dwelling in, 198

Van Bentham, Johan, 219n34
Varela, Francisco, 113n62
virtual-world, 139
voice, 134, 135
Vygotsky, Lev, 177n72, 228

Wallis, Charles, 68n40
Walton, Douglas, 219n29
Weinberg, Steven, 69n61
Wheeler, Michael, 113n67
Williams syndrome, 158
Wilson, E. O., 180n114, 180n124
Wilson, Margaret, 113n50
Wittgenstein, Ludwig, 144, 170, 176n55, 176n59, 217n11, 220n45, 221n52
Woodward, Bob, 219n32
world, 3, 22
writing, 130, 131, 175n42; and abstraction, 234–235, 236; and disembodiment, 234; and orality, 230–238; and reflection, 235; and representational truth, 237; and tradition, 236–237

Yakubu, Tussif, 218n22
Yousef, Nancy, 178n97

Zahavi, Dan, 65n8, 69n69, 70n75, 111n29–111n30
Zahidi, Karim, 113n55

Lightning Source UK Ltd.
Milton Keynes UK
UKHW040801160819
348010UK00011B/3/P